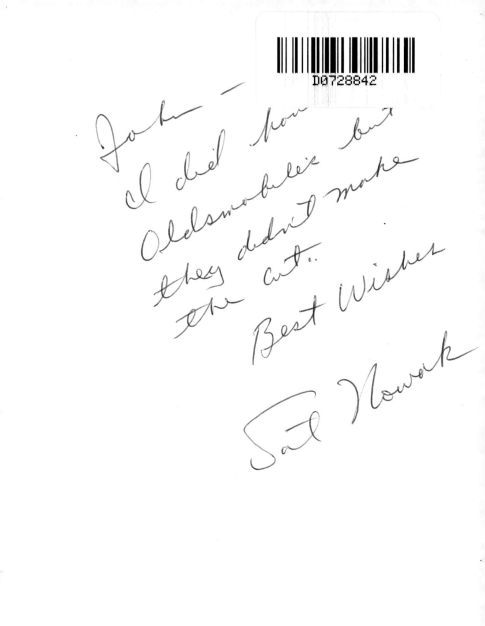

John —

I did three Oldsmobiles but they didn't make the cut..

Best Wishes

Sal Nowak

# Forty Cars That Owned Me

## Patrick J. Nowak

ISBN 0-7414-3736-8

*Published by:*

PUBLISHING.COM

*1094 New DeHaven Street, Suite 100*
*West Conshohocken, PA 19428-2713*
*Info@buybooksontheweb.com*
*www.buybooksontheweb.com*
*Toll-free (877) BUY BOOK*
*Local Phone (610) 941-9999*
*Fax (610) 941-9959*

*Printed in the United States of America*

*Printed on Recycled Paper*

*Published April 2007*

This book is dedicated to my wife, Nancy,
and to our three kids,
Mike Nowak, Joe Nowak, and Jennifer Brady.

# Acknowledgments

I would like to thank the following people who provided timely encouragement, creative suggestions, and helpful comments: Alan Ware, Randy Olinger, Joe Wojt, and my wife Nancy.

Jane Martin and John Harnish of Infinity Publishing provided the needed handholding to bring this project to completion. Cathy Kessler, copyeditor, improved the book with her considerable skills.

In regard to photo credits, I believe that almost all of the photos were taken by family, friends, and crew members with exception of those on pages 1 and 2, taken by Kurt Meister, "der Nashmann" and that of the airborne rally car in Chapter 16, The Red Mist. I would like to give that brave soul credit if he'll step forward.

Men like Don Ensley, Gary Butzke, Craig Weidner, Steve Steeb, John Erickson, and Greg Coleman were all instrumental in helping me become a successful driver at Waterford Hills and on the Pro Rally circuit. Their skills and dedication made the difference. They are all great guys, and I am proud to call them friends.

# Table of Contents

# Forty Cars That Owned Me

## Introduction

My initial intention was to write a brief history of some of the more interesting cars I have owned. What I ended up with is a collection of stories about people: the people involved with these cars and myself. I thought about changing a few names to protect the guilty, but soon realized that I was the one whose good sense and sanity were often suspect. You'll have to render the verdict.

Over the last forty-eight years, I acquired and disposed of more than seventy cars, trucks and motor homes, and those experiences, good and bad, have generated some wisdom about how to minimize the damage to one's bank account when dealing with what is almost always a depreciating asset. The reader will hopefully draw some useful conclusions.

Ladies who are trying to understand their husband's devotion to certain cars and the money spent on them might find some insights to male behavior, but I offer only reasons why, and I doubt that there is a long-term cure. I should add that I was never a collector who bought, restored and sold cars for profit. I bought these road, race and rally cars to drive. When I got done with them, they were definitely used cars.

The savvy auto executive might like to peruse this collection of tales and see if he or she agrees with me on what the "secret sauce" is. What do certain cars possess such that people get passionate about them? I believe there is a very tight relationship between styling and substance that determines a car's perceived value by owners and would-be owners.

By the time you finish this book, you'll have a pretty good idea of what I think a car has to have to be loved and sought after, long after it has gone out of production. I wasn't in love with all the cars herein, far from it. Most of them were fine rides, but a few were disasters. A car can own you, even when you're mad at yourself for buying it.

Have you ever had a car that, after you've parked it, you pause, turn around and look at it, and it makes you smile? You're glad that car is yours. You're proud of it. You feel fortunate that you managed to acquire it. That car makes you feel good.

There are cars like that. You'll know it when it happens to you. I used to say to myself, "I would steal that car, except for the fact that I already own it."

This interest in cars began sixty years ago, way back in 1947. I was eight years old, growing up in Alpena, an old lumbering town on the Lake Huron side of Michigan, about 250 miles north of Detroit.

It had been two years since the end of World War II, and the country was crazy about cars. None had been built during the war, and now Ford, GM, Chrysler, Kaiser, Hudson, Willys, Nash and Packard could not build them fast enough.

Just before the new cars came out in the fall of the year, the dealers would cover their show-room windows with great sheets of white paper. I would ride downtown on my bike to three dealerships—Buick, Chevrolet and Ford—situated within a few blocks of each other. Leaning my bike against a tree by the sidewalk, peering through the small cracks in the spaces between the paper sheets, seeing only a fender, part of the grill or a rear quarter panel, I wanted to be the first to see the new models. If I couldn't see the whole car, which was usually the case, but could see enough to be able to tell it was going to be different from what they had before, oh boy! Then it was off to the other two dealers for more detective work.

After the official introductions of the new cars, I would return to see if I could have a few brochures of the new models. To me, the brochure was the car. I liked the smell of the brochures. I didn't care much to sit in these cars, or pretend I was driving them. The shape of the car is what interested me. The grill, the hood, the sides, the colors and the back end were what distinguished one car from another.

Beginning with that first car, a '53 Nash acquired for $100 in the summer of 1958, I bought more than fifty cars over the next forty-five years. Counting race cars, family cars, company cars, pickup trucks and motor homes, and excluding motorcycles and sail boats, I will admit to being "owned" by more than seventy vehicles.

The 1962 Triumph TR-3B and the first Jaguar, the 1974 XJ6L sedan, were great cars. Why did I sell them? And the 1965 Aston Martin DB-5 that I purchased for $6000, I sold for $9000 and later learned that it had been sold for more than $40,000—the same Aston Martin DB-5 shown at the press conference when Ford bought Aston Martin? What could I have been thinking when I sold that?

Most of the race cars I owned were imports, but the last of them was a classic muscle car, a 475 horsepower 1994 Ford Mustang Cobra hand built from a body shell purchased from Ford Motor Company for $500. Five long years later, it was the car that won the ITE Championship at the Waterford Hills racetrack in Clarkston, Michigan, in my last season of competition.

These are the stories of those cars, the forty cars that owned me.

Pat Nowak
Holland, Michigan
November 1, 2006

# Shouldn't Have Taken Seconds on the Pie

## 1953 Nash Four-Door Sedan

*This is Carol & Kurt Meister's car in Long Grove, Illinois. Mine was red and black and not nearly as nice as the Meisters' car. Photo by Kurt Meister.*

I was 19, working construction in the summertime, earning money for my sophomore year at college. There wasn't much work in Northern Michigan in the summer, but I got a job with the City of Alpena, repairing sidewalks and streets, learning how to operate a #2 shovel when there was work to be done and how to look busy when there wasn't. Most of the time we had to work pretty hard as labor was cheaper than equipment.

College was Michigan Tech in Sault Ste. Marie, about 175 miles away. Getting up there and back was always a hassle, so I decided to buy a car if I could find a decent one for under $200. A new car could be had for about $2000, so $200 would get you something that would run but it wouldn't be too fancy. I bought the Nash off of the used car lot at Louis' Chrysler Sales in Alpena for about $100. Try as I might, I just can't remember any prolonged search or negotiations.

Nashes were not mainstream cars like Fords, Chevys, or Dodges. They looked different, with fenders that almost covered the wheels, particularly the front ones. Nash and Willys Jeep had merged to become American Motors and were eventually acquired by Chrysler. This particular model was a big wide four-door that seemed about as wide as it was long. It was "square" in more ways than one.

The front seats could easily accommodate three regular size people, and the rear seats seemed even bigger. Sometimes we would have seven or eight people in the car. The two front seat backs had a vertical split between them. These front seat backs could be reclined, separately, in about four steps from nearly vertical to absolutely horizontal, as in lying down horizontal. From under the rear seats, there were two little metal supports that swung out and supported the seat backs when they were in the horizontal position. This feature made the car into a double bed for camping purposes or whatever. Imagine being a 19-year-old guy with an automotive double bed.

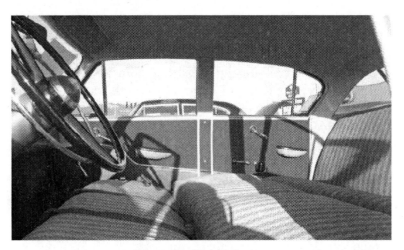

*Photo by Kurt Meister.*

"Forgive me, Father, for I have sinned."

I used to rate my dates on how many steps backward and downward the front seat backs could be positioned. Not many were "4's," as the prevailing moral climate in Northern Michigan in the late '50s was pretty conservative unless marriage was a distinct possibility. I may have been about five years ahead of the times.

The Nash's body was a pretty good shape, just some rust along the rocker panels. I cut those off and went to a sheet metal shop that made ducts for furnaces and had the guy cut two horizontal pieces with a bent over "hem" on the bottom edge for strength, and I pop riveted those on, and with an aerosol can of shiny black enamel paint, I foo-fooed it on to match the black paint of the rest of the main body. Didn't look too bad and the repairs held up over the years.

The body was black and the roof was red, as two-tone cars were popular at the time. I don't remember much about the interior, besides the double-bed feature, except it had what Nash called "The Weather Eye Heater." This heater actually had a little thermostat in it that would turn it on and off depending on how warm it was. The seat back position sometimes affected how warm it was.

Mechanically, it was pretty good. It would stop, turn and generally comport itself like a regular car. The one thing it wouldn't do was accelerate. It eventually gained speed, but you really couldn't say it accelerated. The Nash had a six-cylinder engine and a three-speed manual tranny plus an electric overdrive. I doubt if it made more than 100 horsepower. To make up for the lack of power the three-speed tranny was geared very low. First gear would get it up to about 12 mph, with the engine screaming for mercy. Second gear might make it to 25 mph with cries of pain coming from the engine room. Third gear made it to about 40 with the pistons threatening to change cylinders.

Then the overdrive kicked in. I say "kicked" because the OD unit was geared so tall that it would almost stall the engine. Imagine you were on your trusty ten-speed bike in third gear and you decided to move the derailleur on the crank and rear hub such that you were now in tenth. You could hardly pedal it, right? That's what this little motor had to deal with when the overdrive kicked in.

In any case, once I got it rolling, it would continue to gain speed, but hardly accelerate, to a top end of almost 100 mph. This process would take about three minutes provided I was on the flat or had the benefit of a few downhill runs and had no head winds.

The first big trip was in the fall of 1958 when I sallied forth in the Nash, heading north up US-23 for my sophomore year at Michigan Tech in the Sault, my Weather Eye heater ready for winter's challenges. The Nash had a big trunk, lots of seating and was a comfort machine if there ever was one, lacking only the ability to accelerate.

Speaking of the Sault, short for Sault Ste. Marie, ever notice how lots of things in Michigan have a "The" in front of the noun? There are "The Straits, The Keweenaw, The Bridge, The Thumb, The North, and The U.P." Back then, folks from around here who didn't travel much may not have realized that there were other straits and bridges.

Prior to 1958 the Mackinac Bridge wasn't there, so I had to time my arrival in Mackinac City to synch up with the car ferry that would take me five miles across the Straits of Mackinac to St. Ignace on the north shore.

Now I was in the U.P., which most people think stands for The Upper Peninsula, but we always thought it stood for The Upper Peculiar or maybe The Unusually Peculiar, as the folks up there, good Scandinavians mostly, along with a few Frenchmen, were, well, different.

Eventually, I arrived at the Sault, which, after St. Augustine, Florida, is the second oldest settlement in America, dating back to the early 1600s. Sault, by the way, is pronounced "Sue."

There are actually two Saults: the American one, which is small and old, and the Canadian Sault, which is eight times larger, filled with industry, several colleges and a nursing school. But to get to it, we needed to take another ferryboat across the St. Mary's River, and once across, one needed to get around, which is where the Nash would come into play. Why would we want to go to all that trouble to go through US Customs, Canadian Customs, and take another boat ride across a wide and sometimes rough river? The answer is simple: women.

Socially, the American side of the river was a disaster. Michigan Tech was an engineering school, a very serious college with high academic standards. This two-year school was a branch of Michigan Tech at Houghton, one of the toughest technical schools in the States. How many good-looking warm and cuddly cheerleader type honeys do you imagine went there? Right, very few.

Not only were there no presentable women to choose from, there were more males per square mile than anywhere else in the country. The American Sault, unfortunately, was a military town. And it was a very well-defended town, indeed.

More than 20,000 US servicemen were stationed in the area. The women, you might say, were over subscribed. The US Army had a large base there, The Air Force had a big field; Kinross or Kinchloe, it was called. The Coast Guard had a station there and then there were other small radar squadrons, some Navy personnel, and of course, the Border Patrol.

About the time we were ready to give up hope, we accidentally stumbled onto a social oasis not far from school. We had visited the Canadian Sault on the weekend, mainly because we could drink Canadian beer at the age of 18.

We made a great discovery one Saturday night when we went to what used to be called "blue" films, movies that were banned in the States but OK in Canada. We were standing in line to buy tickets to see a slightly naughty French film when a cab pulled up to the theater's entrance. Four or five women got out of the cab. They looked like a group of finalists for a beauty pageant. Real women, real pretty.

As it turned out, every able-bodied male in the Canadian Sault who did not have a job at Algoma Steel or Abitibi Paper right out of high school left immediately for Toronto or Vancouver, almost never to return. The girls, in 1958, did not do that.

There were pretty English girls with perfect manners, and lots of Italian girls with incredible mammarian structures who would take you to the weddings of their cousins at Marconi Hall. The Nash was the perfect car for this kind of work, and no place above the 45th Parallel could claim more beautiful women that the Canadian Sault.

"Forgive me, again, Father."

Getting back to the Nash, it was a good and faithful servant. Always started, never had any component failures that first year. After completing the two years at the Sault, it was time to transfer up to the main Michigan Tech campus in Houghton, Michigan, in the Copper Country on the Keweenaw Peninsula, a 40-mile piece of former copper mining real estate that stuck out into Lake Superior and received more than 300 inches of snow each winter.

Houghton, Michigan, and its sister-city Hancock were the heart of the copper mining industry, and if you wanted to be a geologist or mining engineer, Michigan Tech was the school to graduate from. I was there as a chemical engineering student, in way over my head academically. My grade point was in free fall after the fall term.

It was a tough school, and I'm not sure what I was doing in chemical engineering in the first place; although at the time I graduated from Alpena Catholic Central, it seemed like a good career choice and the patriotic thing to do. Patriotic because in 1956 the Russians had launched the first space satellite, the Sputnik, and there was a huge push on to get promising young high school students to enroll in technical curriculums. I think it was partly the Nash, which allowed me to escape to Houghton's nightlife, and the extreme difficulty my brain had with memorizing the elements of organic chemistry or complicated chemical process equations that accelerated the decline of my academic record.

I was living in the Newman House, a Catholic boarding house that operated like a fraternity. We had a regular cook and a priest who kept an office there but lived in a nearby rectory. The residents were good guys to live with, but they had a tendency for practical jokes that could have disastrous consequences, particularly in my case.

I had been out running errands in the Nash one day when I stopped in a small grocery store to buy some snacks, and across the counter stood a young girl, perhaps 17 years old, maybe 16. She was so incredibly lovely in face and form, I was speechless. Imagine a young Sophia Loren. Dark hair, big dark eyes, a beautiful smile, oh my, oh my. This girl was as close to perfect as one might possibly be. On a scale of one to ten, she was a twelve.

When I recovered my mental footing, I asked her about herself and began, as the English would say, to chat her up. I wondered out loud if she would go to a movie with me that weekend, and she said she really didn't date much, but she would ask her parents. She excused herself and went into a back office and talked with someone for quite awhile, presumably her mom or dad, and then came out to say that she could go, but I would have to promise to have her home by 11 PM. That would kind of cramp my style, but I had to agree to the curfew, as she was a rare jewel.

Houghton-Hancock was worse than the American Sault as far as good-looking women went. There were no Canadians here, except for hockey players on scholarship, and of the 4000 engineering students, less than 300 were female, and they were serious students who wore engineering boots and carried slide rules in holsters on their ample hips.

But I had found this beautiful dark-haired princess who did go to the movies with me in the trusty Nash that Friday night. When I picked her up, a visibly worried set of parents reminded her of the 11 PM curfew and her father gave me a look as if he could read my mind. Probably could.

There was a tradition at the Newman House that those fortunate few who had a date on Friday night would swing by the house after the movie for some desserts that the cook had prepared and left for this purpose. This would also provide an opportunity to show off the girl, and I had one that was an absolute showstopper. She was really something to look at and be seen with. She was beautiful. She was unbelievable.

While we were eating the apple pie and having a glass of milk to chase it with, naughty boys were doing bad deeds. In the time it took to have seconds on the pie, the guys upstairs had gone out to the Nash, placed the front seat backs in the horizontal position, stripped my bed, made up the bed in the Nash with sheets opened just so with big fluffy pillows all around, put red cellophane over the dome light, ran a power cord with a nightstand light to put on the back shelf, and then waited for us to go back out to the car.

Ever the gentleman, I opened the car door on her side and the red dome light went on. She looked in and went into shock. She started to shake, began to cry softly and would have none of my explanations that I had nothing to do with this and was as mad as she was.

She didn't want to know. "Just tell me where I can find a phone to call my parents and have them pick me up." She called, they came quickly and spirited her away, never to be seen again. She probably was sent off to live in a convent in Switzerland, poor thing.

God, she was beautiful. If there is a moral or two to this story, they might be: Don't be a showoff and don't take seconds on the pie.

In a 15-minute time span I had gone from a guy eating homemade pie with a potential movie star to a guy with a car with a red dome light and no date. My princess was gone for good. I went back into the house, and there was no one around, it seemed. I went up to my room and found 23 guys studying in my room. I slammed the door, and they began to laugh. They laughed until Tuesday. Unforgivable.

Later that winter, my friend Mark Anderson arranged to have his girlfriend bring one of her friends down to Michigan Tech's Winter Carnival as my date for Carnival weekend. Her name was Donna, a pretty girl of Serbian descent, from Minnesota's Iron Range. We had a great time, and we made plans for me to drive up to Coleraine, Minnesota, to see her at the end of the winter term.

Finals for the winter term were going to be a disaster. Several of us had mostly the same classes, and we knew our chances of passing were slim. Somebody had the idea that we might have a chance if we were drunk, something like the one guy who survived the "Charge of The Light Brigade" by being drunk during that epic battle.

Our first exam was at 8 AM, so we set our alarms for about 5 AM so we would have sufficient time to get inebriated. We were pretty well gone by 7:30.

We took a test or two and while we were pretty disgusting and disgusted with ourselves, we gathered up the remaining brews, put them in the Nash and headed west to Minnesota, still half in the bag, for winter break. It never occurred to us to consider going to a warm place.

Mark Anderson was already up there in Grand Rapids, Minnesota, when we got there. He took us over to a bar that was owned by several of his buddies, guys in their twenties. This place was called the Alamo. They had great bands and were doing good business all through the week, and you couldn't get in on the weekend.

I couldn't get over the fact that guys our age could own and run a bar. I took Donna there, and we had a great time. Donna was a very pretty girl, had a deep voice and she seemed to be quite taken with me. I couldn't quite understand that as all these other Minnesota guys looked like John Wayne in his prime and were built like Arnold Schwarzenegger. Could it have been the Nash?

This particular visit came to an end, and it was time to get back to school in Houghton. We were headed back when the Nash had its first mechanical failure. The motor erupted with white smoke and steam, and the engine stopped right then. I managed to get if off of the road onto the shoulder and that was it. We emptied the suitcases out of the trunk, locked the doors, stuck out our thumbs and got picked up by the second or third car that came along.

As far as I could tell, we had grenaded the motor, and since the Nash's initial cost of $100 was more than justified by the almost two years of continuous use, I felt we were about even and that the engine's repair cost was far beyond my means. I patted it on the hood and said, "Thanks." I guess this is how cowboys felt when their horse came up lame and they had to shoot it.

When we got back to the Newman House, a couple of the guys were commiserating with me about the loss of the trusty Nash. As they listened to me describe the motor's last words, I thought I detected some doubt as to whether or not the engine was kaput. I told them that it really didn't matter to me because I had made a decision to leave Michigan Tech while there was a little left of my once respectable grade point average, hopefully to restart somewhere else in a curriculum that I could handle.

They asked if it would be OK if they could drive up to Minnesota and see if the car was still there and they might possibly repair it, as it sounded to them like a blown head gasket or maybe a water pump failure, which wouldn't be that hard to repair. I said, "Be my guest, and if you do get her running, she's yours."

And with that, I dismissed the Nash from my mind, and left Houghton and Michigan Tech for good.

About two years later, I got a call from a guy who said he had some trouble tracking me down, but he wanted to talk to me about a '53 Nash in his possession.

Seems that those guys did find the Nash right where I had left it, repaired the blown head gasket and took the car back to the Newman House in Houghton. There, it served as the house car and was surprisingly well looked after. In fact, as the months passed, the car was slowly transformed from one that was missing a headlight bezel, a door handle, and had a broken tail light to a car that was missing nothing and all of its chrome parts were like new.

I'm told that there was a nearly identical Nash belonging to a Tech professor who discovered to his dismay that his car was losing chrome parts and tail lights. The boys from the Newman House had forgotten their catechism lessons and slowly stripped this guy's car.

The caller said he was the last of the guys who started there when I did, and he didn't just want to leave the car behind when he left. He drove it down to Mt. Pleasant, Michigan, where I was living with the folks, and I took him over to his house in Midland and dropped him off.

I had the Nash with all its useful furniture again, drove it for a few months, and really enjoyed having the old car back.

11

I was finally graduating from Central Michigan University, had a teaching job lined up in the fall in Clarkston, Michigan, and I wanted a new car. I had the hots for a Triumph TR-3B roadster that I was going to get as soon as the loan went through.

When I took delivery of the Triumph, I sold the Nash to a kid across the street for $100.

Sometimes when I think about that 1953 Nash and that dark-haired girl those Newman House guys put into shock and the fact that they rescued the car and returned it to me years later in better shape than ever, perhaps there was some rough justice in it all. But I would have traded the Nash and a few more like it for another chance with that beautiful girl.

# Crime Does Pay

## 1962 Triumph TR-3B Roadster

*Two of my all-time favorites.*

Once upon a time, the English built some interesting cars. MGs, Austin Healeys, Rovers, Jaguars, Vauxhalls and Triumphs were well known on both sides of the Atlantic. A good part of their popularity in the States was a result of US servicemen bringing them back here after their tour of duty in England in World War II.

These were lightweight cars, usually two-seaters, and while a bit underpowered, the exhaust note was quite pleasing to the ear and they handled well. Mostly though, they were fun cars, stylish convertibles that guys liked to drive and women liked to be seen in. Many of the Austin Healey Sprites and MGs were modified for racing, and there are a few still circulating around racetracks in various classes.

These cars would give you the occasional sincerity test by breaking down at inopportune moments. The electrical components were weak and made by the Lucas Company who enjoyed a monopoly position in that country. The headman, Joseph Lucas, was often referred to as the "Prince of Darkness." This weakness would later be, in large part, a major reason for the demise of the entire British car industry.

God may have saved the Queen but not the British auto industry.

Let's get back to the TR-3. I had seen this car in a number of auto magazines. There was something about the swoop of the front fenders, kind of like a French curve, that blended into the door and then a new shorter swoop formed the rear fenders.

The upper edge of the doors was shaped like an armrest and cut down toward the ground at a 45-degree angle. You could easily reach out and touch the ground. The car of cars at that time was probably the Jaguar XK 120, a roadster of timeless beauty. The TR-3 mimicked those flowing lines but didn't look like a copy. It had a stout four-cylinder engine that originally was used in a farm tractor, so it had good torque and was well built.

There had been a TR-2 that had the same body but a little different nose, and it was not quite as mechanically advanced as the TR-3. TR-3 sales were thriving in the States, but the home office back in England was bringing out a successor model, the TR-4, a rather squared-off car that the US dealers thought looked awful as it had none of the graceful curves of the TR-3.

The dealers over here raised such a stink that the factory decided to use up some TR-3 bodies that they had built for spare parts and put TR-4 mechanicals in them which included a better transmission and a bit more power. The car was then named the TR-3B because it was mechanically different from the TR-3 and became one of the most valued Triumphs, and good examples today will bring between $15,000 and $20,000. Triumph built 3331 of the TR-3Bs, and all were exported to the United States.

At the time I got interested in the car, I knew nothing about it except it looked great, all the magazines that covered foreign cars were raving about it, and I wanted one bad. When a guy wants a particular model car and he has the fever, obstacles like money, time or space are swept aside as the car is pursued.

There was a foreign car dealer over in Flint that handled English cars. Nowadays these cars might be called imports, but back then they were "foreign" cars. The dealer was known as Sports Cars, Inc., and he had four different brands in stock at four price points. If I had $1800 he would be happy to sell me a cute little Austin Healey Sprite; for $2400, I could have the TR-3B; $2800 would get me an MG and $3200 was the price for the big Healey, the AH 3000. He had one of each. The TR-3B was white with a black convertible top and a black interior. The whole deal totaled $2584. I managed to get him to throw in an AM radio and bring the price, tax included, down to $2401. The number sticks in my mind because I had to finance 100% of it.

I went to my friendly banker, a young guy named Fitzpatrick that I had met in the bar at the local K of C's. He said the bank would loan 80% of the car's selling price. "How much is the car going to cost?" he asked. I said, "$2400, I mean $3000," and he said, "Fine, we can go up to 80% or $2400 in this case." I said that was great, but there was one more little problem we needed to resolve and that was that while I was working part time in the summer, my new teaching job wouldn't start until September and I wouldn't see a real paycheck until late September or early October. "No problem," he said, "we'll start the clock now on interest and just put that in the calculator so that when your payments start in the fall, they will reflect the interest charged from now up to that point."

I don't know where Fitz is today, but he is either president of some big bank or doing time in a federal penitentiary. Our deal wasn't illegal, just a highly accommodating arrangement that I was grateful for.

So here we are, in the good old summertime, me in my spiffy new TR-3B, King of the United States, well, at least of the Midwest. What a great car. Girls loved it; I loved it. The trunk was just big enough for a beach blanket and a picnic basket and maybe a small cooler with a few brews.

After work or on the weekend, I might have a date with a good-looking girl to go play tennis. She would be dressed in tennis whites, looking great. I was in tennis whites, not looking too bad either. The new tennis balls were white. The King's car was white as well. Mighty white.

A Corvette or T-Bird convertible might have been just as impressive, but I had the only TR-3B that anyone from around here had ever seen. It was beyond cool because it was the only one, *the only one*.

The TR-3B made great sounds. A big part of its appeal other than its looks was the exhaust note. Every time I started it up it made my heart beat a little faster. I once read a slightly naughty book about a girl who had recorded the sounds of Ferraris and Formula One cars and NASCAR race cars and she would play these tapes while making love. I think the making love part would be a distraction from the aural pleasure those tapes must have provided.

I used to go over to Windsor, Ontario, across the river from Detroit, and you could take the Ambassador Bridge or you could take the tunnel under the river. I always took the tunnel and wound that TR up in first or second gear and just let all the sound reverberate off the tunnel walls and drown you in sound. It wasn't real loud, really kind of mellow, and the sound bouncing off the walls, slightly delayed from the sound coming out from the car—well, you had to be there.

The summer flew by, September arrived, and it was time to report for that teaching job in Clarkston. I liked the job and met a girl who liked the jaunty little car and me. She thought the TR was nice but a bit of a pain if the top was down because it would rearrange her pretty blonde hair. I do believe, though, she thought I had money, a notion she would disabused of soon enough.

My doom was sealed with this one on our first date when looking over the menu in some hamburger joint (a big spender, me), I said, "Damn, it's Friday, so I guess it'll have to be the fish for me." We Catholic boys couldn't eat meat on Friday until God changed his mind one day in the late '60s, sent word to the Pope, and then it was OK. This was 1962, so we were still eating fish on Friday.

I was not aware that this fine-looking lady had recently converted from the Dutch Christian Reformed Church to Catholicism, and #1 on her to-do list was to find a Catholic boy who was taller than her and had no criminal record. There I sat, already selected, unaware that I was even a candidate. I ended up marrying the girl almost exactly one year later on 9/7/63, which I can remember only because, as a former math teacher, I recall that 9 times 7 is 63.

The courtship was a real whirlwind deal. We met in September, we were engaged in November, and married the following September. We might have gotten married earlier, but she planned to go to France for the summer and I planned to go up north in the TR for a pipeline job. Looking back, we both characterize our courtship as one of dual

17

fraud, she thinking I had a bit of money and me thinking she was a true blonde. Now, nearly 43 years later, we're still together. Crime does pay.

The school year ended in early June, and the fiancée was off to France to study French as part of her French teaching deal. I went up to Petoskey to work construction. I had been persuaded that, since we both worked at the same school, the sensible thing was to keep her new and paid for Volkswagen Beetle and sell the financed TR that was costing $81.01 per month that I didn't have. I put an ad in the Petoskey paper as the construction job was winding down, and a local guy bought it for his high school son, the lucky little bugger. I think I got $1950 for it, which was about what I owed on it.

I have spent the rest of my life trying to reincarnate that TR3 in other cars.

Three Jaguars, two Austin Healey Sprites, one Aston Martin, two Cadillacs, three Lincolns, numerous race cars, five motorcycles, four Pro Rally cars, six motor homes, six sail boats, and many other fine cars could never quite bring back that sense of excitement that was part of the TR-3B experience.

I see a TR-3B once in awhile in the paper or on websites advertising classic English cars. Maybe one day I'll get another one. I would like to think so. I hate to say this so early in the book, but this car was one of the very best of all the vehicles I have ever been owned by.

# He Brought the Gun up to His Shoulder

## 1947 Ford Sedan

This car was not in the family for very long, maybe about a week or so, but it was an interesting car.

It's the summer of '63. I was still in Petoskey, having just parted with the beloved Triumph TR-3B roadster. I hated to sell it, but I had to as the summer's construction work didn't pay that well and my living costs up there were high. The bottom line is I had been able to save almost nothing, and I was still looking at $81.01 each month. I was getting married in two or three weeks to my lady friend who was on her way back from France. Wondered how I was going to pay for the honeymoon. I couldn't even afford a one-night stand.

One of the guys on the construction site drove a beat-up old '47 Ford sedan back and forth every day. He was the same guy who owned and operated a giant front-end loader that got pretty wet one day due to a moment's inattention. We were putting a pipeline in along the banks of the river that runs through downtown Petoskey and he jumped off of this big machine to talk to a foreman about something. His brakes weren't set just right, or they didn't work, and that thing began to roll towards the river. He saw it and attempted to jump back on as it rolled by but fell back off which was probably a good thing. That beast rolled over the edge and into about 20 feet of water. Made a hell of a splash. He was beside himself, so honked off at his own stupidity. His means of making a living was now making bubbles at the bottom of the river.

They brought in a large wrecker to hoist the loader back up. Divers were needed to find it and attach cables to it. No way could they budge it. They then brought a larger wrecker to try and lift it. Nothing doing. Then they hit upon using both of them. This process took the whole day, but they eventually fished it out and had it running and working the next day.

A couple of days later, he told me he noticed the Triumph was gone and he wondered how I was getting around. I told him I was hitching rides here and there. He offered to sell the black '47 Ford coupe for $100. I said that was more than I had, and the price went to $50 in a hurry. He didn't have a title but he thought he could find one for it. I suspect he just acquired the car somehow and never did have a title. In those simple bygone days, we didn't seem to worry much about titles, license plates or insurance. The car had somebody's plates on it, and when I produced the $50, he handed over the keys and that was that.

It had a flathead V-8 that was really pretty peppy. It sounded good too. The three-speed shifter was on the steering column, common practice back then. The dash had all that tan plastic trim around the basic instruments, most of it cracked, and there was a radio that was stuck on one station and you couldn't change it, but you could turn it on and off. The speedometer didn't work and the gas gauge always showed full so you had to remember when you filled it up and about how far you went. It sounded so good I always had my foot in it so I was probably getting about ten miles to the gallon, tops.

It was a work car. Back in Alpena, guys had work cars to go to the cement plant. These were old Chevys, Fords, or Plymouths that they drove to their jobs in the plant or the quarry. These cars were never washed. They had a permanent coating of white limestone dust.

I liked this car. Guys in high school lusted after these $50 specials because you had so little invested; you could trash it or start to make something nice out of it. I just wanted it to get me back down to Mt. Pleasant or Clarkston.

The job finished up, and I cashed my last check and headed south. Can't remember the highway, maybe it was US 27, but I remember the bar. It was called Spike's Keg of Nails. My dad knew Spike. He and I had stopped there when I was a kid ten years earlier. I was surprised to see Spike there that night, as I thought he had passed away. He seemed to be about 100 years old when I met him the first time. I was just stopping for a sandwich and a beer. Wouldn't be staying long. Yes, the folks were doing fine.

One beer led to another and pretty soon I had a nose full. It was still 125 miles to Mt. Pleasant, so I had to get moving. I could handle the car OK, but I needed to take a leak about every 30 miles. I would pull it over onto the shoulder and water the bushes.

I turned the car off, doused the lights and I could kind of see a building back off of the road but it was dark out there in the country.

I just finished the bush-watering exercise when the lights came on and this old guy came out, brandishing a rifle or a shotgun. "Who in the hell do you think you are, waking me and the missus up, and then we look out the window and there you are, peeing on our lawn? As far as I'm concerned, you're trespassing, and I'm within my rights to shoot ya, which I have a mind to. Now get that car and yourself out of here, now!"

I got back in the Ford and the damn thing wouldn't start. I tried all the tricks I knew, but it didn't want to cooperate. Sometimes these old cars would get vapor lock and the fuel couldn't get from the gas tank to the carb and you're out of business until the engine cools down. I got out and told the guy what I thought the problem was, but he would hear none of it. "It's midnight, damn it, so just get your ass out of here before I have to use this thing." He brought the gun up to his shoulder to make his point.

I grabbed my meager possessions out of the car, but left the keys in the ignition. Somebody else will be driving it tomorrow, probably the guy with the gun. A couple of cars passed by and then an old truck stopped to pick me up. Five rides later I was in Mt. Pleasant, walking the last mile to my folks' house.

I've owned three cars so far, and two of them I've left by the side of the road. I knew I wouldn't see this one again. Too bad, it was a neat car.

# How Do You Suppose the Snowplow Driver Gets to Work?

## 1962 VW Beetle

*The collie "Prince" and his friend.*

You might say this car was part of my wife's dowry. She bought it before we were married. It was her first car. She had earned $4000 as a first-year French teacher at Clarkston High and saved half of it, so she could buy this pretty blue car. She was so proud of it.

Besides the almost brand-new VW, she brought considerably more into the marriage from an economic point of view, than I did. My net worth in September of 1963 consisted of a garden hose, a wash mitt, a soup pot, a wedding suit given to me by my parents, about a week's worth of clothes and all of $250. I still owed a doctor about $500 for some serious medical maintenance, so I would have to say I had a negative net worth. She, on the other hand, had this paid-for car, a substantial amount of money in the bank, a higher paying job than I had, and enough domestic possessions to furnish a small apartment.

My state of impoverishment was such that when, on the morning of our wedding, the florist unexpectedly hit me up for $40 for flowers at the church, my total cash on hand decreased to $20, an amount inadequate to pay for the motel we stayed in across the border in Sarnia, Ontario, during our one-night honeymoon. This was before the age of credit cards. I sheepishly had to ask the bride if she could pitch in to pay the innkeeper, which she did. I'm sure she was having second thoughts at this point. But Nancy hung in there and is still with me forty-three years later.

I liked her VW. It seemed like a businesslike little car to me. Others described it as a whimsical car with flowers on the dashboard, driven gaily around by free spirits. I didn't see it that way. It looked like a serious German-engineering exercise designed to last for many years. It had a business-like sound to the exhaust, reminding me of a baby diesel.

The other "foreign car" being sold at the time was the Renault Dauphine, a cute little four-door job that, while popular in Europe, was a bad choice over here. The main problem the Renaults had was dealer service. It was almost nonexistent.

The VW dealer, on the other hand, was a stand-alone operation staffed by people with a consumer friendly attitude. They had low-key salespeople, no real price haggling going on and outstanding service departments. VWs had such a reputation for reliability; they had to run the occasional ad that implied that these cars might, just might, have a component failure.

After my third year of teaching math at Clarkston High, I decided I had to find a more lucrative way of making a living. Nancy no longer taught French because she preferred to stay home to look after our new baby boy, Michael. Our rent was still under $100/month. Gasoline, which our thrifty VW burned very little of, was about 23 cents per gallon. The car was paid for, and we owed zip at this point. Nancy worked one year after our marriage in 1963, and we saved her salary in its entirety. So, we really didn't have a financial problem, but I could see how the other teachers were doing, the ones who had been here ten to 12 years and they were struggling. I didn't want to have that happen to us. I was making about $5800 now and that wasn't going to be enough to get a house and maybe a second car someday. I still missed my TR-3B.

I was offered a job by Allied Chemical to sell industrial chemicals to their major customers. The job involved moving to Chicago for training for eight months and then a transfer to Minneapolis. While we were living in Park Forest, a suburb of Chicago, the VW had its first component failure. It was nothing more serious than a failing battery. I remember pushing it to start it, slipping on the pavement, and tearing a hole in the pants of my best suit, the one I had gotten married in. There wasn't room in the engine compartment for the battery, so VW had found a space for it under the rear seat.

If the VW had one under-engineered system, it was the heater. The air-cooled engine had two large plenums called heater boxes, which collected hot air from the rear engine compartment, and that air was given a little push by the fan that cooled the motor. I say little push because the volume of warm air coming out of those heater boxes was hardly noticeable until the car was moving at least 50 mph. Therefore, when you were driving slowly through town in the winter, you had better be dressed warm.

The fact that the engine sat directly over the driven wheels at the rear of the car gave it exceptional traction. I recall VW running an ad that asked, "How do you suppose the snowplow driver gets to work?" Then a picture of the car moving down an unplowed street was shown. It was quite a good winter car, aside from the heater.

It remained in our little family, now grown to Mike, Joe and Jennifer, until 1973, a period of eleven years. It was the only car we had until Allied Chemical gave me a company car in Minneapolis, so I got to know it quite well.

The wife used it for her errands and to haul the kids around. The boys tell me that small rust holes began to appear in the floor of the back seat in its later years. When they couldn't hold it any longer, they would try to pee out these small holes, their near misses aggravating the rust problem.

Finally, I persuaded the bride to get a new car. I picked out a new 1973 Mercury Capri for her that she seemed to like, other than the color. She said to never buy her a brown car again. I said that it wasn't brown; it was Aztec Sunset Bronze, or something like that. Wives should come with an instruction manual that states clearly that one of the most important things about a car is its color, and if you don't get that part right, the rest doesn't matter.

I think she paid $1900 for her VW, painted a light blue with a white leatherette interior, equipped with an AM radio and a sunroof. I hated to part with it. Mechanically, it was still going strong, but the rust had won. It certainly owed us nothing. Nancy's VW was probably one of the most useful dowry gifts a husband has ever had the use of.

# If There is a Car Heaven,

# These Three Deserve to Be Up There

## The Company Cars: 1965 Ford,

## 1967 Ford, 1969 Chevrolet

*This is the 1969 Chevrolet in snowy Minnesota.*

These three cars are grouped together because they were all company cars provided by the Minneapolis office of Allied Chemical in the middle '60s while I was employed there as a sales representative. Let's talk about the first of the three: the '65 Ford Galaxie 500.

The '65 Ford had been ordered and used for about 20,000 miles by my predecessor, Rick, and I would have to keep it for another year. It was a burgundy four-door hardtop with a small but willing V-8.

The lines on the '65s were quite straight, with hardly a curve on the car, except for the windshield. Even the dashboard was all horizontal lines.

You could choose the make, among Ford, Chevy or Plymouth, and the color at the time you placed your order with the local manager of the office. The guys had definite preferences on the brand, but they would switch around too. They all had air, automatic transmissions, a decent radio and power everything.

Allied Chemical paid all travel expenses, and the cars were well kept-up. We covered five or six states, and while air travel was permitted, even required for certain longer trips, most of the time we would go out on the road for a week at a time and organize the trip as a large circle route. I had to cover the Dakotas, Iowa, Nebraska, part of Wisconsin, and, of course, Minnesota. I might drive 40,000 miles per year in all kinds of weather and usually in an impaired state.

We were selling tank trucks and railroad tank cars of chemical commodities. These products were also available from DuPont, Union Carbide and others with exactly the same specifications and exactly the same prices, to the tenth of a cent. If DuPont had supplied a product by tank car and the customer was getting low, and I got the order for the next tank truck, our material would be going to go into the same storage tank that held what's left of the DuPont material. They had to be identical.

If the price, product and specifications are identical, which chemical company is going to get the order? The supplier most endeared to the purchasing department and/or plant management is going to get the majority of the orders. And how would this endearment come about? Right again. We did spend a lot of money. In the '60s that meant lavish meals, lots of drinking, nice resorts, pro football games, hunting and fishing trips. We would spend $500 per week when the best steak in the house would cost less than $10.

Another factor was that part of the product line, a refrigerant like Freon, called Genetron, was sold to wholesalers who in turn sold it to big HVAC contractors. These wholesalers were a wild, hard-drinking bunch, mostly World War II vets who had made it big in business in the '50s and '60s. We spent a lot of time with the wholesalers because that product line was far more profitable than the big tank car commodity sales, and their reason to do business with us was the same as with the large volume users of commodities.

All of this background is by way of explaining that we operated these cars, some of us, under the influence or nursing a mammoth hangover, almost all the time. Not proud of that and there surely must be a God and legions of guardian angels who kept us alive. In the three years I was with Allied, no one was killed or injured.

I would leave Eden Prairie, a suburb of Minneapolis, about 5 AM heading west for Sioux Falls, South Dakota, driving fast so I could arrive by 9 AM. My customer in Sioux Falls was a wholesaler who usually had a good bottle of Scotch in his desk in his private office. I don't care much for Scotch, especially at 9 AM, but you did what you had to do. He would usually be good for a small- to medium-sized order of "gas," as refrigerant was referred to in the trade, and I would be on my way, feeling pretty mellow, by 10 AM.

I had to get to Sioux City, Iowa, by noon to meet with another wholesaler who liked to close the place for a couple of hours, so we could take the whole crew over to a roadhouse where we would eat, drink and play some pool with lots of side bets and horsing around. I tried to get out of there by 3 PM if at all possible because I had another wholesaler tentatively lined up for cocktails after work in Omaha, Nebraska.

It would take 1.5 to 2 hours to make Omaha if traffic and the weather cooperated, but lots of time the weather, particularly in the winter, was a real challenge. That cocktail hour would usually become a dinner deal as well, and the party would continue. By the time I parked the car at the motel that night, I had covered 450 miles at a fairly high rate of knots.

This scenario would continue the next day with a couple of stops in Lincoln, Nebraska, and then head back east on the Interstate towards Omaha. There were no speed limits in Nebraska back then, so you could make some time up if the party got extended. I remember knocking back 12 Manhattans one night. The next day I was hurting badly.

I woke up one morning in Des Moines, after one of those marathon-drinking deals, and went out to the car in the motel parking lot to put my luggage in the trunk when I noticed that there was something odd looking about the passenger side of the car. There weren't any scratches or dents, but something was wrong. Then it dawned on me what was different. That side of the car had no door handles. I seemed to recall getting kind of close to the edge of a bridge out on the Interstate on the way back from the last bar. I did remember hearing a couple of clicks just before I made a slight correction in my heading. Took those door handles off like a surgeon. Made for an interesting insurance claim.

Enough of the mea culpas, back to the car. I do credit the '65 Ford with saving my bacon more than once because it was a great handling car and a great road car. The handling was important because it meant that a late correction would usually result in a save, as in save your car and its contents. It had conventional bench seats, which I think are often better than bucket-type seats. Buckets hold you in one place, but the circulation to your fanny is reduced and you get what motorcycle guys call "numb butt." The Ford liked to go fast; that is, it was comfortable at speed. You could just drive and drive and drive. Eventually you got tired and had to hang it up for the day, but if I ever had to drive a car coast to coast, I think that '65 Ford would be one of my top choices. Yet with all the nonsense and high speeds, I never got a ticket. Not that I wasn't guilty as hell, just never charged.

The successor car was the '67 Ford Galaxie 500. It was another four-door with all the goodies, and I picked out a butterscotch paint color with a black cloth interior. It looked pretty good. It was a bit heavier than the '65 and didn't feel quite as nimble, but it was another long distance runner. Three hundred-mile days were no big deal.

My boys, Mike and Joe, put the first dent in that car one Sunday morning on the way home from church. I had stopped at a party store for some donuts and the Sunday papers. The kids were sitting in the front, and one of them pulled on the transmission lever, situated on the steering column and pulled it out of gear. The parking lot was on a slight rearward incline, so the car began to roll backward across the parking lot towards the street. It picked up speed, rolled out across a busy street, and then fell down a paved incline into another parking lot and continued to roll toward a supermarket that, fortunately, was closed on Sunday. It hit that building by the front door and came to a stop. The boys were fine, although frightened. I don't know if they were more afraid during the ride or when they had to explain to the pater familias what they had done.

I rearranged the front end of the '67 more than once, but it was just considered an occupational hazard. At one point I began to suspect that my drinking was getting out of hand. We "had" to drink a bit because we were doing a lot of entertaining. I went to my boss and wondered out loud how much longer I could keep this up. Just possibly I might be an alcoholic. He was a bit of a knob who in turn called his boss back in the Morristown, New Jersey, headquarters and reported our little talk. His boss was an old friend of mine who called me and relayed the conversation. He said, "Pat, we all drink like you do, maybe more. If you're an alcoholic, what does that make us? We have concluded that we are not, so you are not. Now get us some new customers."

The miles piled on, and the company decided to replace the '67 Ford with a new car. I really liked the lines of the '69 Chevrolet Impala, and after two Fords, I felt like it was time for a change.

Big mistake. The car wallowed around like a whale. It was sprung so soft you felt like you were at sea. And when you would turn the steering wheel, it seemed to take a half second before the front wheels got the message. The motor, another small block V-8, was willing, but it just didn't have the "up and leave" like the Fords.

Another problem was that I seemed to get this car stuck in the snow a lot. It, like the Fords, was a rear-wheel drive car, pretty light in the back and heavy in the front. But the Fords seemed to get through, and the Chevy just got stuck. One snowy night I came home from one of these big dinners, again under the influence, missed our driveway and got the car stuck right in front of the house. The village didn't want cars left on the street because they plowed snow every night. I had to try and get this whale out of there. I shoveled a bit, put some sand under it, tried to rock it back and forth, but I was too far into the snowbank.

I did more shoveling and got back in the car for one final try. Nothing doing, I wasn't going anywhere. In my frustration, I just slowly pressed the accelerator to the floor and held it there. I held it down for several minutes. You could start to smell the rubber burning, as the tire finally got down through the snow to the pavement. The transmission was starting to howl, and the motor temp was climbing fast. Then there was a hell of a noise and the rear of the car lifted about three feet off of the ground and settled back down. I shut the car off and got out to survey the damage. The left rear tire had exploded and blew away the inner fender with such force that there was a huge hole where the left side of the trunk used to be. Another interesting insurance claim.

By now I was getting in my cups on such a regular basis I couldn't make it home. I would sleep in the car and then get awakened by the sun and finally get home at 8 or 9 in the morning. Obviously, this was becoming a big problem on the domestic front. To get back in her good graces, I would often buy a new rosebush or rose tree as I asked for "one more last chance." I was looking the rose bushes over one day and was trying to remember which ones were "Honey, I'm sorry" bushes. Of the 60 rose bushes in five beds, about half were of this type. Not a good thing.

In the meantime, I had taken a so-so chemical sales territory that had annual sales of $1,000,000, and after three years of hard work, hard playing, and 120,000 miles of driving, I was doing $3,000,000 in sales.

Those three cars had been through hell, involved in a thousand close calls and near crashes and real crashes, but they managed to help me stay in one piece, especially the Fords. If there is a car heaven, these three deserve to be up there.

# I Was Most Fortunate to Have Been in
# the Care of That Good Cop
## 1962 Cadillac Fleetwood

This was a fine-looking automobile. Classic in looks, it was well cared for by an older Jewish gentleman who had recently retired to live in Florida year round. He had another smaller car down there and had put this one up for sale for the princely sum of $1500.

I was in need of a car because I had recently resigned from Allied Chemical to take a sales position with Honeywell to sell their new line of small business computers. I might have stayed with Allied, but the computer business was just starting to take off and a good salesman could make $50,000/year, which was more than some chemical company VPs were making.

So, some of us had to make a decision on whether or not to stay with Allied Chemical long term. The national sales manager for our division made my mind up one evening when he and I went out to dinner. We both got a pretty good shine on after dinner, and I thought I would ask the big question, namely, what kind of money did this guy, king of the mountain in our corner of the corporate universe, make in annual compensation? He had me promise to keep the information confidential, which of course I would. He paused for dramatic effect, and then confided with obvious pride, "I knock down a salary of about $35,000 per year and with bonuses it gets up to around $45,000." I said, "That's wonderful," but thought, that's terrible.

That's when I decided to leave the bosom of Mother Allied and find a job that had a lot more potential. I would have to part with the '69 Chevy, give up a very generous expense allowance and take a slight cut in pay. I would do that because of the possibilities of big commissions. Some of the guys at Honeywell had been there just a year or two, and they were well beyond $50,000 and doing better every year.

I made the decision to go with Honeywell and started looking around for a car. People were starting to buy smaller cars since the early '60s and the larger cars were going out of vogue. I could get a used five-year-old Buick or Olds for less than half its cost new, and they still had a lot of use left in them. I liked the bigger cars. These cars had a lot going for them in that they had lots of room, they were cheap to acquire, and they were safer than the newer lighter cars because the older units had an actual steel frame underneath the body. The newer cars were called unibodies. They didn't have a frame. They had little sub-frames to sit the motor on, but they derived their strength from the design of the shell of the body. The shell was computer designed to hold itself together without a frame. This saved weight and made the cars a lot less expensive to build, but I wouldn't want to get in a bad wreck in one of them because the laws of physics weren't on my side.

Remember the big outrageous fins on the '59 Cadillac? By '62 they had modified them to where they were still there but much less pronounced. The '62 had a timeless style, like a blue blazer with charcoal-gray flannel slacks. It looked sturdy, stately, and smart. Car prices were going up every year but a brand-new loaded Cadillac Fleetwood, circa 1962, would still sell for less than $10,000.

I looked through the *Minneapolis Star's* want ads for cars, and this '62 Cadillac caught my eye. I drove up to one of the northwestern suburbs of Minneapolis and met the older gentleman who had the Cadillac Fleetwood for sale. I think it had about 20,000 miles on the odometer and probably had never been driven over 70 mph. For a five-year-old car, this Cadillac had to be rated a near virgin. The interior was spotless, even smelled new, and the exterior was unmarked, painted in a metallic light gray/blue. It looked like an expensive suit.

He was asking $1500 for the car, which seemed unreasonably low. I surmised he was given that figure by a dealer, who normally will offer a slightly below wholesale price for a car like this. He may have presumed that was its market value. After a short ride, I decided I wanted the car. I offered $1350 and he said $1400 was his floor. I said done, and we did the deal.

Driving this big car made me feel like a senator who might consider being asked to run for President. I would consider it, as long as I was permitted to drive the presidential limo, and the car I was in would fit the bill.

I drove the car from Eden Prairie into Honeywell's offices in Minneapolis every day, a trip of maybe 15 or 20 miles, depending on which route I took. The ride was always over too soon. The big Fleetwood had climate control, not just air conditioning, and a great radio that would seek and scan and remember. I think the radio antenna was powered as was the steering, brakes, locks, and windows. There was a large V-8 engine up front and a silky smooth Hydramatic transmission. The tires were big Uniroyals with chromed wheel covers, and of course it had fender skirts to cover up part of the rear-wheel openings, almost like a modesty shield they used to put on receptionists' desks in office lobbies.

The headlights would remember to turn themselves off and would automatically dim when they detected oncoming headlights. The windshield was tinted of course, and the interior had more vanity lights than the average showgirl's dressing room table. There were ashtrays in abundance and even electric cigarette lighters in the back seat. This was big stuff back when it was new in '62, and still big stuff in the late '60s. It was just such a pleasure to drive; I hoped I could keep this car a long time.

The Minnesota Twins baseball team was a big deal in Minneapolis-St. Paul, and opening day was not to be missed. I rounded up the usual suspects, and we made a full day and full evening out of it. We met for lunch near the stadium out in Bloomington, probably at Eddie Webster's, ate a little, drank a lot, and headed over to the ballpark to watch the game and maybe have a beer or two dozen or so. I don't recall the outcome, but I think the Twins won, so we went back to Webster's after the game for more of the same. Eventually we had to call it quits, as tomorrow was another workday, and we all headed home, each in his own car.

I was driving the Cadillac, of course, and having driven a lot of miles in an impaired state, this was par for the course. You didn't worry too much about the steering or stopping or maneuvering the car in traffic. The big worry, when you had a bit too much to drink, was falling asleep on the way home. I had never fallen asleep, and it was only about 25 miles out to the house, so I wasn't too concerned.

I woke up just as I hit the guardrail on the right side of westbound I-494. I swerved away from the rail and headed back to the left at a fairly severe angle and hit a bridge wall at about 45 degrees. The Cadillac bounced off of the bridge wall and headed back across to the right. This time when I hit the right side guardrail, the car climbed up on it and did a slow roll over the rail, like a high jumper trying to clear the bar and just grazing it with his fanny.

You only have guardrails along freeways where there is something off of the road that you don't want people ending up in, like a ravine. That's where I was headed, straight down the embankment, rolling once more, I think, and where my head hit the windshield, not going through but giving me a nasty headache, which was the least of my problems. I climbed out of what was left of the car and with considerably difficulty, climbed back up the bank to the road. It seemed like it took about five minutes to get back up the road. It was really steep, and it must have been at least 40 feet from the road edge down to where the car lay. I was sweaty, with dirty hands and dirty clothes from the climb, a little blood on my forehead, and so disgusted with myself.

Son of a bitch. Damn. Damn. Damn.

I stood by the side of the road looking at the bent guardrail, the skid marks and some pieces of chrome that were lying at the point of the second impact with the guardrail. A car was slowing down and pulling off of the road. I could see it was the Minnesota State Police with the lights on the top and their trademark burgundy paint job. The cop walked up and said nothing. He looked at the skid marks and the bent guardrail, and he followed the trajectory of the car down the embankment. He turned and asked me if I was all right, and I said I thought so.

He aimed his flashlight back at the car and asked me what it was. I told him it was a '62 Cadillac Fleetwood. He asked if it had been in good shape. I said it was close to perfect. He said, "I think you totaled it. It looks like you really crashed it three times, hitting the rail back where I've got my car parked, then I can see where you hit the bridge, and then it looks like you hit right here again, and then up and over down into that ravine. That looks like three hits and then up and over. A lesser car would have broken up. You probably don't feel lucky right now, but you are a very lucky guy." I looked at the cop, and I could see he was an older guy, maybe in his early fifties. He seemed genuinely sympathetic: sorry about the car being wrecked and sorry for me for having done it.

Just then another police car pulled up. This was a Hennepin County sheriff driving a white cruiser. He looked down in the ravine and came over and stood right in front of me, barely hiding his contempt. I probably looked like hell and smelled pretty boozy too. "Well, well, well, another drunk tries to kill himself. You're taking him straight to jail, I presume," he said, "unless you want me to, as this is in my jurisdiction as well as yours."

I could see that the old cop was clearly irritated by the presumptuous attitude of the younger officer, trying to take over the arrest. "I have the situation under control here," the State cop said, hoping that was the end of it. The sheriff persisted, saying, "Hey, this is a clear case of drunken driving. What is there to talk about? Let's get him in your car or mine and get him to the cooler." They both stepped away from me to continue this out of earshot. I heard the younger guy say, "Is he a relative of yours or a neighbor's son?"

Now the old guy was getting mad. His integrity and judgment were being questioned. He raised his voice a bit. "I will handle this accident. It is under my control. The man has wrecked his car. He has had something to drink, no argument there. We didn't see it happen, and in fact, we don't even know exactly when it happened. We can only surmise what took place and what condition the driver was in at the time of the accident. I will file a full report that you and your superiors are welcome to read. Now get out of here."

The junior guy didn't say anything for a few seconds, just showed his contempt by giving him a big smile, as if to say, "I don't know why you're doing this, but I hope the driver made it worth your while." He got back in his car, stood on the gas, like a jilted teenaged boy, leaving a couple of streaks of rubber on the pavement. I thought I heard the old guy mutter "Asshole."

"OK," he said, "get in the front seat of the patrol car and stay there. You might want to say a prayer thanking the Almighty for keeping you alive. Your license says you live about five miles from here. Are you married?" I nodded. "Then you better say another one that she doesn't kill you. I'm going to take a couple of measurements of the skid marks and find out what mile marker we're near, so you can send a wrecker out here tomorrow and get the car over to a salvage yard. Then I'll get you home."

He was right, of course. I was lucky to be alive and really not hurt, just that headache. I wondered what was going to happen when we got to our house. On the way to the house he asked what I did and if I had kids and so on. When we got to the house, he said, "I'll just let you out here. Here's my name and phone number on this card. Call later tomorrow and see if my accident report is available. It should be. Listen, kid, you were very, very lucky. You might want to lay off the sauce or cut it all together. If I were you, I'd consider AA or something like that. Good luck."

I knew one thing for sure. I was most fortunate to have been in the care of that good cop.

Now, I had to face the wife. We had a lot of these kinds of encounters where either I did something expensive to the car or stayed away all night. This would be the first time I came home without the car. She could see I had had a nose full, and I probably looked like I been in a fight with my clothes all dirty from climbing back up that embankment. She listened for a little while and then said nothing, just turned and went back to bed. I knew what she was thinking... "How much more of this crap am I going to take? Next time it may be the cop who comes to the door because he is in the hospital or in the county morgue." I decided it would be a good idea to sleep on the sofa since I didn't want to take a shower and wake the kids.

I awoke the next morning and knew from my appearance that what seemed like a bad dream was all too real. Damn, why did I have to wreck that fine ride?

I called a towing company, agreed to meet them out on I-494 and got the car out of there. It was pretty bad. The body still looked straight, but all the glass was gone and not a single panel was unbent. What a damn mess I had made of that car. That old Jewish guy had faithfully done all the maintenance, kept it clean and indoors in a garage, and all of that was for naught. The big smooth V-8 motor, the silky Hydramatic transmission, all the gadgets and features were never going to be used again, at least not in this car. The tow truck guy took it to a salvage yard, and my insurance agent stopped by to look at it. He called and said it actually could be repaired because the frame had taken all those hits but was still straight. However, the economics wouldn't work, as it wouldn't be worth what it would cost to put it back together again. He said they would write me a check for $1700 and call it done. I took the check and bought a used Buick. It was the same color and would get me around OK, but it wasn't half the car that big Fleetwood was.

I called AA, and some guys came by the house to talk to me. I went to a few meetings and said that this wasn't for me. These guys were old drunks who lost everything and I was a young guy who still had wife #1, although I don't know for how much longer, and I was still employed. If I could just remember that one drink was too many, two might be just right, and three were never enough, I'd be OK.

Coming home one night in that Buick a few weeks later after I had a half-dozen martinis, I saw the lights of an oncoming car go out and then on and then off, flashing on and off every four seconds. As I got closer and more irritated, I sped up a bit to get past this idiot. Then it dawned on me what I was looking at. The oncoming driver was on the other side of a freight train that was crossing the road between us. The lights appeared to turn on and off because of the gap between the freight cars. Sweet Jesus! I hit the binders hard and stopped just a few feet short of the train. That was close.

The next day, I tried a different AA group, consisting mostly of young hotshot salesmen, like myself. I could relate to these guys because we all were on top of the world or fighting the depression that comes with the rejection that is always there in the world of sales. In any case, AA and these guys helped turn me around. You really have to decide to give it up for your own self-interest. You don't stop drinking for somebody else. You do it because it finally gets through your hard head that you're juggling dynamite and your very life depends on making a change.

Would you drink a tall cold glass of gasoline? Why not? Because you know it is likely to kill you in about ten minutes. The booze just takes longer.

It finally sunk in. I could die. The 50,000 men, women and children who do die horrible deaths in auto accidents every year were just not as lucky as I had been up to this point.

On October 8, 1970, I had my last drink. I hadn't wrecked my last car, as I would tear up a lot of hardware on the racetrack and out on the professional rally driver's circuit.

Nonetheless, I was now free of the demon booze. From the age of 15 to the age of 30, I had dissolved a lot of neurons in my brain, no doubt dropping my IQ by at least 25%. But the sauce didn't own me anymore.

Freedom!

# Thank You, David D. Buick

## 1965 Buick Super

*1965 Buick Super.*

This car had a tough act to follow. It was the replacement for the beloved 1962 Cadillac Fleetwood that I had totaled out in a bad crash on Opening Day of the Minnesota Twins baseball season.

I bought the Buick off of a used car lot with the insurance money from the Cadillac, and while it inspired no great passion on my part, it was a solid car, conservatively styled, and really never had a repair that I can recall.

Buick Supers were Buick's hot rods. They had the big motor out of the Roadmaster and the smaller body of the Special. More power and less weight did wonders for performance. This car was a real "sleeper" with its plain Jane steel-blue paint job, four doors, whitewall tires, low dollar wheel covers and a bland interior. You might be at a stoplight next to some kid with his buddies in a hopped up Chevy Camaro, a Plymouth Barracuda, or a breathed-on Ford Mustang, and when the light changed the old family sedan up and left, with the big four-barrel carb feeding about a gallon per mile into 400 cubic inches of V-8 muscle and they would be looking at your tail lights until you lifted. I didn't want to push my luck much further, so I would make my point off the line, accelerate rapidly up to about 70 mph and back it down. At the next light, they would look that car over and just shake their heads. They might have thought the car was on the bottle, that is, nitrous oxide injection, but it was bone stock.

Under the skin, the Buick was mechanically similar to the Cadillac and to the other Olds '88s, Pontiac Catalinas, and Chevy Impalas. They all had big bodies, ladder frame construction, large Uniroyal tires, powerful V-8s, and a nice blend of styling that was conservative but with a little sauciness to the design as well. They might have a little fin, a scallop out of the side, large rear-wheel openings, wrap-around windshields, and provided a ride that made you feel as if you were floating about six inches above the road.

In retrospect, I think that these, the cars of the middle '60s, were among the best cars that General Motors ever designed and built. You felt that you made a good practical decision when you bought a General Motors car. Ford had some decent cars, especially the Ford Galaxie 500, that had such great handling, but they didn't quite have the luxury and opulence that was part of the charm of the GM line. Even Rolls Royce was using GM Hydramatic transmissions.

Gas prices were starting to increase at an alarming rate and the big domestics couldn't match the imports' fuel economy.

Sound familiar? Typical miles per gallon on a full-size GM car might be 8-10 mpg around town and 14-16 out on the highway, if you kept it around 55-60 miles per hour. The imports, on the other hand, like the VW Beetle and the Toyota Corona could deliver 20 mpg around town and 30 mpg on the highway. In effect, if you drove an import, your gas mileage was double that of the domestic cars, and therefore your cost of gas was half that of the domestics. These imported cars were much smaller, and therefore much lighter in weight.

Weight is the enemy of good fuel economy. Aerodynamics are important, especially at higher speeds, but most cars are driven at 40 mph or less most of the time, and the weight of the car, particularly when accelerating up to cruising speed, is the critical factor. In the world of drag racing, a well-established rule of thumb is that every 100 pounds of weight differential between two otherwise equal cars will make a difference of a 1/10 of a second in a quarter mile drag race. In the world of racing, 1/10 of a second is quite significant. This difference in performance gave a good indication that heavier cars are less efficient to operate.

People started to worry a lot about the price of gas and how high it might go. They began to dump their big cars and buy imports in greater volumes every year. GM countered with the Chevette and Ford with the Pinto, but these were cheaply built cars, and while they were better on gas than their big full-size cousins, they didn't have the build quality of the imports.

Back in '62, when I was burning premium gas in the TR-3B, I was paying about 25 cents per gallon of premium and regular grade gas could be had for 18 cents per gallon. Now, gas had passed 40 cents per gallon for regular, and there was no end in sight. Even a big car man like me couldn't argue with the twin economic trends: namely, gas was becoming more expensive each month and the noble Buick was depreciating at an alarming rate.

The Buick was a good car, gave good value for its price, and the cost of a new car half its size would wipe out any savings in gas for years to come, provided that gas prices didn't get much higher. Most observers of the gas price trends were concluding the same thing: namely, there was no end in sight and you might as well take your loss now on the big car trade-in and hope to get some of it back in lower operating costs.

We still had the wife's VW Beetle all these years, so we were a bit ahead of the curve with her car, but our main ride, the one we took on vacations and trips back home to Michigan, had to change. I looked over the current stock of imports and small domestics and decided the car for us was the '69 Toyota Corona, a car about half the size and weight of the Buick Super and twice the gas mileage. And the price wouldn't be too bad. I think the Buick brought $1200 as a trade-in, so I had to pony up another $1000 to buy the little emerald-green Toyota.

Thank you, Mr. Buick.

# "And What of the Kids?"

## The Toyotas: '69 Toyota Corona, '70 Toyota Corona Mk. II Wagon

I had pretty much made up my mind to buy a small "foreign" car. The wife's VW had been with us for eight years now and, aside from some rust problems, hadn't really given us any trouble. I didn't think I wanted another VW, because aside from the VW Squareback or their Westphalia bus, I didn't think they had a car that was big enough in the back seat for my two kids, with a third one on the way.

I looked 'em all over: the Toyotas, Volkswagens, and the early Hondas. The Subarus and Mazdas had not yet arrived in any quantity on our shores. VW, with the Beetle, was the first to become popular here and had a dominant position in the marketplace. Renault had retreated to France by this time, defeated by poor service from an inadequate dealer network.

Toyota was setting up several dealers in Minneapolis, and we found two of them less than five miles apart. I bet those dealers liked that. We went back and forth between them until we got the best deal on the little Toyota Corona that kind of appealed to me. Rear window defrosters were standard and AM/FM radios were standard, while on American cars these features were an extra cost. One of the dealers gave me a rather good quality football to help make up my mind that I promptly handed off to my oldest boy. When the number two son began to whine, the dealer had to provide a second football. I couldn't make up my mind between the white one the "football" dealer offered and the turquoise model offered by his nearby competitor. Their prices were nearly identical, both around $2000 out the door.

We decided on the turquoise unit. I called the first dealer back and told him of my decision and asked him if he wanted his footballs back. He said, "No, you can keep them. Good luck with your new car." As a salesman myself, I couldn't be that gracious in defeat. But I remembered it and told myself that when I was beat by the other side, no point in blaming the customer.

The little car had a black vinyl interior. It didn't look cheap, though. It looked "integrated." The knobs were soft, the controls were small to my big Midwestern hands, and the radio was great. It had some pep with its four-cylinder engine. The mileage was amazing, usually around 30 mpg out on the highway. With domestics getting about half of that, it seemed like we were driving for free.

I had to admire the overall quality of the car. The paint was perfect, the seats and carpets had no loose strings, the trunk was finished off, and the jack and tire-changing tools came in their own neat little bag. When you looked under the hood, it was very tidy: there was the battery, there was the fuse box, and there was the distributor. It was all so neatly laid out.

I drove it for about a year, quite happy with my purchase, until temptation beckoned in the form of another Toyota, the Corona Mark II wagon that belonged to a friend of mine in AA. He bought it new, but had recently been given a company car by his employer and he wanted to sell it. He knew I liked the Toyota I had, so he approached me.

The wagon was going to be difficult to resist. It solved the one shortcoming of the Corona sedan, and that was a small trunk. I was a little hesitant about the fact that it was used, but it only had about 10,000 miles on it, and it would cost considerably less than a new one. I succumbed, once again, and it was now in our driveway. I cannot, for the life of me, recall what we did with the Corona. I think we just sold it privately through an ad in the paper, but I'm not sure.

We were now driving the "big" Toyota and enjoying it immensely. If GM or Ford bought one of these for evaluation of the competition, which they surely did, they must have wanted to cry. How were they going to compete against a product that was so complete and yet didn't cost that much to acquire, never mind the lower operating costs?

Again, the quality of the interior appointments, the pretty powder-blue paint job, and the efficiency of the design were all quite remarkable. We would put two of the kids in the back seat and the third one behind that seat in the "trunk" area, and they were as happy as clams because they didn't have the space fight that almost always occurs among kids on long trips. The gas mileage was a little less than the Corona, but we liked having more sheet metal around us and more room.

We were still living in the Minneapolis area, and we would drive once or twice a year to Holland, Michigan, through Chicago to see the wife's folks and mine, who lived farther north in Owosso, Michigan. The run from Minneapolis to Holland took about 12 hours. We would start out after supper, maybe at 9 PM and drive through the night, arriving at 9 AM, more or less. The kids would sleep most of that time, so it passed quickly for them. On one of these trips, I was running about ten over the limit and was pulled over near Black River Falls, Wisconsin, by a Wisconsin state trooper. He ticketed me, and we went together to a judge's office in the middle of the night to pay the fine. We didn't have a lot of cash, maybe $100, and the fine was $60. I asked him what would become of us if I couldn't pay up then and there. He said that the wife and I would be put in the slammer until the money was sent from elsewhere. "And what of the kids?" I asked. They would be taken temporarily to a county home for foster children. This was nuts. The trooper was serious. I imagined that resisting arrest might cause an automatic response, resulting in a fatality, maybe mine. We paid the fine and left. What an abuse of authority!

I didn't speed in Wisconsin for a long time, or ever consider it for a vacation.

The only mechanical problem the pretty blue wagon ever gave me was a water pump failure just outside of Alpena, Michigan. Actually it was the belt that failed, and we were able to find a replacement belt to limp back to Ann Arbor. The pump itself was also failing, so we had a new one installed for $85. That was the only expense other than gas and oil that occurred with that car. But it did cause a couple of other problems that hastened its eventual departure from the fleet.

By this time, we had moved back to Michigan from Minneapolis, and I was in the employ of Scan-Optics, a Connecticut-based manufacturer of optical character recognition (OCR) systems. These systems were used to read data directly off of input forms. If a customer and/or our staff would design its payroll or order forms in such a manner that they could be optically read, you did not need expensive data entry personnel, or at least you needed fewer of them.

One of the biggest market segments we went after was manufacturing. They had tons of paper in use for everything from inventory to sales orders to personnel matters. GM, Ford and Chrysler were big targets for us, and we spent a lot of time with their various divisions. We did have a lot of success with GM, selling systems to GM Parts Division, GM Corporate, and Buick Motor Division. Arriving at one of these facilities in my Toyota Corona Mark II wagon was not a good idea. The parking lot guards were openly hostile and UAW (United Auto Workers) union workers would threaten you verbally from time to time. At one Chrysler facility, I was refused admission.

This was beginning to become a pattern and a problem. We had a good solution for the elimination of the expense of excess data entry personnel. These systems cost the customer about $400,000, and my commission was about 6%

or $24,000 on each sale. If my $3000 Toyota was going to cost me even one such sale, it had to go. I thought about buying a used GM car just for calls on the Big Three auto manufacturers, but decided I would just go with the flow and buy a new one and sell the Toyota, whose only sin was it was such a good car that people wanted to buy them at the expense of a union guy's job. If we fast forward to 2006, we find the same two companies in a very similar situation. My father used to say there were no new games, just new players. The 2006 players are the same as the 1970 players. Thirty-seven years is a long time to come up with a competitive alternative to the Japanese, no?

It wasn't that the union guy could not assemble a car that was the equal of the Toyota. The management of the auto companies themselves were at fault by not competing head on with the Japanese. We called them copycats, which they were, but where they really beat us was on the plant floor. Their manufacturing systems were much more efficient than ours, probably due in large part to their listening to Dr. W. Edward Deming, the American who taught them. Their designs were easier to build. The difference in labor costs was a factor, no doubt. Yet Honda and Toyota began to manufacture cars in this country, and while they were paying somewhat less than the Big Three's union wages, they were paying the US worker more than their homeland workers, and they were still making money.

I didn't need any rough stuff from union guys or objections from plant managers to impede making the sale of the big profitable OCR systems to the manufacturing segment of the market. I was off to the local Chevrolet dealer to order a new 1973 Chevrolet Monte Carlo.

# Grosse Pointe Gothic

## 1973 Chevrolet Monte Carlo

*One of the best GM cars ever built.*

Monte Carlo. What does that make you think of? Princess Grace and the casinos in Monaco? The French Riviera and Grand Prix Formula 1 racing? All of the above? It is a neat name for a car, and a name you wouldn't want to waste on an ordinary car.

The 1970-72 Monte Carlo was a nice upgrade from the standard Chevelle. It shared the same body style but had a nicer interior and was available only in a two-door. It was quite conservative, however, compared to the new 1973 edition of the Monte Carlo.

It seemed odd to some observers that Chevrolet brought out a totally new car that really looked nothing like the 1972 Monte Carlo, yet Chevrolet continued using the same name. It was a big hit because it was a great-looking car that had a solid 350 cubic-inch engine that made considerable horsepower, had excellent handling, and had no real competition. It had the secret sauce: styling plus substance. Ford had nothing like it, and while the other GM divisions had the Pontiac Grand Prix, Olds Cutlass, and Buick Regal, they didn't have the overall styling appeal of the Monte Carlo.

*Car and Driver* thought the styling was a bit over the top and called it "Grosse Pointe Gothic" as a bit of a putdown. It had all the usual styling cues of a classic rich man's sports car, only larger. You know—long hood, short trunk, tight cabin and enough muscle to back up its sporty looks. *Motor Trend* named it their "Car of The Year."

I decided that if the Toyota Corona Mark II wagon was going to be replaced by American iron, you couldn't get more American than a hot new Chevrolet. I took my two young sons, Mike and Joe, with me over to Rampy Chevrolet on the west side of Ann Arbor to get some brochures and look at the one they had on the show-room floor. Joe noticed the badge near the quarter panel window on the side of the roof, and it made a big impression on him. He would touch it and stare at it for a minute or two. It was kind of a medieval shield that he can describe to this day.

I decided to buy the Monte Carlo and made a deal with the sales guy. My big problem was the Monte's color. Chevrolet had about three or four different bronze or taupe paint colors that all looked good. I finally narrowed it down to two, and the sales guy made it easy by placing orders for one car in each color with the options I wanted, and I could decide which one I wanted when they came in.

Six weeks passed, which seemed like six months, and I finally got a call from Rampy Chevrolet. Both cars were in.

I waited until the boys were out of school for the day, and we headed out to the dealership. One of the reasons I brought the boys was to get some input on the color, as I would still have a tough time deciding.

Thinking back, it didn't occur to me to ask my wife Nancy what she thought. I guess I just didn't involve her in these matters, and she didn't seem to mind.

But let's get back to this year's excitement. After serious consultations with my six- and seven-year-old boys, we decided on the lighter of the two bronze colors and got the delivery process started. You can begin to ruin your kids at an early age, and I guess I launched the process that day. They have been into cars ever since. I think there is something in the Torah about the sons paying for the sins of the father. Their sons will have to pay too.

This was a great road car in that you could drive it all day and not tire of it. It had big tires, BFG Polyglass, which were a big technological leap forward at the time. These glass-belted tires would wear longer than those that had been available, and they would really stick to the road, rain or shine.

I got a great opportunity to explore the limits of its handling one day in what could have been a life-ending situation. I was following an old pickup truck down US-23 just north of Ann Arbor when the tailgate came loose and the contents of the truck began to unload. This guy must have been moving all his possessions to some place, as he had a stove, a refrigerator, a washing machine and maybe a chest of drawers. These large objects came off in rapid succession and bounced crazily across both lanes, almost like a bunch of footballs might. I had to weave between these while they were still moving, left and right, up and down. The stove was a particularly close call. If any of those had come up onto the hood and through the windshield, it wouldn't have been pretty. More than likely, it would have been fatal. I was steering a slalom course, hard left, hard right, and hard right again onto the shoulder. It was over in a matter of just a few seconds, and I really believe Mr. Monte played a big part in my survival.

My business travels took me across five states; the Monte was made for that kind of freeway travel. I would occasionally take a "blue highway," a two-lane asphalt road with some twists in it to have the opportunity to play race car driver. For a front engine, rear-wheel drive car, it was one of the best handling cars available at that time.

Speaking of engines, the Chevrolet 350 and 327 cubic-inch engines were and are some of the best engines ever made. They're really the same motor, except that in the 350 the piston travels a little farther, increasing its displacement by 23 inches. This increased piston travel is called "stroking," and it is made possible by making the connecting rod between the piston and the crankshaft a little shorter so that the piston has to go farther down in the cylinder. The displacement increase means that the motor can ingest a larger volume of gas and air, thereby making more power.

For many years, almost all of the racing engines in sprint cars, racing stock cars, and even some Indy cars were based upon the Chevy 327/350. The 800 HP engines used in today's NASCAR stock cars are direct descendants of these engines. Ford built 289, 302 and 351 cubic-inch engines to compete with the Chevy mills, and they did make equivalent horsepower. Mopar (Plymouth, Dodge and Chrysler) also made strong V-8s, displacing 318 and 360 cubic inch, as well as the mighty Hemi, that they installed in very light street cars that did well at the drag strip and on Woodward Avenue in Detroit. It has always been less expensive, however, to make horsepower out of Chevy parts because so many aftermarket components were built for the 327/350 engines. Think of Chevrolet as the Microsoft of V-8 engines in the racing world.

These 327/350 engines could easily make 400 HP without a great deal of expense. They were called "small blocks" to distinguish them from the "big blocks" that Chevy and Ford and Dodge also built. These "big blocks" would displace 427, 428 and 460 cubic inches. With size comes weight, and weight is always the enemy of performance, so the "small block" was almost always preferred for racing applications.

The Monte Carlo had the 350 engine with all its potential for mayhem. The neat thing was you didn't have to hop it up to make it perform. It would smoke those big BFG Polyglass tires at the slightest provocation. When a car looked good, performed good and made you feel good, you were a happy customer. The Monte Carlo sold well. Young guys bought 'em and old guys, like my father, may his memory be for a blessing, bought them as well. It never came out as a convertible. That may have been an oversight on Chevy's part. I think it would have sold well. It might have been tough to duplicate the shape of the top and its "opera" windows that were part of its charm.

Covering my five-state territory, I believe I put in excess of 50,000 miles on it in the 18 months I owned it. At the same time, the Arabs were getting restless, forming something called OPEC, and the price of fuel was going up rapidly and the supplies were beginning to get scarce. I was beginning to think small again, and my next car was probably going to have an engine half as big as this one. I knew I was going to miss it, all that power, the surefootedness and the looks. *Car and Driver* magazine had kidded about its styling clichés, but Chevrolet had a big winner in this car. I don't believe I ever purchased another GM car that was as satisfying to own as the 1973 Chevrolet Monte Carlo.

If you ever want to hear "The Song of The Small Block," just stand on the gas and wind up a Chevy 327/350 to the red line on the tach. The acceleration is breathtaking. It might take a block or two for your ears to catch up to your head.

You might not remember the words, but you won't forget the melody.

# You Don't Get Smart All at Once

## The 1973 Capris:

## '73 Mercury Capri 4, '73 Mercury Capri V-6

*Nancy and I are pictured about to leave for a U of M football game in the Capri V-6 in September of 1974.*

I had seen Mercury Capris running around for several years, and the design intrigued me. If I ever needed to replace my wife's aging '62 Volkswagen, this might be a good candidate.

There was a rumor going around the household that the demon rust had been eating away at the floor of the VW to the extent that one could actually see, through a very small hole, the road passing beneath the car.

Upon investigation, I discovered two disturbing things. There was indeed a hole, and the back seat floor had a funny smell, not unlike that of an outhouse. I asked the boys about it and they said it had been there for some time, and that on occasion, when they could no longer hold it, they would tinkle in the hole. And since it was difficult to aim accurately at that small hole, especially when the car was moving, well, that's where the odor came from. I decided it was time to replace the VW with something I thought I would like to have, if I were my wife, which is quite a different thing from what she might like to drive if the decision were hers alone to make.

That VW had been a good and faithful servant for the past ten years. After we bought its replacement, we sold the VW to our mailman. I understand he never drove it, just parked it on his farm. He did mention that he noticed that the battery, located under the rear seat, was now resting comfortably on the ground. I guess the rust caused in part by road salt from below and inaccurate aim from above had finally consumed most of the rear floor.

Nancy just needed a small car to get back and forth between classes at the University of Michigan and trips to her job at St. Thomas Catholic Church. She probably drove less than 25 miles per week. It seemed to me that the Capri would be perfect for this kind of work.

Devon Lincoln Mercury sold Mercury Capris in Ann Arbor. The cars were built in Germany and were the first imports sold by a Ford division, soon to be followed by the German-built Merkur. I never have figured out why Ford Motor Company thought the Lincoln Mercury Division was the place to sell small foreign cars. I suspect Ford Division didn't want competition from these cars in their Ford dealerships, but L/M sales guys and L/M customers were buyers for Lincoln Town Cars, Lincoln Continentals, and Mercury Marquis, not little imports. Those dealers would have preferred to sell fancy trucks to small foreign cars. The Capris and Merkurs were all metric, so the mechanics had to buy metric tools in addition to their regular English measurement wrenches.

There was a two-word description for Merkur owners, and that was "Ford Employee." I'll bet they didn't sell more than a few thousand of them to non-employees. Ford people could buy them under Ford's A Plan, which was below dealer cost, and Ford encouraged their employees to buy them. They were good cars, but the styling was kind of homely, the name was dumb, and the Merkur was introduced around the same time as the Ford Taurus/Mercury Sable, cars that people were excited about and both versions were sales successes.

I went over to Devon L/M and persuaded an overweight salesman to get out of his comfortable chair and find a set of keys for a new Capri. He gave me the keys, a magnetic dealer plate, and said I could find the car around the back of the dealership. The car was a bronze-colored coupe with a four-cylinder engine and an AM radio and a four-speed manual transmission, no air, no power anything. Dealers sometimes called these stripped cars "beer cans" because they had very little in them. This one was priced that way too, with a window sticker of about $3000.

I took it out onto Stadium Boulevard and headed out to the freeway, I-94 westbound, where I would see how it ran up around 70 and then exited to a small twisty two-lane road that would take me back to Ann Arbor and the dealership. The little car was impressive. The small four-cylinder engine was willing; the shifts were smooth with a nice "snick" sound as you changed gears. The English say that they "select" the next gear, where we "shift" to it. The dash had a big tach, actually the same size as the speedometer, and I loved the bucket seats. Nothing fancy, but it all worked nicely together. The back seats looked pretty roomy too. I liked the car and was sure the wife would like it too, as it would be a lot like the VW in size but had a lot more pep and room inside than the VW Beetle did. And it was German built as well, meaning good quality.

I brought her over to the dealership the next day and asked her what she thought of it. She said it was "nice," but she wasn't crazy about the color, which she referred to as brown. I said it was bronze, but she said it was a brown car and she couldn't get too excited about a brown car, but she didn't put up too much resistance. We took it for a ride, and she said it was OK. Talk about "damned by faint praise." She did like the fact that it had a manual shift. Her only other car had been the VW, and it was a manual and she thought automatic transmissions were invented for those uncoordinated types who could not master a manual tranny, which I guess is partly true.

I noticed that the Capri also came in a fancier version. This was the V-6 edition that also had air conditioning, a nicer interior, a better radio, and a better-looking dash. It was four or five hundred more than the base four-cylinder under consideration.

She said that since we still had the Monte Carlo for trips to Grandma and vacations, the lesser Capri would be OK, if only it wasn't brown. We looked around the lot, and there were a few other colors, none of which she liked any better than the brown, I mean bronze. We haggled a bit with the sales guy and got him to take a few hundred off, so when the taxes and whatever else were tacked back on, we were out the door for around $2900.

After we had the car at the house for a few weeks, I noticed that I was borrowing it more and more to run errands in because it was so much fun to whip around town, going up and down through the gears. And the little car would get 28-32 mpg, which wasn't bad, as the Arabs were taking more and more of our disposable income each month, at least the part spent on gas and oil. The Monte Carlo was still the better highway car, but I had put 50,000 miles on it already and it was beginning to show a little wear and tear. No dents or scratches or missing hubcaps, just the usual stuff, like tires and shocks needing replacement. And as there was no end in sight for gas price increases, that Chevy 350 V-8 was starting to look pretty thirsty to me. Worse than that, the trade-in value of GM and Ford cars with big V-8s was in free fall, so I thought I better make a move.

I went back to Devon L/M and took out a loaded V-6 Capri for a ride. The V-6 transformed the car from being peppy to being fast, all the way up over 100 mph. It sounded nice too. I have always wondered why the sound of a car has been important to me. It just is. I think a car's sound is like the aroma associated with delicious food. The smell isn't the food, but if the scent is good, the food is good. If a car sounds good, it generally is good.

I have this theory about engine sounds. These are all four-cycle engines that make their noise on the third cycle, the power stroke, right after the fuel is ignited. When there are four cylinders, one of the cylinders is on the third cycle or power stroke. If it is a V-8, two cylinders of the eight fire at about the same time, giving a deeper sound and a more solid beat. If it is a six-cylinder engine, each cylinder fires at its own time, and no two cylinders fire at exactly the same time. So the beats are closer together than on a four-cylinder and make the engine sound busier and a bit noisier. If you listen to an engine closely, you can usually tell how many cylinders it has. You can also tell by class. Almost all mid-size and larger cars have V-6s today, especially General Motors. Late Ford Mustangs have either V-6s or V-8s. Earlier versions were either fours or eights. If the Mustang has a single exhaust on the left side, it is surely a four or a V-6, never a V-8. If it has two exhaust pipes, it is always a V-8. Ford's big cars like Lincolns, the Crown Victoria and the Mercury Marquis have the same V-8s.

The V-6 Capri had dual exhausts as well, and they sounded pretty rorty. The Capri charm was working again, and I could see us having two Capris in the garage, which is exactly what happened. My V-6 had a light green exterior with a black interior. It was pretty well tricked out with A/C, plush interior with nice bucket seats, AM/FM cassette radio, and on the exterior there was a black stripe on the rocker panel below the door to further distinguish it from the four-cylinder model.

The wife noticed the differences and didn't seem to mind, except for the color of course, which would remain an issue for the life of that car. I learned a painful lesson in that deal, namely, the color of the car is much more important to the fairer sex than I had ever realized. That car's venial sins, of which there were very few, became mortal sins, because of the bronze/brown color. I can think of only two problems her car ever had. One of which was the clutch cable, which broke twice. This was a cable between the clutch pedal and the clutch itself. We replaced it twice, as I think some kind of corrosion took place, and it eventually would snap. The other problem she had was a chronic one, and that was the passenger side door. It would come out of adjustment and fail to lock, although it appeared to be closed properly. I think the poor lady suffered with that door for several years before it eventually got fixed. You don't get smart all at once.

The V-6 Capri was getting lots of miles on it, as I covered a five-state area for my employer. I would organize trips so that the prospects and existing customers would be visited in a pattern that was roughly a circle that started in Ann Arbor, down through Toledo, over to Columbus, west to Dayton, on to Indianapolis, maybe a run out to Terre Haute, and back up through Ft. Wayne to Ann Arbor.

That swing would put a thousand miles on a car in one week. You might wonder how any business got done if I were driving an average of 200 miles every day, which would take three to four hours. The secret was to meet with a customer or prospect or two early in the day and leave for the next town late in the day or even after supper. I didn't mind arriving in the next town at 9 PM, as it was just another motel, probably the same one I had stayed at three weeks previously. You became a creature of habit, knowing where the good restaurants were and which gas stations usually had the lowest prices. As a generalization, gas was always cheaper in the big cities and meals were cheaper in the small towns.

The Capri V-6 was more than a "business coupe" for me. I used to drag race it too. One of our service engineers, Bob, whose last name escapes me, bought a Capri V-6 identical to mine, except for color, as his was bright red, a color my wife admired, of course. Bob and I would drive our cars down to Milan Dragway just south of Ann Arbor and have some fun drag racing each other. When we got there, we would take the spare tire and jack out of the trunk and the air cleaner off of the carburetor. Removing the tire and jack was to save weight and we would arrive there with no more than a quarter tank of gas for the same reason. Taking the air cleaner off allowed more air to enter the carb and that would result in a slight increase in power. Did you know that *carburetor* is a French word that means "Do Not Adjust"?

Bob was about 40 pounds lighter than I was and ten years younger. I mention all this weight stuff because it is an article of faith among drag racers that, all other things being equal, every 100 pounds difference between two identical cars will cost the heavier vehicle 1/10 of a second in a quarter mile drag race. A tenth of a second is significant because at 60 miles per hour you're moving at 88 feet per second, so in a tenth of a second, the faster car has traveled almost nine feet farther than the slower car. We would cover the quarter mile distance in 17 seconds and change, traveling about 80 miles per hour, as we crossed through the timing lights at the finish line. Our cars were about 15 feet long, so that tenth of a second made a difference of just about half a car length, leaving no doubt who won the race.

This was cheap fun. I think it was about $10 to gain entry to the track, and while we did toast the rear tires a bit, the launching box at the starting line had a lot of rubber laid down, we really didn't leave much of our tires there, as they just spun in the previous driver's rubber. I would never light up the tires in town at some stoplight grand prix. It just wouldn't be worth it to leave two streaks of black rubber and possibly fry the clutch or damage the gears in the tranny through some ill-timed speed shift. But when you're sitting in the starting box at a drag strip, you're in a different world.

When Bob and I raced, it was side by side all the way down the track, and the outcome was in doubt until you crossed the finish line and a light came on above the winner's lane. You had another quarter mile to slow down and turn to the right off of the track and head back to the pits to talk it over. Halfway back to the pit area you drove past a small booth where a track worker handed you a timing slip with the elapsed time and your speed at the finish line as well as who won your race. We would talk about it for 15 minutes, with the winner laughing and joking and the loser saying, "Let's have another go."

It was pretty even, although Bob would win about 60% of the time. He was quicker off the line and that usually was enough of an edge to take the win. Then one day the equation was altered. Bob showed up with some new rear tires that were just slightly wider than stock. The additional traction his car had meant he now won 100% of the time. We raced a few more times, but we knew we were no longer equal, so we started racing other guys who had Ford Pintos with V-6s or other smaller foreign cars. That was OK but not nearly as much fun. I think Bob regretted his decision, and I guess I could have popped for tires like his, and we would have been equal again. He got in some kind of wreck with his Capri later that year, and I think he fixed it up enough to sell it and went back to a pickup truck.

I went to Milan in the Capri occasionally the next season to race whoever showed up in my class, accompanied by a real character I worked with named Billy Cotton. He had a fire-breathing Chevy Nova with about 500 horsepower that either won or broke. That car would make incredible noise, and the ground under it seemed to tremble.

Billy and I worked together for about five years, and we eventually got involved in another kind of racing, sports car racing. But that story is a few cars down the road.

The little bronze/brown Capri that the wife was driving would last her until 1979 when it was replaced by a new Subaru wagon. Somewhere late in the Capri's life, it needed a new muffler, so I put one on her car that gave it kind of a sporty sound. That was around Christmas that year, so I recall that before it was put on the car I had it wrapped as one of her Christmas presents, along with whatever else I gave her. When she took the wrappings off, she was not amused. Thank God I had some other stuff she did like, or I might have been wearing that muffler.

The miles kept piling up on my V-6, as I circulated around the five states I covered for Scan-Optics. There were close to 40,000 miles on that car in just 15 months. I thought briefly about trading it in on a new '74, but they put more emissions stuff on the '74, heavier bumpers, and a slightly bigger motor, yet the car magazines said it was slower and heavier than the '73s. So, I started to look around a bit. I was also beginning to make some big sales for the company, and the commission checks were substantial. I discovered that if I wasn't careful I might make over $100,000 that year which was a lot of money back in '74. I wasn't careful, the money kept rolling in, and I felt like I was hitting the big time.

I told the wife it was time to get something more substantial to reflect our new prosperity. She has always been a believer in living below our means, and a good part of the reason we had a bit in the bank is that she didn't like restaurants or country clubs or flashy clothes. I had no such inhibitions. I was off to get a new Lincoln or Cadillac.

Nancy did offer the observation that every guy who owned three liquor stores or a fleet of trucks had one of those American luxury cars, but the people with serious money drove foreign cars like Mercedes and Jaguars. I was quite taken back by that observation and had been burned before driving foreign cars while trying to sell systems to the Big Three auto companies. Nonetheless, I knew she had an eye for style, so I headed over to the Mercedes and Jaguar dealers in Detroit. The Mercedes left me kind of cold. They were good cars but were so conservatively styled. The Jaguar sedan was another matter. It was beautiful. It knocked you down. I took one out for a test drive on a parkway that ran along the Rouge River, and I was hooked.

The green Capri's days were numbered. It was about to be replaced by one of the best cars I have ever owned (or been owned by): a 1974 Jaguar XJ6L sedan.

# "All Singing, All Dancing"

## 1974 Jaguar XJ6L Sedan

*The Jaguar XJ6L parked at the Concours D'Elegance.*

Jaguar cars were the pride and sorrow of England. Beautiful to look at, finely sculpted objects of envy, they carried a reputation for general unreliability that tested the loyalty of all but the most die-hard owners. Few faults could be found with the motor, drive train or suspension, but like many English cars, the electrical components were sadly out of date and temperamental, particularly vulnerable to moisture. Aside from the electrical faults, they were beautiful cars and a joy to drive.

Jaguars had been around since the 1930s under the leadership of Sir William Lyons and were known for winning the 24 Hours of Le Mans, the famous race held each year in France. Cars like the original XK 100, the stunning XK120 roadster, and the Jaguar XKE secured Lyon's and Jaguar's reputation for beautiful cars that were surprisingly affordable for their pedigree. I believe that the Museum of Modern Art in New York still has a Jaguar XKE roadster on display as one of the most beautiful cars ever built.

Besides the roadsters, they produced a number of attractive sedans with both six and twelve-cylinder engines. These were "fitted," as the Brits would say, with all the amenities, including burled walnut dashboards, Connolly leather upholstery, power everything, and a sophisticated suspension that made these large, rather heavy cars handle as if they were lightweight roadsters. The V-12 engine offered more power than the straight in-line six-cylinder motor, but the six had been under continuous improvement for 30 years, so it was rock solid with tremendous low end torque. In England, versions of these cars were sold under the name of Daimler and Vanden Plas with differing trim levels. The cars exported to the United States were loaded with everything.

Sales in the States were slow. Fewer than 3000 Jaguars were sold here in 1974. Part of the reason may have been price. A new Cadillac or Lincoln could be bought for under $10,000, and Jags ran between $12,000 and $15,000, depending on which motor was in the car. Mercedes were priced in line with Jaguars, and there was very little movement (negotiation potential) in their pricing, at least at the dealer I had visited. But Mercedes' reputation was pretty solid, so they didn't have to do "deals" with the unwashed who came in looking for a better price.

I drove into metro Detroit one fine day, flush with recent prosperity, and stopped first at the Mercedes dealer on Woodward Avenue, out near the tony suburbs of Birmingham and Bloomfield Hills. He had several on the showroom floor, but he must have made the judgment that I was just another dreamer who wanted to waste his afternoon. A demo ride was out of the question, and discussions of price were terminated with "The price for that particular vehicle is displayed on the right rear window. Do you have any other questions?" It was implied that if you hoped to bargain, you obviously couldn't afford this car.

I had two reactions, the first being, "You haughty little prick, you just cost yourself a sale." I thought I should tell him, "Look, pal, I can buy and sell your ass and that French waiter act just brought your commission down to zero dollars." Then I thought, why should I educate this guy? Hopefully, he will blow many more sales like this, and that will be justice done. Besides, I wasn't crazy about the cars he had there. They looked nice on the outside, but the interiors were so plain and the seats looked like the kind of black leatherette one might find in a low end Toyota.

It was off to the Jaguar dealer in Westland, Bob Owens Jaguar/MG/Subaru. This dealership was a bit less pretentious, I think, in part because they handled a range of cars at completely opposite ends of the economic spectrum, and partly because it was on Ford Road in Westland, a blue-collar suburb if there ever was one. I met a charming Englishman there, one Eddie Atkinson, who was exactly the right guy to explain the merits of the car and who had no qualms about letting me have one to take out for a demo ride by myself.

Just a quick aside about Eddie—I believe Eddie has finally retired from the car business. In later years, I would stop at the BMW dealership in Ann Arbor where he was the sales manager and reminisce about past adventures like the impromptu 72-hour trip we took to Florida to see the 24 Hours of Daytona. We left Detroit at 3 PM on a Friday, arrived in Daytona for the 3 PM Saturday afternoon start, left shortly after the 3 PM Sunday afternoon finish, and arrived back in Detroit by 3 PM on Monday. Ten of us went the 2400 miles in 72 hours in a small Winnebago, stopping only to take on beer and fuel and empty the toilet's holding tank. Good times.

The Jaguar on the show-room floor was the XJ6L model. "XJ" meant sedan, "6" was the engine size in cylinders, and the "L" meant "Long Wheelbase." This model had more back seat legroom than a standard XJ, and the longer body stretched the horizontal lines in a pleasing manner.

The exterior of the car was a color I hadn't seen before. It was gold with the slightest hint of a green in the gold. The interior picked up the green with medium-green leather seats. The ceiling and floor carpet were tan, and the dashboard was a combination of dark burled walnut and black leather. There was an enormous console between the front bucket seats with a thin chrome plated shift lever above the transmission's detents. The console was topped with a large glove box compartment, and at the very back of the console there were air conditioning/heating outlets for the passengers seated in the rear. The bucket seats wrapped around you like a baseball player's glove would cradle the ball. You got the feeling that this car was well thought out and built by craftsmen.

This model was loaded with every feature Jaguar offered. It was "All Singing, All Dancing," a phrase we used to use to describe a car that lacked nothing. The XJ Series first appeared as a standard length model in 1969 and had five years of improvements before the long-bodied version was exported to the States in 1974.

It didn't seem like too much trouble for the dealership to open up a side door to the show room and roll this car out to the parking lot. They took down my name, looked at my driver's license, and said that I shouldn't put more than 25 miles on the car. I asked Eddie if he wanted to come along, and he said he had to take care of some other things just then. "Just be careful, we don't want to have to put it in the body shop when you return," he said.

I pulled out onto Ford Road and headed east. Was it my imagination or were people staring at me like I was driving a spaceship? I could see that this car would have an impact on people, people who weren't necessarily car people, for two reasons: namely, it was quite different from anything else on the street and it was beautiful. I turned off of Ford Road and went north to get onto Hines Drive, a parkway that twisted back and forth, as it followed the Rouge River as it wound its way towards Dearborn.

The car was in its element in the twisty stuff. As a curve came up and I slowed a little for it, the car seemed to say, "Don't do that, keep the speed up a bit, so I can show you my stuff." I would take the next curve a bit faster, and the car handled that just fine with no heeling over, no squeal from the big Dunlop tires, and no drama. The acceleration was brisk, and I was surprised to find that I was driving 20 mph over the limit.

I didn't want to take it back. It gave me the kind of kick in the pants and activated the grin muscles in a way I hadn't experienced since my first new car, the Triumph TR-3B, twelve years earlier. Reluctantly, I drove back to the dealership and tried to park it defensively, so it wouldn't get a door ding. I was already beginning to think of it as mine.

Eddie was out of the store when I got back, but another guy stepped up and said he was Eddie's buddy and he would answer my questions. Car sales guys often do that, that is, cover for each other so that Eddie's sale would still belong to him. The favor would be returned when this guy asked Eddie to cover for him.

I wanted my interest in the car to be taken seriously, but I didn't want to look too eager either. When I inquired about the price, he said they didn't discount much but the price was somewhat negotiable. Fair enough. The window sticker was around $12,000 plus taxes, dealer prep, license and registration, and options. There weren't any options to haggle about, so we just postponed the price negotiations until I returned.

I took some brochures home to look over and sell the wife on the car. The brochure had a picture of the car in the gold color and green-leather interior, so I was able to say, "Just like this one." She liked the car, and she liked the color too.

I think she liked the idea of a Jaguar, but if she did, she kept that thought to herself. She did say something along the lines of, "Now the neighbors will think we have money, and that might not be so good, might make them envious." I reminded her that we did have a lot more money than we had ever had before, and I liked to be envied. I also reminded her that she was partly responsible for my looking at Jaguars in the first place. I had told her that we were doing well financially, and I was thinking about replacing the Capri V-6 with a Cadillac or Lincoln. I reminded her that she was the one who said that all the guys who owned three party stores drove Cadillacs, but the fancy women in the automobile ads in her haute couture magazines were all pictured as drivers or passengers in Mercedes or Jaguars.

The other vote for a Jaguar came from my boss, Alan Ware, another Englishman. We had just signed a big contract in Toledo and were driving down to Columbus in the Capri where we were to pick up another contract the following day. He wasn't crazy about the Capri and suggested I think about another car. I replied that I was thinking about a Cadillac or Lincoln. He said that I should consider the Jaguar as a possibility. So, both of my bosses were in agreement that they would prefer to see me in a fancy foreign car, with one of them having an obvious preference for English steel.

When I mentioned to Alan that English cars in general suffered a bit of a bad reputation in this country, he said it was a different deal in England. There, every Sunday morning about 11 AM, men trotted out to the curb, tool kit in hand, lifted the bonnet, the hood to us, and tightened all the electrical connections, checked the battery, and topped off the dashpots on the downdraft S.U. carburetors. After an hour of this, the car was pronounced ready for another week's service. After visiting the pub for one or two quick pints, the husband was late for Sunday dinner for the hundredth consecutive time, but all was well within the British Empire.

The wife wondered how I would dispose of the Mercury Capri V-6. We just happened to live on a cul-de-sac, Cayuga Place, that came south off of Stadium Boulevard, the main east/west artery across the south side of Ann Arbor. Between 10,000 and 15,000 cars came by each day of the week. On a University of Michigan football Saturday, perhaps 20,000 cars drove slowly past our house, once headed west and then heading east after the game. We lived there from '71 to '99, and I must have sold 30 cars off of that corner.

I never wanted to trade a car in to a new car dealer because he can only pay wholesale or less and still remain in business. Selling it myself could be a pain, but I got closer to getting the retail price, which was usually 20% better than using it as a trade-in, where you only received its wholesale value, if that. The secret to getting my price was to spend a weekend really detailing (cleaning) the car, inside and out, and especially under the hood. The oil would have to be changed and the wipers replaced with new ones. I would make sure the interior was spotless. When there are no issues with the car, the price paid will be pretty close to what you were asking. I should expect to be bargained down about 10%, but figured that all in when I set the asking price. I had paid about $3300 for the '73 Capri V-6 and probably got $2500 for it. It ran well, looked good, had a spotless engine bay, clean interior, and had no chips or dings on the body. Clean 'em up, lads, and you'll get top dollar.

Back at the dealership a day or so later, I asked for Eddie. Again, he was away from the store, out sick or maybe he took a vacation day. I was going to have to deal with his buddy, and hopefully he would take care of Eddie. The car with taxes and dealer prep totaled up to around $13,800 or thereabouts. I managed to get the price down to $12,000 OTD, that is, out the door. I had saved $1500 to $1800 over the full retail but would have paid more if necessary. I never bargained hard for a car that I wanted badly because I knew that, in the long run, $200 to $500 one way or the other didn't matter to me, and if the dealer made a bit more of a profit, good for him. He would treat me right.

The deal was done, and he said to bring it back when I had a thousand miles on it, and they would inspect it and fix anything that was wrong with it. I called him four days later and said I had a thousand miles on the "clock," as the English would say, and I wanted to schedule an appointment. He laughed and told me that most people bought these cars to be seen in and usually wouldn't have a thousand miles on them in a month. He asked if I had turned it off since I bought it. I had, reluctantly.

I made the appointment for the next day and brought it back to the dealer. There were no problems, so they just changed the oil and filter and sent me on my way. The service manager said I might have accidentally discovered the secret to a happy relationship with English cars and that was to drive them a lot so that the electrical components wouldn't fail from just sitting around. I knew that from my Triumph TR-3B days. Drive these English cars every day, and they'll be happy.

He didn't have to tell me to use the car. I drove it everywhere, and it didn't get turned off much. Thousand-mile weeks were common. I have never been crazy about flying on commercial airlines, so if I had to go to Ft. Wayne or Indianapolis, I would often drive. It's about 150 miles to Ft. Wayne and another 115 to Indy from there. Columbus was just three hours away; Cleveland about the same, maybe another hour. I would stick an Olivia Newton John tape in the eight-track and place a fresh cup of coffee on the flat part of the console, from which it never seemed to spill or even slide sideways, and I was again king of the known world, well, at least of the Midwest. It was good to be the king, again.

One of the big sales I had made a little earlier that year was to a fulfillment company in Indy. It was one of the fastest sales I ever made. The whole campaign to sell a half million-dollar scanning system took about four days, instead of the usual twelve to eighteen months. They had a competitive scanner that wasn't working just right, and I managed to make a friend out of the competitor's maintenance engineer. He was frustrated because that machine had some design flaws, and neither he nor anyone else could make it read as well as ours could. I happened to be there in the computer room one evening when he was working on it, and it had a very high reject rate on his test deck. I told him we could do a lot better than that. In his frustration, he gave me a pile of the rejected test deck documents, and I had them sent overnight by plane to headquarters out east and our scanning system read 95% of them correctly. I had those guys put the documents and a complete printout of the records scanned from the test deck on the next plane back to Indy. I was able to march into the Operations Manager's office a day later with solid proof that we had the system that would solve their input problems.

I'm not sure why the competitor's engineer shared his problems with me and gave me the test deck to see if we could do better. I think he was just at his wit's end. We won the day, and his machine was tossed out. He still had his job, as he had other customers in Indy. We eventually hired him, not as a quid pro quo, but because he was a good service engineer.

I had left Indy in a Mercury Capri V-6 with a big contract and returned a month later in a new Jaguar. The fulfillment people said they felt they had bought the car for me, and I said, "Absolutely." We went out to lunch, and I let the Operations Manager drive the Jaguar to the restaurant and back to the office afterwards. He tried hard not to show that he was impressed, but his grin gave him away. He talked about that for years afterwards. And when I left the company in 1999, they were still customers. I'd like to think the Jaguar got us off to a great relationship, but our system's performance had more to do with it, I'm sure.

As I toured the territory and took customers to lunch or dinner, often offering them the opportunity to drive the car, which most accepted, I would worry that they thought we charged too much for our systems, and the Jaguar was the result of excessive commissions paid out of huge profits. I never heard a whisper of envy from a customer. I was still reporting to Alan Ware, and of course he enjoyed the car except that he wished the steering wheel were on the side it belonged on, namely the right side, as it would be in England. He used to say I was the only one of his men who didn't drive a foreign car.

I drove the Jaguar for about three years. It had some little accidents but nothing major. One such mishap occurred in our driveway when the wife was backing her Capri out of the garage and managed to turn her car enough to hit the Jag in one of the rear doors and push it in. She came in the house in tears and told me what happened. She knew it was there and tried to steer away from it, but turned the wheel in the wrong direction.

Easy to do, not so easy to fix, but I knew a good guy named Steve at Import West Collision in Inkster, near Detroit, who was pretty good at matching paint and he took care of it for a few hundred dollars. Nothing more was said about it. I had Steve fix a lot of my cars over the years. He was of Russian descent and intense, very intense. A hundred years ago, he would have been leading the charge against the Czar's army. He would have been tough to work for, but I noticed he had the same guys working there year after year.

On another occasion I was driving from Albany, New York, westward on the Interstate towards Cleveland when a ferocious wind came up and what seemed like a sandstorm pelted the car head on. It finally abated, and when I stopped to clean some white stuff off of the windshield, it wouldn't come off. I also noticed that there was no paint left on the nose of the car. The wind was so strong that the car's front surface and the windshield were virtually sandblasted. The front had to be repainted and the windshield replaced. My man in Inkster made it look like new again.

I never tired of driving the car, but after three years, it had close to 100,000 miles on the clock. I was thinking about what to do about that when a friend of a friend told me about another Jaguar that he owned that he was storing in his parents' garage in Detroit. He knew I liked Jaguars and wondered if I would be interested in looking at it. Usually when you go look at one of these stored but non-maintained cars, you want to weep.

Much to my surprise, he had a very nice '70 Jaguar XKE Roadster stored there, with a Primrose Yellow exterior and a black-leather interior. XKEs are often referred to as "E Types," and this was the genuine article. It was all there, no rust, no mice living in the upholstery, and it ran without blue smoke coming out of the exhaust. We got together on price very quickly, around $6250 as I recall, and I knew now I was not going to sell the big Jaguar right away because now I could really show off. His-and-her Jaguars, I could say.

My wife knew she was welcome to drive the E Type, yet she preferred to drive the Capri because she was afraid an accident might happen, not a good thing, in such a beautiful car. I took the XKE on a few trips, but it wasn't as comfortable, by a long shot, as the XJ6L.

The big sedan was getting tired after 100,000 miles and three hard years on the road in all kinds of weather. I sold it off my little corner for about $9,000 to a local engineer. I would see it around town for a year or so. When the guy moved away, it left town with him.

Of all the cars that have owned me, I would have to count it in the top three. It had the secret sauce: style plus substance. It was better than the brochure, and it delivered on its promise. You can't ask more of a car than that.

# It Is Difficult to Be Rational in the Presence of an Idling Jaguar XKE

## 1970 Jaguar XKE Roadster

*The epitome of cars with the "secret sauce."*

I still have a model of this car sitting on my bookshelf. It possesses a timeless beauty, a balance between raw power and elegance. When it was introduced at the Geneva Auto Show in 1961, it was the hit of the show. Every man who looked upon the XKE's curves was seduced on the spot. Nothing else looked quite like it, sounded like it, or performed like it.

Like most sports cars, it had the long hood symbolizing a powerful engine and the most abbreviated of trunks, implying that one need take along only the barest of necessities, as this was the car of choice for mad dashes down to Brighton from London with your paramour. The

cabin space was cozy, and the dashboard was filled with a dozen round gauges, like that of a small private airplane.

The XKE or "E-Type," as it was commonly referred to, was no poser. The long hood was needed to enclose a hefty 4.2 liter six-cylinder engine. Granted, the hood was perhaps two feet longer than it really needed to be but that provided enough of an extended nose to curve inward towards an opening that resembled the open mouth of a large predator, like a shark.

Early '60s XKEs were equipped with triple carbs, one for each pair of cylinders. These were large side draft S.U. carbs that looked like small coffee pots hanging off of the intake manifold. By 1970, the US Government had mandated stricter emissions rules, causing Jaguar to change over to two smaller Stromberg carbs, costing the car at least 50 horsepower. Even with the Stromberg set up, the car produced more than 250 horsepower, a tremendous amount of power for a sports car in that era.

I was driving a Jaguar XJ6L sedan at the time and was introduced to the XKE by a friend of mine. He owned this '70 model that he bought as an investment and had no place to keep it. His folks had some space in their garage, but they lived in Detroit in a neighborhood that was going downhill and he worried about the car being vandalized or stolen. I read a report a few years back that about 35,000 cars are stolen each year in the Detroit metropolitan area. That's about 100 per day. There are shops in that area that offer "steal to order" services. You specify what year, model and color you're looking for, and they can generally satisfy your requirements in a week or so. My friend was beginning to worry about his investment.

He started looking for a buyer, and it occurred to him that since I had one Jaguar, I might like to have another, particularly an XKE roadster. I got a call from him, and after some discussion I agreed to motor into a rough part of Detroit with him to look at this car. I had made trips like this before, and they usually were a waste of time, as the car was normally in pretty bad shape, beyond repair. He was worried about the neighborhood getting worse, and it seemed to me that it was pretty bad already, with vacant vandalized houses here and there and absolutely no one walking about. It seemed like a ghost town. His folks had a very small house with a detached one-car garage. They no longer drove and had sold their car. They were really prisoners there, dependent on their kids or friends to get around.

We undid several locks on the wooden garage door to get it open. A couple of cars drove slowly past the house, trying to get a look at the contents of the garage. I could see why he was worried. We turned a small light on inside and quickly closed the garage door. He took the cover off of the car, revealing a light yellow car with a black top. Fortunately, I had brought a flashlight to look closely at the car. I couldn't really see anything obviously wrong with it. No rust on the rockers or lower parts of the fenders, no rust under the trunk floor, and only a small amount of oil appeared on the floor under the engine.

He got it and pulled the choke out, crossed his fingers, and turned the key on. The engine turned over slowly, and then a little faster and then it fired up. It coughed a few times, and we too began to cough, as the exhaust filled the closed garage. "Open the garage door, or we'll get gassed in here," he said, as he blipped the throttle a few more times and then released the choke, as the engine now had enough heat in it to idle smoothly. At idle, it sounded like an airplane sitting at the runway's end waiting for clearance from the control tower. The sound was savage. A serious sound from a serious car.

We took it out for a short drive around the neighborhood. The ride was a little harsh on these bad streets, but there weren't any rattles to speak of. The oil pressure looked good, and it wasn't smoking or leaking anything when we got back. It had passed its physical.

I had to think about this car rationally as we didn't really need another car at the moment. The wife's Capri was running okay, and other than its genetic defect of being painted bronze, or brown in her view, and having a door that occasionally opened when she didn't want it to, she was reasonably happy with that car. My big Jaguar, the XJ6L, was getting a little long in the tooth but was still turning heads and still getting me around the territory in style.

It is difficult to be rational in the presence of an idling XKE.

Pick a movie star of the period, say Natalie Wood or Ann Margret, and imagine her inviting you out to dinner and who knows what after dinner. Of course you would go. We are mere men, not gods. I asked him how much he thought he would have to have to part with this beauty. He said he had paid about $6000 for it and had done a few things to improve it, so he would like to see $6500. I told him I had to think about it, but I had already made my decision. He would come down some because if what he was worried about came to pass, he might have nothing.

At $6500, it was a depreciation-proof purchase. I wouldn't pay quite that much, because it would make him feel bad. Anytime you pay what someone asks, they feel terrible because they think they should have asked for more and might have gotten it. I would not pay his asking price, and he would be happier because of that. Besides, it would be a good idea to time the purchase of this with the arrival of a commission check. The wife never knew when commissions were coming, or how much they might be for. I didn't know either, although I could call the home office and occasionally get some advanced information. I learned that a big one for something like $10,000 after taxes was in the hopper. The checks always came to the house, and she would handle them so I would say that I wanted to buy this or that out of the next check that arrived and assure her that there would be some left over for savings.

After I saw the XKE, I let her know I wanted to buy a very special car, and it would take six big ones out of the next commission check, but she would have four big ones for the savings account and that seemed to go over OK.

The check showed up a few days later, and I got hold of the guy. He was anxious to unload it but said he really had to have $6500. Usually in that situation, the seller will invent another potential buyer he'll tell you about, but he didn't do that. He had probably told his wife when he bought it he would make a killing, and now he had to tell her he was just going to get his money back, period. I sympathized and offered $6000. He said he just couldn't go that low. At this point in the negotiations, for a car or anything else, the next person who speaks loses. I didn't say anything, and he didn't either for maybe a minute. Then he offered to split the difference. Deal. We both had earned our price.

People would see both of the Jaguars sitting in the driveway and ask me which I preferred. It was a hard question to answer. They were built for different purposes. The XKE was great for a drive down twisty roads by myself in the summertime and taking the kids to the Dairy Queen. The XJ6L was the car of choice to get to Columbus in a hurry and in comfort.

I came across a three carburetor intake manifold setup for the XKE and bought it for $250 from some guy at a swap meet. I wasn't sure I could install it correctly, but I took my time and got it all to work. These S.U. carbs had two-inch throats, compared to 1.75 inches on the Strombergs that came with the car, and the "new" intake manifold was a straight shot into the cylinder head. Three larger carbs versus two smaller carbs made a huge difference in the engine's power. I believe it added close to 50 horsepower and made the car a real thrill ride. On the north side of Ann Arbor where Plymouth Road crosses over US-23, there is an on ramp heading south down to US 23. It isn't very long and has two wiggles in it, so it's not a straight shot onto the highway. Nonetheless, I could have the car up to 100 mph as I pulled onto the southbound lane. Granted, it was a slight downhill grade, but the acceleration was awesome.

On another occasion I was driving at a high rate of knots through the Irish Hills about 30 miles west of Ann Arbor on US-12, maybe running around 80 mph on the short straights and almost as fast through the curves. Just as I crested a hill, a State Police car was coming at me. His red light went on immediately, as he slowed down, turned around and gave chase. I pulled over and waited for him to come up behind me. He asked to see my license and walked around the car. I could see he admired the car. He just stood there, looking at it.

He said he was going to have to give me a ticket because I didn't have a license plate on the front bumper, as was required back at that time. I was stunned. He was going to give me a ticket for a minor technicality and was ignoring the obvious, namely the speeding. I was greatly relieved and decided to see if I could explain why it wasn't there. Maybe I could escape a ticket all together, knowing he was really letting me off the speeding ticket because he liked the car.

I explained that the car really didn't have a front bumper that was large enough to hang a plate on, so the manufacturer had attached a small bracket right in the middle of the large air intake for the radiator to attach the plate to. However, if you did that, the engine would overheat in traffic because of insufficient air going to the radiator. I had the license plate and its bracket in the trunk, so I took it out and handed it to him. He took the plate and stuck it in that opening, and he could see how restrictive that would be. "You're right; this could cause overheating," he said, as he handed the plate back to me. "I won't give you a ticket," he continued, "but other cops might not see it that way, so you might want to engineer some kind of bracket elsewhere on the front. If I had this car, I might be tempted to speed. You wouldn't do that now, would you?" As I pulled out, and looked back through the rear-view mirror, I could see him just standing there by the side of the road, watching, listening, until I was out of sight.

On another occasion, I actually lent this car to a friend of mine who was going to his high school reunion. I must have been out of my mind.

The guy was Steve Steeb who worked down at Ernie Weaver's Marathon station on the corner of Packard and Stadium Boulevard. He was paid to work on my cars, but he had gone out of his way more than once to help me with my car or the wife's car. I knew he lusted after the car, who didn't? I suggested that he take the car to this reunion party, which was to be held in the afternoon and would last three or four hours.

Steve couldn't believe his ears. He promised not to drink anything, and he would be especially careful and so on. I knew he would be careful but would probably toast the rear tires at least once, but other than that I knew he was smart enough not to take any real chances. That was the longest four hours. I kept asking myself why I just didn't give him a $50 tip for all his extra effort and be done with it. What if another one of his buddies ran into him, or he was hit by lightning or a dragon rose out of the earth and swallowed him and the car whole? The car came back in one piece, and he was grinning from ear to ear.

I have to admit that I bought this car out of pure lust and because this was a particularly good one. Speaking of buying a car, how about buying the same car more than once? A friend of mine, Paul Nielson of Nielson Florists, also had an XKE, but his was a '74 I believe, and was "fitted" with the V-12 engine. What was unusual about Paul and this particular car was that Paul would sell the car in order to buy something else, and then a year or two later he would buy it back. I believe he did that six or seven times.

I had the XKE for several years, and while I would never tire of driving it or just looking at it, I was beginning to think about another kind of vehicle, a much larger one, that the whole family could be in at once and travel together and even sleep in.

That's right; I was getting the RV bug. We started going to RV shows and making comparisons and talking about which kind we might get. We eventually settled on a Southwind 26' Class A motor home that would set us back about $14,000. I really struggled with whether or not to sell the XKE to offset some of the cost. You hate to sell one toy to have another if there is a way to keep both. Finally, I decided that I would sell the XKE, and if I couldn't live without it, I would buy another—maybe even buy this one back, like my friend Paul.

I put it up for sale for around $9000. A local police detective purchased it. That was about 25 years ago, and I understand he still has it. I don't blame him, and if I had it to do over again, I would have kept it. It was beautiful, unique and very fast. Like the TR-3B and the Jaguar XJ6L, it represented British craftsmanship and styling at its very best.

# Long Live the Queen

## 1976 Jaguar XJC Coupe

*Misty, our white Afghan hound, her friend and a silver cat.*

This car was a rare bird. I guess rare cat would be more appropriate. I don't think I had ever seen one before I noticed the XJC in a British auto magazine.

Jaguar had been making the XJ four-door sedans since the late '60s. In 1974, they lengthened the car and changed the styling slightly. Now, they offered a long body and continued to offer the standard body with the new styling changes. So, there were two bodies available, very similar in looks, differing only by the chassis length. Either the standard six-cylinder or a new V-12 engine could be "fitted" to either car, as the Brits like to say.

This XJC was something different than either of the above. Jaguar took the standard length four-door body and modified it to have just two doors. Now you had a fine-looking coupe with a reasonable back seat, and since the XKE roadster had been discontinued in '74, at least this coupe was available for the "with it" British executive who wanted to dash from London down to Brighton to spend a weekend with his lady at a seaside resort.

This one was silver with a blue vinyl top. Honest, a vinyl top on a Jaguar. I've been trying to remember where I acquired this car, and I think this was one of those that I had seen in a "pulp," those $1 magazines that are a collection of car ads that come out each week. I probably bought it from some guy in one of the tonier Detroit suburbs, who bought it for his wife, and she didn't care for it, or it wouldn't start or some half reason like that. Seems like I paid $7500 for it, which was a reasonable price. I drove it as my main ride in all kinds of weather. That dog in the picture was an Afghan hound named Misty, one of my wife's favorites, ranking slightly higher in the family pecking order than yours truly.

I had sold my '74 XJ6L a year or two before, and it was good to get back in a Jaguar again. I have always found this brand of car to be a satisfying car to drive. Yes, that's the word: satisfying. There were other cars that were more hip, faster, more efficient, and certainly more reliable, but other brands didn't bring "satisfaction." In a Jaguar, you didn't feel rich or even ostentatious. You felt fortunate, and you felt satisfied. You had to get used to people staring at you, and it might make you a bit self-conscious at first, until you realized they weren't looking at you, they were looking at the car.

I think what Jaguar had then, and probably still has today, is the secret sauce. The secret sauce to me had always meant style plus substance. Maybe I should say the secret blend: a blend of style, power, comfort and handling. The last one is the hard part, the handling. You can make a car corner quickly and keep four wheels glued to the pavement, and it will handle like a race car. But the stiff suspension and stiff walled tires needed to make the car handle usually provide a hard ride, an uncomfortable ride, a noisy ride, and it isn't much fun to be in on a long trip. My first and last Corvette was like that.

Jaguar mastered the handling without the hard ride. They were heavy, weighing about two tons, but there was no wallow like you might find in other heavy cars, such as Cadillacs and Buicks and the like. The rear brakes were inboard, that is, the half shafts coming out of the rear end had disc brake calipers in close to the differential. Independent suspension at all four corners plus big oversized Dunlop tires made for a great ride. The engine was the venerable in-line 4.2 liter six-cylinder that Jaguar has been building and refining since the late Forties. The only weak spot was the three-speed Borg Warner transmission that was just adequate. It seemed like you always could have used another gear, either off the line or at the top end. The car deserved better.

I liked the way the XJC handled and looked. It was one of those cars that as you walked away from it, you might turn around and take another look. It had the cozy cabin, the burled walnut trim, firm leather seats, and the huge center console, upon which you could place a cup of coffee, and it would not spill except under extremely hard braking.

I drove it year round and was driving quickly down to Fort Wayne, Indiana, one winter day when a sudden snow squall began to reduce vision to where you could see no more than three or four car lengths in front of you. I was tooling along about 35-40 mph, just a little north of Coldwater, when out of the storm I saw a large domestic car sitting right in the middle of my lane, not moving at all. I hit that Buick pretty hard. The poor XJC crumpled up from the front bumper back to the windshield. The Buick suffered a scuffed bumper. Nobody admitted to being hurt. The lady driving the Buick said it was beginning to be difficult to see, so she just stopped. I asked her why she didn't pull off rather than stopping right in the lane, and she said that maybe she ought to have.

In any case, I was out of business. I got out the mobile phone and called ahead for a wrecker. They used to be called mobile phones, came in a bag the size of a small backpack, and cost $2500. The wrecker got the car into town, and I acquired a rental car to get on down to Ft. Wayne. On the way back I made arrangements to get the car trucked back to Ann Arbor and make the rounds of the body shops.

The bump and paint guys weren't crazy about working on the car, and their estimates reflected that. My insurance guy said he would total it if I liked. That just didn't seem right. Here was a rare car that I had mucked up because my reflexes or judgment were inadequate. I finally found a shop in Ypsilanti that would work on it, but he cautioned me that it was going to be a long process, like five to six weeks, and if he couldn't reshape those beautiful front fenders, he might have to get new ones from England.

Three months later he had the car done. It looked pretty good. I had to buy something else in the meantime, and it needed to be able to haul race cars around. Race cars? Yes, I'm afraid so. I had been hanging out with bad company, as you'll learn in the next chapter. That meant a pickup, van, or maybe a station wagon. Either of the first two choices made sense, so there isn't much mystery about the one I took: the station wagon. Not only a station wagon but also a diesel station wagon. If I were to say it was a Mercedes diesel wagon, you might say good choice. But no, GM seduced me again, and I purchased an Oldsmobile Cutlass wagon with that unusual GM engine that had diesel heads grafted onto a 350 cubic-inch engine originally designed as a gasoline-powered engine. Oh, the shame. Oh, the noise and smell, and lack of power. What was I thinking? In defense of GM's diesel, they seldom failed. My friend, Moe Bronson, of Van Eck Diesel here in Holland, MI, tells me that GM passenger car diesels were generally long lived, with many of them running for more than 200,000 miles.

I decided that the Jaguar XJC had lost its virginity in the crash and wondered if the subframe on that unibody chassis had been compromised.

I sold the XJC to a young couple. His wife looked pretty good in it. She looked pretty good not in it. They liked it, and I saw it around town for several years. The last time I saw her in it, the XJC was getting to look kind of rough, with the power antenna broken and a dent in the trunk lid. She still looked pretty good, though.

On a purely prejudicial note, I have concluded that some folks don't look like they belong driving Jaguars. Oh, they're worthy enough, might have even paid for it themselves, and anybody should be able to drive anything they can buy, finance, lease, or acquire in a divorce settlement.

These same people, often quite good-looking trophy wives and athletic-looking young men, seen in a Lexus or Mercedes with one hand holding a phone, appear to be in their element. They're ensconced in a luxury car, enjoying its opulence and comfort, air conditioning on, premium sound playing some CD, one hand on the wheel and enjoying life to the fullest.

There it is. There's the problem, the one hand on the wheel, a cell phone in the other, with most of his or her brain working on something else. The Jaguar is a car you drive with both hands and with 80% of your brain operating the car, appreciating what the car is doing, or could do, on a second's notice. Yes, I've made phone calls from this car, but they were urgent and short. One would never call up somebody just to visit on the phone while driving this car. I suppose it's done, but shouldn't be.

You don't eat at the symphony, or write postcards while at the opera, or take a call while in your church or synagogue. You don't do these things because they would diminish the pleasure from the primary activity, and you wouldn't do it out of respect for your surroundings. Now that I think about it, I normally don't play the radio when I'm in a good car because it's a distraction.

Women like the Jaguar, I think, because it seems to me to be a feminine car. There is a big difference between a feminine car and a chick car. Jaguars have always had fine lines, an understated look, a subtle car that shows its beauty in stages, like a demure librarian who, when her glasses are removed and the bun in her hair comes undone, reveals herself to be a beautiful woman.

The wife used to say that she thought the Jaguars I owned seemed like mistresses to her. Maybe she could see the feminine side of the Jaguar as well.

I believe that you don't really see a car until you hand wash it and dry it, and there is an innocent pleasure in doing so.

Wouldn't you have loved to be the artist who first drew these lines, the craftsman who formed the body panels, and was one of those Englishmen, who, looking upon the finished car, smiled with pride at what they had built?

Long Live the Queen. Long Live Jaguar.

# Hanging Out With Bad Company

## 1965 Austin Healey Sprite Race car

*Here are three cars in one picture that merited inclusion in this collection of stories: Nancy's 1973 Capri, my 1974 Jaguar XJ6L, and the first race car as it looked when I bought it. How about that semi-hippie haircut? Long hair was in style in the mid-seventies.*

As usual, I had been hanging out with bad company. We would talk about racing a lot, and while drag racing had its appeal, we were starting to think about sports-car racing. I had been over to the Waterford Hills racetrack near Clarkston a few times, and the racers looked like they were having a great time tooling around a 1.5-mile course that had 11 corners, front and back straightaways, and several elevation changes.

There were crashes and equipment failures, but nobody seemed to get seriously hurt. There were all kinds of cars running in about 20 different classes. You could divide the cars up into four groups: purpose-built race cars, larger V-8 powered domestic cars modified for racing, small imported cars modified for racing, and "showroom stock" cars.

Most of the purpose-built race cars were open wheeled; that is, they had no fenders. They looked similar to an Indy car or a sprint car, but these were much smaller with tight little cockpits. Guys over six feet tall, like me, weighing in around 200 pounds just didn't fit in the car. There were exceptions to that, but most of the pilots of the open wheel group reminded me of jockeys.

The second group was known as the "Big Bore" cars, because the cars had large V-8 engines with "big bores," that is, large cylinders. These cars were anything but boring, and their races were usually the most exciting of the day. Corvettes, Camaros and Mustangs made up this group.

The third group, the small imports, probably had at one time the most cars and made up about half of the classes. The reason for their popularity was mostly economic. They were relatively cheap to acquire, cheap to maintain, and the initial supply was plentiful. MGs, Triumphs, Fiats, Austin Healeys, and other "small bore" imports made up this group.

Showroom stock or "SS" cars could be almost anything imported or domestic. The three ideas behind the "SS" cars were to lower the cost of racing, get more domestic brands of currently produced cars on the track, and have drivers competing in identical cars within a class so that the best driver, not the biggest bankroll, won. Showroom stock meant exactly that. You weren't allowed to modify the car's engine or suspension or tires for racing. Roll cages, competition grade seat belts, window nets and fire extinguishers were required for safety, but nothing more. While these cars were required to remain stock, some folks did modify their engines illegally to get a competitive edge. For some competitors, "SS" came to mean "slightly stock," but for the most part, it was fairly clean and eventually became the most numerous group of cars.

I had read about an Austin Healey Sprite race car for sale in the Lansing area. I got a hold of my friend Billy Cotton, and we drove up to look at it. We met the seller and went out to his barn and took the cover off. Here was a small black car with a white oval on each door with a black number inside of the oval. It had Dunlop racing tires on it, but they weren't much wider than stock and had seen better days. It did have a roll cage and fire extinguisher, but the driver's seat was a stock bucket and the steering wheel was one of those large diameter wheels meant to compensate for the lack of power steering. I should mention that Austin Healey Sprites and MG Midgets were absolutely identical, except for the name on the side. This practice was known as "badge engineering" because the only thing that needed to be engineered for the "new" brand was a new badge on its side or hood.

I sat in it and could see that I would fit. I got out and asked him to start it up. He fired it up, and it settled into an easy idle. I suspected that he ran it some before we got there which is always a good idea when selling a car. He got out, and Billy took over. He watched the oil pressure gauge, and with one eye on the tach, revved it up pretty high. I thought the motor might explode. The seller was not amused but said nothing. Billy brought it back down to idle, blipped the throttle a few times, and turned it off. He asked to look under the hood and under the car. It looked pretty tidy under the hood, with four cylinders, two carbs, a radiator and a battery. The car sat pretty low, so it was difficult to look under. We rolled the car back and stared at the pavement. There were a few small oil spots but no puddles.

He then took us to a storage area in the barn where he kept the car's spares. There were four more tires, mounted, an extra transmission, an old engine block and two extra carburetors. None of these spares looked all that great, but the seller said the transmission was worth at least half of what he was asking for the car, and all these spares were included in the $500 asking price.

It wasn't getting any warmer in the barn, so we retreated to the house to talk about the car a bit more. Like most sellers, this guy didn't want to tell outright fibs, but he did want to manage the news. He said he hadn't had the car for more than a year or so and just ran through a competition driver's school last summer and ran two races in the fall. Prior to that, he had the engine's head cleaned up some but couldn't vouch for the strength of the motor's bottom end. The oil pressure looked good when we ran it, but there were lots of tricks out there for getting a motor to indicate good oil pressure when in fact the engine might have oiling problems.

You would always ask, "Why are you selling?" and the usual answer was domestic pressure. That is as good of an excuse as any and probably valid most of the time. What wife in her right mind wants her husband to risk his life for some grins and memories? The risk/reward equation is too unbalanced and that probably explains why there are very few women race car drivers. It's not a matter of skill or background or gonadials, rather it's a matter of intelligence. Most women are too smart to do this.

We left the seller's house without making a commitment because Billy and I wanted to talk it over. The hour was getting late, so we agreed to have that conversation tomorrow. When you are buying a used car, used boat, used bike or used race car, you are hoping two hopes: It isn't all used up, and it won't cost a lot to get it a little better. In other words, what will be the cost of repairing undisclosed faults and what will be the cost of modest improvements? If you can buy one of these older race cars and go racing without writing too many more checks, that's a good thing.

We discussed it at length the next day and decided that while we hadn't looked at other candidates, the price of this one was such that unless we grenaded the motor right off, we could get our (my) money out of it rather easily. I called the guy up and offered $400, and he was somewhat insulted or so he said. After the hurt feelings subsided, he countered with $475. I offered $450, but he wouldn't budge. I said OK to $475, and we would be up on the weekend to pick everything up. When we got there, he had all the spares boxed up, the car looking clean, sitting on the trailer, ready to go. He looked so sad, but his wife was smiling. Couldn't blame her.

I have often wondered how I ended up with so many English cars. My first new bicycle was an English bike, a three-speed Raleigh; so maybe there was some seminal connection between mobility and English conveyances.

We brought it back to Ann Arbor and began to make a list of things we needed to get to make it past technical inspection at the track. Aside from the tires, which we would wait on, it had to have new seat belts, and a new fire extinguisher. We didn't have any illusions about winning right out of the box. We just wanted to have a car that could get through the first weekend without major problems.

Racing organizations don't just let you show up and go racing. The first thing you need to have is a checkbook in good operating condition. Generally, you have to join the racing organization, pay a fee to enter the drivers' school for new drivers, pay for a license if you get through the drivers' school, and pay an entry fee to enter the first race. One other item for a new guy…you need to visit a farm implement dealer and buy a red triangle indicating that you are operating a slow moving vehicle and affix this to the rear of the car.

Most drivers' schools operate under a format where you attend a classroom session lasting most of a day, and then the following weekend you're on the track for two full days. Each driver has to take a written test after the classroom session to make sure they have some idea of the "line" around the track as well as basic safety procedures. The "line" is the ideal path around the track, where the cars just touch the apex of each corner and use the entire width of the track to provide the largest possible radius for each corner. Each rookie driver is assigned an instructor who looks after two or three student drivers.

When the on-track session begins on the next weekend, he'll begin by taking you around the track in his street car at relatively low speeds, showing you the line and why driving on the line or very close to it is so important to achieving competitive lap times.

The instructors varied a great deal in their ability as teachers. Some were kind, reassuring in a fatherly way. Others tried to appear to be "Top Gun" instructor material and had a very competitive style. It was important to them for "their" drivers to look good and stand out. After the instructors finished driving their cars around the track for four or five laps with you as a passenger, it was time for you to get into your car and go out onto a racetrack for the first time, along with a dozen other first timers who had cars similar to yours. Open wheelers and closed wheelers (fendered cars) never ran together. The instructors would signal you to come in after a few laps and critique your driving, especially your ability to be driving on the "line." Then you were sent back out and observed again. You would gain some confidence and start passing some of the slower cars, but what you really wanted to avoid was wrecking yourself or being caught up in some other driver's mistake.

Our little Austin Healey Sprite was doing OK. The car had an 1100 cubic centimeter (cc) engine that probably made no more than 60 horsepower, so it was a bit anemic in that department. No matter, it was circulating around the track just fine. When you don't have much power, you try to be very smooth around the corners so that you don't have to slow down hardly at all. If you slow down much, it will take quite awhile to build that speed up again, and you don't want that. The old Dunlop tires were pretty hard, like wood they were. This meant it didn't have much grip, but I found that if I could slide the rear just a little, it cornered pretty well. I highly recommend starting out in underpowered race cars because you learn the value of being smooth.

Saturday's practice sessions were in preparation for Sunday morning's work that would consist of race starts and what to do if there was an accident. You needed to remember what the corner worker's flags meant, that is, what commands or messages they were giving you.

Our car was classified as G Production, which was one of the slower groups. We would be on the track at the same time with other groups like H Production (even slower) and maybe F Production who were slightly faster. You only had to finish well within the G group, but if you could beat an F Production car, and not get beat by an H Production car, so much the better.

Sports car races are usually rolling starts with the car on the pole, first row and inside, setting the pace as the two columns of cars approach the starting line. All the drivers look up at the starter who stands on his elevated platform with the green starter's flag behind his back. You usually can see his elbow sticking out behind him, and you watch for it to move as that means the rest of his arm is about to appear and wave the flag to start the race. You want to stand on the gas and hope the guy in front of you, if there is one, does likewise. As you're all accelerating down the short front straightaway, the moment of truth is approaching, that is, the first corner. Everyone's tires are cold, all drivers are operating under an adrenaline overload, and rookies who have forgotten most of what they've been told surround you. More races are lost on the first corner of the first lap than anywhere else during the race.

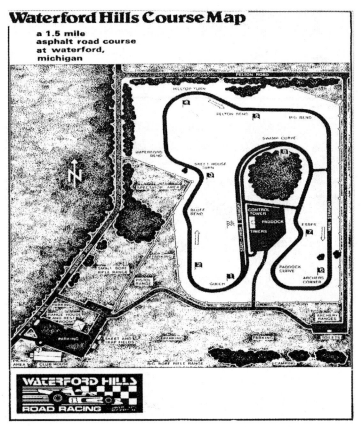

*Track map provided by Waterford Hills Road Racing, Inc.*

You just want to get through those first four or five corners with all of your fenders still attached. After that things will settle down and you can try to concentrate on the line and smoothness and looking a long way down the track and not passing on the outside if you can help it and checking your gauges on the straights and looking for pit signals and watching your mirrors if you're being overtaken and listening to your engine and watching the exhaust pipe of the car in front of you because you know that when he lifts off the gas a little smoke usually appears, and you know he's about to hit the brakes and maybe you can pass if you can brake one second later and still get through the corner without sliding off.

Your brain is processing all that input, and you really don't have time to be frightened. If someone starts to spin in front of you, you aim right at him or her because they'll generally spin off the track. Usually, but not always. What you're really trying to avoid is getting caught up in a chain reaction wreck involving a half-dozen cars. Those can be nasty and expensive. There is no insurance on these cars and no liability on the part of someone who wrecks your car. Did I mention there are very few women involved in this kind of recreation?

These first races are ten laps or less, and you hate to see the checkered flag unless you're in first place. Out of ten cars in our group, I think we finished fourth. Not bad, not great, and we passed the training course, so now we could enter the car in the first race of the season, which would be in about two weeks. I knew I had better get some new tires as these were starting to show their age.

The instructors gave us our rookie licenses, and those who passed, which were most of us, all felt pretty good. Our new white drivers' uniforms had some sweat and dirt on them now, and the car had a couple dents but nothing major. All right!

My crew consisted of two guys: Billy Cotton and Steve Steeb. Billy and I still worked together and since he was involved in the original selection of this particular car, he was willing to invest his weekends for a while. Steve worked at Ernie Weaver's Marathon gas station down the street and did the oil changes and tune-ups on our family cars and agreed to volunteer his services on the race car.

On race day, everyone had to unload their cars and push them over to Tech Inspection for general safety checks. The reason for the car push is that they won't let the engines be started before 10 AM due to some local noise ordinance. If the Tech guys don't like your roll bar or the catch cans for overflowing liquids, like antifreeze, you have big troubles. You need to get that problem fixed and return to Tech

Inspection and go through it all again. This could make you late for the first and only practice session you will get all weekend. If you don't have that practice session, you have to go out for the Qualifying Session not knowing how the car will behave that day. Qualifying is a race against the clock, and those with the lowest lap times start up front in the actual race. Qualifying is probably the most important event of the weekend.

The regular class races are all fairly short, that is ten to fifteen laps. If you start up front, you're driving with the better drivers. Two things were important to getting a good qualifying time: warm tires and a clear track.

Qualifying in sports-car racing is often done en masse. Thirty cars in related classes will be sent onto the track at the same time, and they will circulate around the track for twenty minutes. Somewhere in those twenty minutes, you need to nail a good lap time. After an initial warm-up lap, maybe two, you drive the car at about 80-90%, looking ahead and across the track to see if you would have clear sailing through the slower corners. If you came up on a slower car, you hoped it would be on the straights. You just didn't want to get hung up behind one or two cars in the corners that were driving on the "line" because that's where you wanted to be to get the fastest time.

So, you would see an opportunity and go for it. It was important to be coming across the start-finish line at maximum speed and try to be smooth and on the racing line all the way around for 1.5 miles. I would drive three hard laps, hoping for a clear track, and then take an easy lap, cooling the tires down. In the early days we didn't have much in the way of crew-to-driver communication. Some of the more sophisticated teams had pit boards to signal their driver, but no one had radios. I would then look for another clear track situation and go hard for two or three more laps and then a cool-off lap and go on in to the pits. The team would have recorded the lap times, but they weren't official.

Those times were kept up in the timing tower and would be posted shortly after the session ended.

If you qualified well, you were likely to start race #1 in a good position and finish near the front. The finishing order for the first race set the grid for the Sunday class race, so success would likely insure more success. For reasons I will never understand, Sunday's second race, the Feature, was gridded by the fastest lap time posted during the first two class races and had nothing to do with finishing order in either race.

The racing itself could be pretty wild, especially early in the season, as the rookies were still feeling their way, and the more experienced drivers were getting through the rustiness caused by the winter layoff. The cars of a given group like G Production were close in performance in terms of top speed on the straights and top speed through the corners. The big difference between the frontrunners and those who would be stuck in the middle or bringing up the rear was in braking ability. As you came to a corner where speed needed to be reduced to get around it without sliding off of the track, he who applied the brakes last and smoothest generally would win the corner, that is, either pass a car you had been alongside of, or extend your lead. It can be pretty tricky, as you can't wait too long or you'll be past the point of rescue and will go straight while the road turns.

Braking in a straight line is the best procedure, as you want to keep the car headed straight. You do want to have to do just a little more braking in the early part of the corner to keep the weight transfer forward. It's called trail braking. That weight will push the front tires downward, causing them to stick better to the road and therefore help turn the car. If the front tires don't stick, the car goes straight ahead and you have a problem. In racing circles this inability to turn is called "push" or "tightness." If the front sticks so well that the rear end of the car starts coming around, the car is said to be "loose."

If you were coming up on a car and he was about to brake, you would notice that color of his exhaust gas would change from grey to blue, as he lifted off of the gas just before braking. His brake lights were another clue, but you couldn't always believe them, as there were ways to turn them off altogether or turn them on without actually braking. Going through a corner side by side with another car and not touching it but remaining just inches apart takes a bit of skill and is a thrilling experience for both drivers. The inside of the track is generally the preferred lane for side-by-side stuff. If you make a mistake and slide into him, he may be leaving the track and will probably discuss it with you after the race. If you're the guy on the outside, it could be happening to you.

I wanted to do well on Saturday and finish well in the finishing order, so that Sunday would be more of the same. Each team had their problems with these older race cars such as overheating, electrical gremlins, transmissions not working right, and the worst of all, low oil pressure in the engine. Low oil pressure meant that critical parts weren't getting lubricated and engine failure was likely.

We learned early on not to mix with other teams. We didn't want to let them know what our problems were, and we weren't interested in working on theirs. If another racer came over and asked to borrow a wrench or ask advice, we would be friendly enough and lend the wrench or part or whatever, and we would sometimes need to borrow something ourselves. We just didn't want to socialize much. We wanted to beat these other teams, and we might buy them a beer Sunday night after the racing was done, but buddies we weren't. We were friendly and went to the work bees and club meetings, but we just didn't have the time to schmooze the officials. That probably had some hidden cost over the years, but we were too focused on our own deal.

As the first season wore on, we weren't doing that badly. We hadn't wrecked yet, as we had invested in some new

Goodyear racing tires and some new wheels. New tires on a race car make all the difference in the world. Unlike the big professional NASCAR teams who might go through four or five sets in a single race, we would make four sets of tires last for all 18 races of the season, so it was critical to break them in right and make them last. They were "uncured" to begin with, and when they heated and cooled 16 times, they were cured and harder. The tires might have plenty of rubber left, but they became quite hard and the lap times went way up.

One of the hot shoes in our class, G Production, was Hugo Carlson whose lap record of one minute, 18 seconds has never been equaled up to this point in time. The usual lap times for the fastest G Production cars were around 1:20 to 1:22. Occasionally, it would rain on a race weekend, and if you could afford rain tires, you were likely to finish well, as most of the regulars didn't have them.

We raced this car for about three years, never winning, but usually placing respectively, meaning third through fifth in a ten car class. I was beginning to wonder if I would ever win. It was becoming more clear to me that in order to win I was going to have up the ante considerably. The big expense would be that of a new motor. The top teams had motors that likely put out 25-35% more horsepower than we had. We could hang with them in the corners, but they would leave us on the straights. If a car could do a lap just one second faster than you, in a ten lap race, he would be ten seconds ahead or practically out of sight.

I was starting to get a bit discouraged, and I think my crew was too, although they seemed to remain enthusiastic and hard working. We saw less and less of Billy Cotton, but Steve Steeb hung in there for a number of years. He was lusting after a Bug-Eye Sprite that would run in H Production. When that happened, he would have his hands full with that and I would lose his services at the track, but he would still help me work on the car in between race weekends. Aside from the occasional bodywork repair, the engines needed a fair amount of care. The twin carbs had to be synchronized, valves adjusted, radiators flushed and so on. Brakes and our 5.33 rear gear needed a lot of service as well.

I began to think about selling the Sprite and getting into Showroom Stock. The newer cars were much more reliable and that meant more time in the car and less time under the car fixing whatever.

Changing classes in race cars is a little like changing colleges. Some things transfer, and some don't. The Austin Healey Sprite experience had taught me a lot. I had learned how to race, and I was hoping to learn how to win.

By the end of the third season, I had convinced myself that in the world of Showroom Stock, my chances of winning would be better.

My Austin Healey Sprite race car was easy to sell, as it looked good and was a respectable performer if not a winner. A local guy, Virgil Darga, was just starting out, and he bought the car in the fall to get it ready for the next season. I hated to see #9 hauled away on that rickety old trailer, but it was going to a good home. I think I sold it for around $2000, which would be leaving my pockets shortly for a "new" race car.

In buying any car, anticipation and discussion of all the options is a big part of the purchasing experience. I looked at a lot of cars and read everything I could get my hands on about the available choices. Just as the English bicycle experience predisposed me to like English cars, favorable experiences with German-built Mercury Capris pointed me towards my next race car: a fairly rare Capri V-6 known as a John Player Special. If that car had known what I was going to put it through over the next four years, it might have refused to run the day I first looked at it.

# I Honestly Forgot to Tell the Wife About It

## 1976 John Player Special
## Mercury Capri Race Car

*This is a picture of the car in rally form. I haven't been able to locate a picture of it as a race car. On the left is one of my heroes, Don Ensley, crew chief. On the right is John Erickson, co-driver, a very brave guy who I believe is now with one of the Penske NASCAR teams in some capacity.*

This Mercury Capri was long lived, serving as a road racer and as a rally car. I'll have to break this up into two chapters. This chapter is about the Capri as a race car, and the next one will be about the Capri as a rally car.

I had been racing an Austin Healey Sprite for several seasons but had yet to win a race. When you first begin to get involved in racing, the excitement, the competition, and the inherent danger all combine to provide an experience unlike any you have had before. Just to be racing was enough. That eventually came to an end for me.

We had begun to envy the guys who had switched from English Production Class cars, like ours, to the new Showroom Stock (SS) classes. They were driving new or nearly new cars that couldn't be legally modified and were much more reliable than our 10- and 15-year-old cars. All they had to do was fabricate a roll cage, buy a window net, fire extinguisher, and a set of competition grade seat belts.

They had tire bills too, but they were running regular street tires with most of the tread shaved off to make them stick a bit better. All of the SS cars were sedans with windshield wipers and even heaters and defrosters while all of our cars were open roadsters without windshields, just a little bug screen in front of the driver. The SS cars might not go as fast as we did or make as much noise, but their races were close and they were having a good time. A number of these cars were driven to the track with all the tools and spare parts in boxes in the back seat and trunk.

The Opel Manta Ray 1900 was the hot car. They had a big motor, good aerodynamics, and good handling. Now, 28 years later, the Opel Manta Ray 1900 is still a winner in its class. Showroom Stock cars that are more than five years old are reclassified from SS to IT, that is, Improved Touring, and are permitted a few additional changes in the interest of safety and reliability. The only problem with the Opel in the late '70s was that there were very few used ones available.

I admired the Opel, but I was interested in a different car. I had owned a '73 Capri V-6 that was a great little car for the money, and the only reason I sold it was a sudden influx of prosperity that caused me to go into showoff mode and buy a new Jaguar. I still had a thing for Capris. They had that kind of effect on people. There was a guy in Detroit who became known as Capri Carl who went overboard on Capris. He bought a lot of them and sold a few of them. He stockpiled parts for them in such quantities that I believe his wife might have left him, and he just got further and further into Capris. Last I heard he owned a field out on the south end of Telegraph Road that was just filled with Capris.

The car that caught my eye was the latest Capri: a 1976 special edition called the John Player Special. John Player, a popular brand of English cigarettes, sponsored a Formula 1 Team in the FIA World Championships. Their race cars were all black with gold pinstripes and gold-colored wheels. Ford had built a special version of the '76 Mercury Capri that copied that look, all black with gold accents on the exterior and interior as well. It came equipped with a 2.8 liter V-6 and a four-speed transmission. It had the three things I always seemed to go for: good looks, a reasonable amount of power, and some potential to be better.

I started looking through the want ads in the pulps for this particular car, the John Player Special. I found three or four in about a week's time. I picked the best of the lot, that is, lowest miles and best appearance, paid about $1900 for it and brought it home. I honestly forgot to tell the wife about it. It had been parked on the curb for a day or two when she mentioned that I should call whichever buddy owned the car and get it out of there. I told her I owned it, and it was the next race car. She asked why I would take a perfectly good car with low miles and make a race car out of it. She walked away before I could explain how Showroom Stock was such a neat deal.

It was indeed a shame to start welding a big old roll cage on the inside of such a pretty little car with its black and gold interior and black exterior with gold pinstripes and gold alloy wheels.

We soon had the roll cage in, a window net, competition seat belts and a fire extinguisher installed. Putting all that in the car added about $700 to my initial investment, and I would eventually have to get some new tires, but the ones that were on there were pretty good. One of the more financially painful things you have to do is take your nice new tires over to a shop and pay to have a few thousandths of an inch of rubber shaved off of the tread. This is permitted under the rules, and the shaved tires do stick much better. Obviously, they're not going to last very long, but they are faster for a while. And faster for a while is what racing is all about.

The other advantage to SS cars is that they must remain street legal; therefore, I could make use of it as a go-to-work car or an errands' car or maybe a winter beater.

The car was completed in time for the first race of the season in May and off to the track we went, full of hope and promise. We soon learned that SS cars had one main fault and that was that they weren't race cars. If you keep it stock, it won't stop like a car that has been modified with the addition of big brakes. It wouldn't accelerate like a car that has had its engine breathed on. You gave up all those attributes for reliability and a lower cost of operation. It seemed a little like giving up a good-looking, warm and willing girlfriend, of uncertain loyalty, for a plain girl who would never leave you.

The general equality of the cars made for close racing. In other words, we were all kind of slow. Many of the competitors were new to road racing, at least newer than we were. This made for a fair number of collisions. Fortunately, we were seldom in them. You learned who had their cars under control and who the lunatics were.

I have always been amazed at how little damage occurs when two cars come together on the track. If some of these dust-ups occurred on Woodward Avenue in the evening rush hour, both cars would be totaled. Here, if somebody rear-ended another car, the car ahead would sustain some trunk or bumper damage, but mostly of a cosmetic nature. It was the same with the car who did the hitting. He would have bent something up front but could usually keep running. Part of the reason may have been that the speed differential between the cars was only five to seven mph, and if either car went out of control and spun off of the track, they often slid across the grass alongside the track until they regained control. We had some guardrails and cement walls where spectators and officials gathered, but 90% of the track had open fields on both sides, so you would "go agricultural," until you got the car back under control.

One of the most popular places to leave the track was at the end of the back straightaway. Waterford Hills, as I may have mentioned earlier, is mostly short straights connected by sharp, flat corners. The back straight is the one place where you keep your foot down for more than just a few seconds. In these SS cars, we might get up to 85 to 90 mph before we had to brake for the 90 degree flat right hander at the end of the straight. This was the moment of reckoning, as the longer you waited to brake, the better, provided you didn't wait too long. In fact, most of the passing was done under braking. The other car would be right beside you, and you could easily look over at the other driver's face, as he was only four or five feet away. He might look over at you at the same time you're looking at him.

At 90 mph, you're traveling at 132 feet or 44 yards per second, nearly half a football field in just one second. You have to make up your mind when to brake, send the message to your foot, have the brake pedal send the fluids in the hydraulic cylinder through the brake lines to the little pistons in the brake calipers, which will in turn press the brake pads against the brake rotors, which will then slow the wheels down to reduce your speed. If your competitor does this a half second before you do, you will win the corner, provided of course that you are not going too fast to make the corner. The track authorities wisely provided a long run-off area at the end of that back straight. Great clouds of dust would rise up from that corner whenever the driver's calculus was in error. If you went off, it would take another four or five seconds to get the car stopped and turned around. By the time you got back on the track and up to speed with your confidence in your abilities somewhat damaged, the other guy would be maybe a half mile ahead.

Before every race, all cars had to submit to a technical inspection. The inspectors were mostly looking for safety-related problems, like leaky fluids or bad welding on the roll cage. They really weren't looking for cheating by the teams. And there were lots of ways to make some SS cars a bit more "equal" than others. A little work on the cylinder head to allow it to flow more air/fuel mixture would mean more horsepower, and these kinds of engine enhancements could only be seen if the motor was torn down. If you protested another driver's equipment, you had to pay a protest fee and pay for the teardown. If you were right, your money was refunded, and the other guy was shown the gate. If you were wrong, you forfeited the protest fee, and you had to pay for the teardown and the reassembly.

Since we were just racing for trophies, very few protests were filed, unless it was really a blatant infraction, like oversized tires or an extra wide tire track. Trophies have a lot of importance to some people, so there was a fair amount of cheating going on. These little touches could be found in all the cars, and we began to say that Showroom Stock had become Slightly Stock.

The strongest evidence I saw of enhancing a supposedly show-room stock car was during a race one afternoon in which several categories of SS cars raced together. We were in the class called SSB, or the middle level of speed potential. SSA cars were faster than us, and SSC were somewhat slower. In this particular race, the SSBs and the SSCs were running together. Our V-6 Capri had a 2.8 liter engine, which made good power. I think the only naughty thing we did was have it balanced and maybe the balancing made the flywheel a gram or two lighter. These things wear, you know. I was going down the back straight at a pretty good clip, only to be passed, as if I were parked, by an SSC car, a Chevy Vega with a much smaller 2.0 liter engine. This guy had to have really worked on that car to make it perform like that. He was going 20 mph faster than I was.

Some racers like to say it's only cheating if you're caught. That's nonsense. I think it comes back to the old saying, "Morality is mostly a matter of opportunity."

These racers, myself included, saw an opportunity that they could not resist, and made little bitty enhancements that might mean a half second per lap, which translates into a ten-second lead in a 20-lap race.

We did OK in SS racing, but we could see that there really wasn't any such thing as true Showroom Stock. We were all naughty in varying degrees, and nobody could really protest everybody else because lots of these things were too well hidden and would never be found out unless a drunken crew member spilled the beans a year or two later.

We did not look forward to the next season at Waterford. We were thinking about doing something else with the car, like drag racing or gymkhana racing, where you race around cones in large parking lots, racing against the clock. Then we found out about rallying.

# The Red Mist

## 1976 John Player Special
## Mercury Capri Rally Car

*1976 John Player Special Mercury Capri Pro Rally Car*

We heard about a new kind of automotive competition, a form of racing that our V-6 Capri might be fairly good at, and it wouldn't take too much (famous last words) to convert it over. This was road rallying or SCCA Pro Rally as it became to be known. Michigan was a hot bed of rally activity. Rallies like the Grayling Sno-Drift or the most famous of all, the Press On Regardless, held in the Upper Peninsula, were gaining a national following.

This kind of rallying was not the Sunday afternoon rallies where old guys wearing Harris Tweed sports coats and golf caps drove their ancient MGs and Jaguars sedately around the county, trying to cover a specific distance in a precise amount of time. Those genteel events were called time/speed/distance or TSD rallies that placed a premium on map reading and speed calculations to avoid penalty points. Those events ended at some fine-dining establishment or winery where the good life was toasted and youthful exploits remembered, with enhancements.

No, the rallies we had heard about were performance rallies, in which cars raced down gravel roads and logging trails. The objective is to travel down a series of special stages running flat out so as to take the least amount time to complete the stage. Rallies are scored like golf in that low time wins, and every second you're on the special stage is a point scored against you. The organizers of a performance rally negotiated with the citizens who lived along these remote roads and the local sheriff, to close these secondary gravel roads to the public for certain hours on the day and night of the rally. The rally organizers then recruited "marshals" to patrol the intersections of any publicly traveled roads that intersected with the rally roads in order to keep the public from straying onto these "roads." Additionally, all speed limits were lifted for the duration of the event on the special stages. If you were caught speeding by the High Sheriff on the transit roads between the special stages, you were thrown out of the rally and given an expensive ticket.

A rally route consists of transit roads to and from the special stages—special stages where the actual racing is done—and service areas. There is also a headquarters, usually a Holiday Inn where everyone stays and the rally begins and ends at. Every entry is assigned a car number, according to their ranking in events held in the recent past. The top seeds, the real pro teams backed by the factories such as Audi and Mazda, were assigned the lowest numbers and were first on the road.

The teams would consist of a driver, a co-driver who was the navigator, plus the support crew who were charged with keeping the car running under adverse conditions. The teams would roll out of the hotel parking lot in two-minute intervals, headed for the first special stage that might be ten miles away. We were given a time to appear at the start of the first special stage. Let's say we left the hotel lot at 5:00 PM and were expected at the first stage at 5:40. We would get out there a little early and wait until it was 5:40, at which time we would pull up to the start and check in with the official there. He or she would say, "You're starting the special stage at 5:42," so you would drive another fifty yards down the road to get lined up with the starter who would count you down to 5:42.

We would tighten up our belts, get the engine revved up and wait for the starter's countdown to finish at which time that official would yell, "Go!" The car would launch out of there with gravel flying, wheels spinning, a few spectators cheering, and I would be driving as fast as I could down a road I had never seen before. These roads would sometimes be smooth and fast, but often they were rough and strewn with big rocks. The co-driver held a route book in his lap that provided instructions called tulips that would tell which way to go if there was a fork in the road.

Co-drivers are either the bravest or dumbest guys in the world. Can you imagine riding with some guy who is not really sure where the road is going but is driving as fast as he can? These kinds of events are held in Europe all the time, but there the teams can run the route ahead of time and produce pace notes which tell the driver about every curve and dip in the road. Not here in North America, so pre-running is an impossibility.

Rally driving, with the car always sliding sideways, is a combination of the TV series *Dukes of Hazzard* and of the film *Deliverance*. I pushed hard, but I knew if I slid off into the woods and crashed, I was unlikely to be able to continue and therefore have to withdraw as a competitor. I was hard on the gas or hard on the brakes and always hard on the equipment. The cars have skid plates on the underside to protect the motor, transmission and gas tank. And these plates take a mighty beating. Tires get cut and go flat. If this happens in the middle of a special stage, I would try to drive on with the flat tire until the finish of the stage so as not to have extra time scored against us. Once I crossed the finish line for that stage, we would stop and quickly change the tire and then drive a transit stage to the next special stage to repeat the process. After three or four special stages, we're low on gas and probably need repairs. The organizers would have set up a service area in a roadside park where your support crew awaits your arrival. The crew had about fifteen minutes to fix our problems and get us underway to the transit to the next special stage.

During the first three or four stages, somewhere between 10% and 25% of the cars will crash or stop running for one reason or another. Wreckers would enter the stage after the last car has run through it and pick up what's left of the car and bring the driver and co-driver into headquarters. Sometimes in the middle of a special stage we would catch a car that had started two minutes ahead of us. This happened when the car ahead has had a flat or is overheating and can't go at top speed. We had to find away around him, which can be difficult on a narrow logging trail, but you need to do just that. When I would first see those taillights and realize we've caught a car that started two minutes ahead of us, a chemical change took place in my brain and a phenomenon known as the "Red Mist" took over.

I believe the term "Red Mist" was first used to describe the color that the air took on after those great medieval battles where soldiers whacked and hacked each other to the death until one army was victorious. The bloodletting and gore created an atmosphere: a fog above the battlefield that remained there and it was red in color. So the term "Red Mist" came to mean that the warrior in me took over my brain, and I would do almost anything to achieve victory. And that's how I drove. I couldn't actually hit the car in front of us in the rear. The rally rules prevented that. But if I were to get alongside him and two cars were trying to fit into the space normally occupied by one, well, I did what I had to do. Most of the time, the caught car would move over, as that was the gentlemanly thing to do, and as a group rally drivers were pretty good about not engaging in rough driving.

This "Red Mist" thing happened a lot in road racing at places like Waterford Hills. My driving went up a level or two when I was overtaking someone in my class, and we were both running for first or second place. I became one with the car and the shifting, steering, braking and accelerating were done without conscious thought. I relied on instincts to control the car, and time seemed to slow down. I knew I was doing everything possible to gain a foot here, a yard there. I calculated risk, but fear never entered my mind. My focus on the task excluded everything else. There was only the moment, no future, no past. I listened to the car, smelled the fluids, felt the heat. The car talked to me, said it couldn't do this much longer. I bargained with it, telling it to just keep it up for a couple more laps. If I made the critical pass for victory or held off the guy who was catching me, I thanked the car, and thanked my crew chief, as we were riding around on the victory lap.

Rally cars were subjected to a lot more abuse than road racing cars. The rough roads encountered on a rally could be really hard on tires, shocks and suspension hardware. We still had to go fast even if it was rough. The twin dangers were that if it was really rough terrain, the road would take the car out, and if it was smooth, we would really be flying and a high-speed mistake by the driver would take the car out. Which do you prefer: to be beat to death by a rough road or to hit a tree at 70 mph?

At the end of a Special Stage, typically seven to ten miles in length, we would cross a "finish line" in the woods, and an official would record a finishing time. As soon as I crossed the line, I slowed the car down and drove up to another official standing 100 yards beyond the finish line who, having been told our time via walkie-talkie by the finish line official, would hand us a sticker with our time on it.

The typical SCCA Pro Rally event would have 70 to 100 cars entered. It might have 125 miles of Special Stages, that is, the racing part, and 75 miles of Transit Stages. The Service Areas were located on the Transits. After three or four stages, the cars needed service. The crews would wait, looking down the road, waiting for their car to come in. About 20% of the cars would not have survived these first Special Stages. When we pulled in, the other crews would come around and ask if we'd seen Bill and Fred in Car #47. If they had crashed, and we saw them standing outside what was left of their car, we might slow down and make sure they're OK, but usually they would just signal that they were all right and I would put my foot back in it and the co-driver noted that #47 was done and that was too bad for them.

The service crew really had to hustle to refuel, change worn tires and fix something that was loose or worse. They had 15 minutes or so to do all this. If they took too long, I would have to really hustle on the Transit in order to start the next Special Stage at the assigned time, and we hoped that the High Sheriff wasn't waiting for us. If we got a ticket on a transit, we were out of the event.

The crew chief on our first rally car was Don Ensley, one of the nicest human beings on the planet. He was a huge guy, quiet and smart. I don't think I ever heard him swear. We would bring in a badly abused rally car for service with some serious problems like a nearly severed brake line or a leaking fuel hose. He would crawl under the car, lying in the mud or snow, fuel dripping on his chest, working in the dark, making do with limited parts and maybe one frozen helper. Never complained.

He owned a shop called English Motors in Utica, Michigan. He only worked on MGs, Triumphs, TVRs and Jaguars. I think the shop might still be there. Hell of a guy, one of the best. A man's man.

I have got to remember to tell a story later on about how Don's driving skills saved our lives during a long haul up to the Upper Peninsula of Michigan when a guy pulled out in front of us. Well, let me do that right now.

We were headed up to the POR, the Press On Regardless rally held in Houghton, Michigan, up in the Copper Country. The POR runs for two days, and covers over 700 miles of the roughest, meanest mining roads you ever subjected a car to.

We were driving all night in order to cover the 575 miles from the Detroit area up to Houghton. There were four of us: Don and his helper; John Erickson, my lunatic co-driver; and myself. We took turns driving my Olds diesel station wagon, which pulled the rally car on an open trailer. Don was driving, holding a cup of coffee, and ahead of us was a local guy in an old pickup. The local was slowing down to make a left turn but couldn't quite make the turn, so he pulled off onto the right shoulder to make a U-turn to get back to his turnoff. As we approached, rather than waiting for us to go past, he pulled out right in front of us. Don turned the wagon slightly to the right to go behind him, so the local would be able to cross in front of us. The guy panicked at the last second and decided to stop crossing and began to back up to return to the right side shoulder. This all happened much faster than I'm describing it. We were heading right for his driver's door, and if we hit him, he's dead and we're likely to die too as that rally car was going to leave that trailer and come right through the back window of the Olds wagon.

Ever so gently, Don got our little train turned just enough back to the left to miss this guy's front end by the thickness of a coat of paint. We were now headed for the opposite ditch, and we went down in it. The trailer overturned and dumped the rally car on its side, but it was OK except for some cosmetic damage.

We're OK too. In all of those maneuvers, Don never touched the brakes, thank God. He was a pretty good race car driver in his day, and his driving skills saved us from what could have been a deadly disaster. And he didn't spill his coffee, either. Naturally, the local was nowhere to be seen.

Our very first rally in the Capri was the Sunriser, held in Chillicothe, Ohio. We had installed the required aluminum skid plates under the motor, transmission, and gas tank. I don't think they were legally required, but you wouldn't last more than ten minutes on a rally's special stage without skid plates. Large Hella lights were added up front to put more light farther down the road.

The other important piece added to the car was the navigator's odometer. This device provided the distance traveled within 1/100 of a mile, provided it was correctly calibrated. The "odo," as it was called, ran off of a non-driven wheel. Since the Capri was rear-wheel drive, we ran ours off of one of the front wheels. The wheel spin of the driven wheels would have thrown the mileage reading way off. The display of the odo sat right in front of the navigator. Before the rally started, we drove a test route around the town with mileage known for each landmark we passed. This was needed because the rally organizers set up the route using some unknown vehicle, and we needed to get in synch with that car. The more modern odos allowed us to insert a software factor to calibrate our odo. Older Halda units came with a series of small gears that we would put in certain combinations to make the unit compliant with the organizer's mileage.

So we tooled around town and compared the mileage we had run with the "official" mileage, and if our odo showed 10% more miles than the "official" mileage, we would reduce our software factor by something like that and then re-run the town course so that we were spot on. Having our odo and our watch in exact agreement with the organizers was critical.

When we were waiting for the start of a Special Stage, we would be checking our belts and gauges and I would be asking the co-driver how he's doing. John Erickson, Little John, we called him, was always a bit under the weather. Not from heavy drink, but from heavy food. I think his mom fed him pretty healthy fare at home, and when we went on these road trips we ate at truck stops or greasy spoons and his stomach was not up to it. Poor John would get so sick. Imagine having a bad stomach, feeling car sick, and then having to ride as a helpless passenger in a hard riding, noisy car, taking some BIG chances, for seven to ten hours on end.

After one particularly bad stage down in some rally in southern Ohio, he was so ill he was beginning to pass out just as we crossed the special stage finish line and headed for a service area. You have to have a co-driver or navigator in the car with you, and he has to be the one you started with or you can't continue. We tossed poor John in the back of the service van like a broken doll and put Don Ensley in his seat and put John's helmet on Don's extra large head, and it came down to about the top of his ears. Don is a very bright guy but looking at the navigator's route book and a complicated odometer for the first time was beyond his training and understanding, especially while traveling at a high rate of knots.

We started the next Special Stage okay, but after about three miles we made a bad choice at a fork in the road and became hopelessly lost. We wandered about in the woods, driving like lunatics trying to find the rally route again. The rally gods must have had admired our efforts, because they directed us back onto the rally route just a half mile from the finish line. We may have knocked five to ten miles off of the official route because we finished with a very good time, much better than we expected. Could we have been slightly naughty, taking inadvertent short cuts with an illegal guy in the right side seat? What's a parking ticket to a couple of bank robbers like us?

As I was saying a few paragraphs back, you always had a moment before the start of a Special Stage to check the gauges over and talk to the co-driver about what was coming in the next stage. The rally route book wouldn't really tell us much about the route, but it would say how long it was and if there were any especially dangerous sections like a road with a stream running over it, a road along the edge of a cliff or maybe a steep hill that dropped off sharply right after you crested it. The co-driver would look ahead and tell me, for example, that at 3.65 miles in, there will be a deep water hole in the middle of the road. These locations were where photographers and spectators like to gather to see how the teams would manage the obstacle.

We were running a rally out of Grayling, Michigan, one night and Little John noticed a danger warning on one of the Special Stages that indicated a steep climb up a hill followed by a very abrupt drop-off. If I took it easy, we would still get airborne but knowing it was there would slow me down and save us from becoming automotive equipped ski jumpers. Little John always had a tendency to take a chance, especially if it was going to possibly be caught on film. He decided we're going to set a new record for flight in a car. He says he thinks its straight after the crest, which he has no way of knowing, and he advises to just keep my foot in it.

Well, we crested that hill doing 50 to 60 mph and literally flew for a while. I lifted off of the gas, and it got quiet. I looked out the window like a bush pilot looking for a break in the terrain to put this thing down. I saw some people off to the side looking up at us. A very brave photographer caught it on film.

*Here is the picture. If the photographer who took it*
*recognizes it, I'd like to give him credit for it.*

The Wright Brothers first flight was something like 12 seconds. Ours wasn't that long, maybe three or four seconds, but we came down hard about a half a road width off of the road. Fortunately, there were just some small saplings there and no people. We plowed through those small trees and charged on, with the front suspension badly hurt. The front tires both pointed out about ten degrees and leaned inward about ten degrees. Poor car. Great picture, though.

After the stage, I mentioned something to John about those SOB organizers who should have warned us in the rally book about that ski jump. He agreed with me at the time, but confessed on the way home.

Those were great times in that car. Little John figuring things out on the fly, big poppa bear Don putting the car back together, doing in 15 minutes what should take three or four hours. Sliding the car around, trying all the tricks you knew when you found yourself just about past the point of rescue and somehow saving it, as the tires caught the road at the last second, saving a slide off the road into some cedar swamp in the middle of the night. When you were pretty convinced that the car was going to crash, you looked over at the co-driver to see if he was aware of what was about to happen. He would seem serene and then somehow you managed to save the car, so why bring it up?

The fatigue factor was probably responsible for many late rally crashes. We would have driven 300 to 600 miles the night before just to get there for the Friday night party and registration. On Saturday, we had to get through tech inspection, attend a meeting or two, run the odometer check around town, eat some more bad food, and get the car ready for the Parc Ferme, a closed-off area where you couldn't work on the car after a certain time. We would leave the hotel headquarters about 4 PM for the transit to the first Special Stage. If we were assigned car #28, we would be the 28th car leaving the hotel, and the leaving was almost always done with some kind of ceremony. Maybe the local press or a SCCA Pro Rally photographer might take our picture.

In any case, we would drive transits and Special Stages from 4 PM until about midnight, at which time there would be the dinner break. We could get out of the car, get something bad to eat or drink, while the crew worked feverishly to put the car in shape to run until about 8 in the morning. After about 4 AM, my eyes were in pretty bad shape. I began to see things, like deer that weren't there, and not see things, like big boulders right next to the road that were there. If we finally brought the car back to the finish at the hotel in one piece, we were junk. We couldn't talk very well, were so tired, so hungry, so thirsty and our hearing was pretty well gone, not to mention my eyesight. After most rallies, we felt pretty bad all over until the following Wednesday.

Of course, if we crashed or had so many flats that we began to run more than 30 minutes behind the time the rally master had established for the last car to finish any particular stage in the rally, we were out. If we showed up at a subsequent stage too late, we were informed that, sorry, we are not allowed to continue. This was always heartbreaking, especially if we were still going strong late in the rally and then I stuffed into some swamp, and by the time we got it out, it was too late. If you don't finish a rally, for whatever reason, it was like you weren't there. DNF, Did Not Finish, carries the same points as DNS, Did Not Start. If we were to go out, better to do it early.

One of the things we tried on the Capri was a big foam bumper attached to the front of the regular bumper. This helped some when we went off into the tulle bushes and ran into small trees. The foam bumper kept the hard stuff from breaking our rally lights or messing up the hood and fenders. That worked pretty well, so we then went to a pneumatic bumper, one filled with air. I found a small manufacturer of inflatable boats who made me a tube that could be glued onto a plywood board that was bolted onto the regular bumper. It worked pretty well. We hit a lot of trees, mostly small ones, fortunately, and we never had any sheet metal damage. I do remember hitting several big trees at relatively low speeds, say less than 15 mph, and we would just bounce backward. The reason for the low speed crashes is that we would have done about everything we could do to get the car to turn or stop, and having run out of tricks, we finally went off of the road and hit something.

Forgive me if I've said this earlier, but when the crash or wreck was inevitable, and there were those milliseconds before impact, there always seemed to be just enough time to do three things. First, I would give a sideways glance at the co-driver to see if he was aware of the pending doom, and I might have time to say, "Hang on." Simultaneously, I would begin the assessment of which parts were likely to be damaged to the point where we couldn't continue, such as a radiator, clearing memory on my mental calculator to start adding up the cost of the repairs, and thirdly, I would be thinking about the story to be told of how this happened. All of this is occurring just before the big hit.

It might be suggested that I would have been better served to use those brain cycles to try some further move to save the car. Maybe so, but I had run out of tricks. We were beyond the point of rescue. Usually I didn't feel fear just before the wreck, but rather anger. I was mad at myself for making the mistake, mad that I wasn't a bit smoother, mad that our rally is over, and that the guys behind us, who weren't running as fast, are now going to be going past, giving us the obligatory look-over to make sure we weren't dying, barely concealing their glee as they continue on.

The Capri had rear-wheel drive, which is my preference, but if we got off the road a bit, getting out could be a real problem. The engine was in the front, and the driven wheels were in the rear, so traction could be a real problem, especially in snow. When we're moving fast down the road, the rear-wheel drive was the ticket. I could toss the car around, use the gas pedal to get the rear to come around, and all the front tires had to do was to steer and stop the car. But when we went off, we had a big problem getting back on the road.

We even fashioned an electric winch that we could attach to either end of the car and with the winch's cable wrapped around a nearby tree, pull ourselves out. In practice, it wasn't much good because the tree we needed was usually across the road and couldn't string the cable across the road with another car due to come by any minute.

We were starting to think about a new car, maybe a front-wheel drive model that might not be as tossable but would have a much better chance of extracting itself from a ditch.

The Capri was getting a bit tired too. When a car is sentenced to rally racing duty, it is a little like being one of the galley slaves who rowed those big Roman warships in ancient sea battles. If you don't die of exhaustion, you'll probably drown if your side loses the battle.

We put the word out on the street that we were thinking about offering our "rally proven ride" for sale and who should show up on my doorstep but Capri Carl. He had some guy in tow that was looking for a Capri he could race as a Showroom Stock car. Our Capri could do that.

You would just have to take the four extra rally lights off of the front, remove the skid plates from underneath, and take out the electronic odometer, and you're back to Showroom Stock. Well, almost. I had that engine balanced and the heads cleaned up, so it probably made another 30 horsepower over stock. We hinted that the engine was a particularly good one, but by not disclosing any specifics, the guy could go SS racing with a clear conscience, although he might have suspected we had done something naughty because the car was quite fast.

In any case, Capri Carl, midwife of commerce in his specialty, and the new owner left with the car, and I had something like $2000 in my hand.

I had a pretty good idea of what to replace it with. I had an inside angle to get a new front-wheel drive VW from a fellow who had done some co-driving for me and who worked for VW of America in their Troy, Michigan, office. I can't remember what I paid, something less than $10,000 for a brand-new VW Scirocco.

We sent the car over to Don Ensley's English Motors in Utica to be made into the next rally car.

While Don is working on the new VW Scirocco Pro Rally car, let's talk about several street cars I acquired about the same time. These were two 1980 Chevrolet Citations and a 1965 Aston Martin DB-5.

# The X-11 Had the Same Effect as Jeans Day at Alpena Catholic Central

## 1980 Chevrolet Citations:

## A Standard Two-Door & an X-11 Sport Coupe

*This 1982 Citation X-11 is owned by Jerry Brownell, Gobles, MI who has converted it from an ITA road racer to SCCA Club Rally.*

I was impressed by this new line of compact cars from General Motors. They looked different from anything else and were launched with great fanfare by GM. General Motors, like Ford, hadn't been particularly good in the past at building compact cars. They were much better at Buick Roadmaster 225s, or as our black brethren called them, "Deuce and a Quarters." GM and Ford always confused economy cars with cheaply built cars, a mistake Toyota or Honda did not make.

GM went to war against the imports in the '60s with the Corvair. Ford offered the Pinto and later the Mustang II, a thinly disguised Pinto. Now it was 1980, and GM wanted to have another go at the growing market for small economical cars, against some pretty strong competition from Toyota, Honda, Datsun (now Nissan), and Subaru.

The new GM cars were favorably reviewed by the domestic automotive press, and one might suspect that advertising dollars might have had something to do with that. Yet, they were a breath of fresh air after the dull designs of the '70s.

*This 1980 X-11 is owned by Erik Feldmanis, Indianapolis, IN.*

They were called "X" bodies for some reason, probably an in-house name for that platform, and came equipped with front-wheel drive, V-6 or straight four-cylinder engines, and four-speed manual or automatic transmissions. The four-doors were not very attractive, but I liked the lines of the two-door version. Pontiac, Olds, and Buick offered variations on the theme with slightly different body styles but the same mechanical components. A large plant in Ypsilanti, Michigan, built the Chevrolet, Pontiac and Olds models.

There was also a sport model of the Citation offered called the X-11. I test drove an X-11 and was impressed with its handling and acceleration. I put one on order at Rampy Chevrolet in Ann Arbor and waited my turn for delivery.

The delivery times began to lengthen, and I wasn't pleased when I checked on my order several times and could only find out that it hadn't been built yet. That was particularly frustrating because I see whole fields of these various GM models parked by the plant in Ypsilanti when I drove into Detroit on business, just waiting to be delivered to dealers. Apparently there were special parts not yet delivered for the X-11, like the better bucket seats.

In my frustration, I scanned the want ads in the *Detroit News* and was surprised to find a standard green two-door Citation, with a V-6 and a four-speed manual, with less than 15 miles on the clock for sale. I called the guy to get the story why he was selling the car so soon. He said it was a case of very bad marketing of the car to his wife. "How so?" I asked.

He said that he told his wife he was buying her a car as a surprise, and it would be delivered next week and he would just provide her with a hint or two as to what it was.

"I told her it was a two-door, four-speed on the floor, metallic green in color and kind of sporty, and it was a new model from Chevrolet. She jumped to conclusions and prepared herself to receive from me, her generous and loving husband, her very own new Corvette. Naturally, my gift of this nice little Citation fell flat. She's heartbroken, won't even get in it, so the car's for sale."

He was selling it at a pretty attractive price, considerably less than dealers were getting for the same model, its only sins being 15 miles on the odo and his bad marketing. My X-11 was still in limbo. I said, "What the hell," and bought it. I figured that when my X-11 came in, I would either give this one to the wife or trade it in on the ordered car.

It did take months and months for the X-11 to finally turn up. I'll bet I had 10,000 miles on the little green car by then. The wife was still quite happy with her Subaru wagon. I traded the green plain Jane in on the hot X-11.

I don't believe there was much difference between the two Citations mechanically. 1981 and later X-11 cars had work done to their cylinder heads and a more aggressive cam, but the 1980 models had the same V-6 as the plain Jane version. I think they might have picked up some zip from a freer flowing exhaust system and a lower final drive. The X-11 did have wider tires, better bucket seats, full instrumentation, and some stiffer suspension pieces. The exhaust was "rorty," with a raspy note and the close together beats of a six-cylinder engine.

Have you ever noticed how four-cylinder, six-cylinder and eight-cylinder engines sound different? With a four-cylinder, each cylinder fires with enough time between pulses that you can hear the distinct explosions, like a tap, tap, tap, tap. With an eight, the cylinders fire distinctly but two cylinders always fire close together so you get a tap-tap, tap-tap, etc., with kind of a backbeat. But with a six, each explosion is distinct but much closer together than with a four, so the beats kind of step on each other and the engine sounds busy, even at an idle. The X-11 V-6 sounded nasty, and I liked that. I have always been easily seduced by neat sounding exhaust systems, going way back to the original Triumph TR-3B roadster, which had one of the best sounding exhaust notes of any car I have ever listened to. Especially in the tunnel underneath the Detroit River that took you over to Windsor, Ontario.

*Jason Hornung, Spotsylvania, VA is selling this X-11 because the village says he has too many cars.*

Whatever it was, the two Citations had completely different personalities. I just don't think the decal job could have made that difference. They say beauty is in the eye of the beholder. Perhaps performance is in the right foot of the beholder. I drove the standard Citation like a normal human with an eye for fuel economy and preservation of its mechanicals. I drove the X-11 like a lunatic.

The X-11 brought out the bad lad in me. It kind of reminded me of how we behaved in high school when they occasionally loosened up the dress code. Alpena Catholic Central was run by a hard-nosed priest and no-nonsense nuns. There is good reason why all the pictures in the yearbook show the boys with khaki pants and button-down shirts. That's about all that was permitted. About once a month, we were allowed to wear jeans, just the boys, not the girls. When we had those jeans on, there were always a few fights, louder banter in the halls between classes, a bit more aggressive attitude towards the girls, and a general feeling of pending rebellion. The X-11 had the same effect as Jeans Day at Alpena Catholic Central.

If I were at a stoplight and some other guy in a Mustang or Camaro pulled up alongside, I would gun the motor a bit as an invitation to an impromptu drag race. Usually they would ignore me because they knew they had me covered with their more powerful V-8 engine cars. Just the same, when the light turned green, I would nail it and leave them behind.

Now the muscle-car guy was a bit irritated, especially if he had his girl with him, so when we pulled up to the next stoplight, he was ready. When the light changed we both got on it, and usually I could get away first, being lighter and with better traction, but he would soon catch up and go flying by me. I had made him work for it, though, and a lot of muscle-car guys liked to beat you with potential and not exert themselves.

When we hit the third light, he was back to taking it easy, so when that light changed, I nailed it again and left him behind for good. I made a lot of friends that way.

Speaking of stoplights, have you ever pulled up to a light and looked over to the left or right and seen a pretty girl driving her car? I could never help but smile at the sight of a real fox. Once in a while the girl would look over and notice my big grin, and she would smile back. That would make my day, and we called that "The Double I Love You." In fact, I recently wrote a poem called "At The Stoplight" about this phenomenon. Here goes:

*The light turned red*

*Doggonit, I said.*

*Looking to my left, a new silver sedan*

*Pretty lady driving, cell phone in hand*

*She in a Lexus, me in a Lincoln*

*She saw me stare, wondered what I was thinkin'*

*I gave her a smile and she smiled back.*

*How about that?*

*Couldn't wait to tell a buddy*

*And a few others too.*

*We have a name for this.*

*It's "The Double I Love You."*

I had inflicted considerable wear and tear on the X-11, and it held up pretty well. No clutch or drive train problems at all. That little 2.8 liter V-6 was a willing engine. I love an engine that just winds and winds, and it did.

While I had the X-11, I bought a couple of other vehicles. One was a simple Dodge van that remained in the family for almost ten years, making it the single longest period of ownership for any vehicle I have ever owned. The other car was an exotic that I probably shouldn't have bought, yet I sold that one way too soon. That was the car James Bond made famous: the Aston Martin DB-5.

So at that time, I had the X-11 for everyday driving, a Dodge van for hauling a rally car around, a '76 Capri V-6 rally car, and the Aston Martin for general showing off. My wife was beginning to question my sanity, again.

The X-11 was getting a bit tired and was eventually replaced by a 1984 Oldsmobile Cutlass Supreme, but let's talk about the Aston Martin DB-5 next.

# Twenty-Four Seconds to the Mile

## 1965 Aston Martin DB-5

*This is the model of the Aston Martin line made famous by James Bond, Secret Agent 007, of Her Majesty's Secret Service in a series of popular movies.*

I came across this car one evening when I was visiting a guy I met at a Jaguar club meeting. We were at his house looking over the two Jaguars he owned. One he had had for a while, and the other was a recent addition.

Over in the corner, looking somewhat neglected was another car, a burgundy coupe, with the left side of the car just inches from the wall, as my friend needed all the space he could get for his active projects. I remarked upon how difficult it would be to get in the driver's side to move that car, and he responded with, "Not really. Look again, that car has right hand drive."

What was I looking at, I wondered? He read my mind and volunteered, "It is an Aston-Martin DB-5 Coupe that I bought in England the last time I was over there. I just haven't had time to spruce it up, but it runs OK, looks good, and just needs a bit of detailing and maybe a tune-up, as sometimes it takes a bit of patience to get it to start. I think the choke only works on one of its three carburetors, so I have to sort that out."

"Three carbs, you say?" Now, my curiosity was beginning to increase, usually not a good thing around cars.

"Yes, Aston Martins came with a straight six-cylinder, 4.2-liter engine with double overhead cams, just like Jaguars. This beast has so much torque, it almost doesn't matter if you start in first or second gear and then shift to fourth gear before you get to 40 mph because it just pulls and pulls all the way up to about 150 mph."

"No kidding, it will really go 150?"

"Well, it would when it was new fifteen years ago. I don't know that it wouldn't do that today, tuned up, but I think I might worry about going that fast on these old tires."

I looked at the tires, and the tread didn't look too bad, but there were some aging cracks in the sidewalls, as you might expect. The tires were tall and thin, mounted on chrome wire wheels, and they had a great name embossed on the sidewalls. They were called Avon Turbo Speeds. I could just see them forming an oval or ellipse at high speeds, like an old-time poster of an early race car.

"It says *Superleggera* on the side panel. What does that mean?"

"That's Italian for super light, as the body is all aluminum."

"How about the *DB*?"

"That stands for David Brown, an Englishman who rescued the company after the war and has kept it going all these years."

Who couldn't help but be interested in this car, a 150 mph aluminum bodied coupe that was the same brand and model that James Bond himself had selected as the epitome of British automotive class?

Sensing that the hook had been set, my friend said, "Oh, by the way, I'm thinking about selling the car rather than keeping it. My original plan was to have the one Jaguar and the Aston Martin, but then I couldn't turn down the deal I got on the other Jag."

"Does it have any problems that you know about?"

"No problems, but there are two things I wish were different on the car: namely, the right hand drive setup and the lack of air conditioning. There were left hand drive Aston Martins built for export to the States, but this one was meant for the home market where right hand drive is an obvious requirement and air conditioning isn't, given their climate."

He continued on. "Luxury cars always had A/C, but this car was considered a high speed touring car, and it could be had with or without the air. Over here, the car can be pretty warm in the summer, so I found I was just driving in the spring and fall. Also, I just could never quite get used to right hand drive. In theory, what's the difference? But the gear shifter is in your left hand, the turn signals are in your right hand, and you're looking around the right side of the car in front of you to see if it's OK to pass him. I hate to sell it because it is so unique, but I only have so much room in here. The wife's car has to be in here in the winter too, so I'm going to have to find another home for it. I had it appraised for $8000, but I'd be happy with $7000 as that's about what I paid for it, and I really haven't done much to it."

I wasn't quite ready to part with $7000 for a unique piece of merry old England, but I was certainly intrigued. I said that I would think about it and perhaps I might come back on the weekend and look at it in the daylight. He thought that would be fine and said to call and set something up, so he would have it out of the garage and ready to go when I showed up.

Astrologers often talk about the planets being in a certain alignment, and when that occurs, unusual things can happen. There are three elements rather than planets that, if aligned, and present in sufficient quantities, make it difficult for me to resist buying a car. These are the unique beauty of the car, the sounds the engine makes, and a sufficiently large commission check from a recent sale of computer systems for my employer. The last part occurred several times per year as business was very good from 1970 to 1983, and I was often "sales guy of the year" for our little company. If I got a commission check for $18,000, say, I could often persuade the wife to take $12,000 for the household and let me have $6000 for my automotive pleasures. We received a regular salary, and the commission checks were always a big surprise to her.

Naturally, I took advantage of the situation. One of these checks arrived while I was thinking about the Aston Martin. I got in touch with my friend and set up the demo drive for the next weekend.

When I got there, he had it out of the garage and ready to go. I knew he would get it started and warmed up ahead of time, so there would be no embarrassment with starting it. I put my hand on the hood and could feel the heat from the engine's recent warm-up. I also looked in the garage where it had been parked to see if I could see any oil spots on the floor. He noticed that and said he hadn't found any leaks either. We both laughed, but I was a little embarrassed.

I suggested he drive it first. That way I could look around at the interior and listen and smell and get an overall impression as to how the car moved down the road. It was very odd, at first, to be sitting on the left hand side as a passenger with the driver to the right.

The car sounded very mechanical, that is, you could hear the motor's rising revolutions clearly and the transmission's whine was quite apparent. It sounded like straight-cut gears, and the ratios were spaced far apart. The engine had a ton of low-end torque.

Most modern engines need to turn at fairly high revs to make good power, but not this one. It reminded me of one of the Jaguars and the Triumph TR-3B that I had owned in that these were all low revving engines that had long strokes. Modern engines have very short strokes. That means that the piston doesn't travel very far up and down in the cylinder, and the engine's internal components will remain in balance so they can be run at much higher engine speeds. With a long stroke, you make a lot of torque right away but you can't rev them very high or the engine's internal balance may fail. I think the Aston's engine had an upper limit of about 6500 revolutions per minute. The transmission was matched to the engine's torque and operating range so that it could indeed approach 150 mph in the right state of tune.

The other desirable characteristic, especially of English cars, is a distinctive exhaust note. It has to sound like it means business without being too loud or obnoxious. It should sound unique and hint strongly at latent power, like a distant thunderstorm, slowly approaching.

The Aston Martin DB-5 held a PhD in exhaust notes. Six cylinders, with three large carburetors, one for each two cylinders, flowing massive amounts of air and fuel, meant a large volume of hot gasses rushing out through the exhaust headers down to the mufflers, out through the resonators to the end of the exhaust pipes, making a glorious sound that rose as the car accelerated smartly up through the gears, and then a steady exhaust note as our speed leveled off. He made the shift to fourth gear when we were around 50 mph, but I noticed we could slow down to 35 mph, in traffic, and he might not downshift as the car would pull nicely even though the motor was running barely above idle. He drove for about five miles and pulled off on a side street and asked what I thought thus far. I just grinned, as we got out and switched sides.

I buckled up my lap belt and looked things over. The shift setup looked normal with first gear upper left, second lower left, third upper right and fourth gear down to the lower right in the classic "H" shift pattern. The steering wheel was big, with lots of legroom under it, and the turn signal stalk was on the right hand side. I adjusted the rear-view mirror to my liking, looked over my left shoulder to see if anyone was coming, and seeing no one, put it in first gear with my left hand, and pulled out onto the street. The clutch took some effort to push in and release gradually, but the gear shifter was buttery smooth.

He had driven around on suburban boulevards, and I wanted to see what the Aston was like out on the freeway. As I accelerated down the on ramp in third gear, it just took off, almost like a small plane reaching a speed where liftoff occurs. We must have entered the freeway at 80 to 85 mph. He gave me a nervous smile as we overtook cars driving at the normal five or ten mph over the speed limit.

It is an unwritten Michigan law that you are not to drive at the posted limit on the freeway for to do so invites ridicule and anger. In fact, when they passed the 55 mph after the '73 gas shortage, several socialist professors from the University of Michigan attempted to enforce the law by driving side by side from Ann Arbor to Detroit, thus blocking all three lanes and preventing anyone from passing. Well, talk about instant civil unrest, cars and semi-trucks were passing them on the shoulder, traffic was backed up for miles, and the air was blue. The State Police arrested the profs and charged them with disturbing the peace. I think they let them off with a slap on the wrist, and that was the end of that kind of foolishness.

I slowed down a bit and just drove, looking at the water temp and oil pressure gauges, which were in the normal range. I noticed another switch on the dash, unlabeled, and asked my friend what it was for. He said, "That's kind of a neat feature. It controls how much air pressure there is in the rear shocks. You probably know that most shock absorbers, or dampers as the English would say, are filled with oil and they work by forcing oil through a small aperture inside the shock body when the car hits a bump and the wheel rises up, compressing the shock which dampens the impact, hence the name "dampers." How much dampening depends on the size of the oil aperture. The smaller the aperture, the stiffer the shock. How stiff the shock is affects the ride quality and also affects how loose the rear end of the car is. If you want a comfy ride, you want a soft shock, but if you are racing or driving fast and you want to steer the car around tight corners with the gas pedal, you need the rear end to be able to break loose, and so you need a stiff shock. What Aston Martin did was add an air chamber to the shock, so it could be made soft or hard by the switch on the dash that controlled a small air compressor. Kind of neat, eh? I usually leave it on the soft setting, but it is fun to fool around with on a twisty road when you want the rear end to dance a bit."

I can't imagine I would throw this relatively heavy car into a corner and then depend upon the rear end breaking loose with a massive application of power, but you never know.

By the time we got back to his house, the die was cast. The car looked great, sounded great, and I had the money. So all the planets, I mean elements, were in alignment. My resistance was gone. If we can improve the price, I'm a buyer. Now came the fun part, the haggle.

Some folks don't like to bargain. They don't like the tension, the possible hard feelings and the fact the final price depends in large part on their ability to haggle. They would rather pay a fixed price with no room for negotiation. Not me. I enjoy the experience, but wish I were better at it. I'm better at getting the other guy to lower his price when I'm buying than I am at holding my price when I'm selling.

Everyone knows that you want to buy low and sell high, but the more important thing is to know that you assure your eventual profit, if any, when you buy, not when you sell. You want to buy the car or boat or house at such a price that a profit is guaranteed if you had to sell it the next day or five years from now. That's why new car dealers always offer you a little less than wholesale when you trade your car in. That way they can wholesale it out tomorrow with some profit.

You don't want to buy something worth $5000 for $3000 that needs $1500 worth of repairs. The repairs could be much more than that, as they generally are, and the selling price is a guess as well. But, if you buy something this morning for $3 that can be sold for $5 tomorrow afternoon without further expense, then you have made your money at purchase time.

He was asking $7000, and he thought it was worth at least $8000. He said he hadn't put any money in it, just wanted out of it what he had in it. You never really know if a guy is being truthful. A car salesman once said to me, "A priest is not a priest when he buys a car." He meant that normally righteous people shade the truth or tell outright fibs in car buying negotiations. I can put my hand on my heart, standing on my mother's grave, and say that I never did that. What I will admit to, though, is managing the news. I would disclose any known weaknesses, such as a tendency to overheat if you just let it idle on a summer day, and I would say that the tires have so much life left. I wouldn't bring anything else up, and I wouldn't claim that the engine is good for another 50,000 miles because you never know. Also, I would always put on the bill of sale: "Sold In "As Is" Condition."

I was hoping to buy the car for $5000, so I would be in a position to sell it at a profit if I tired of right hand drive or the bloom came off of the rose for whatever reason. He countered with $6500 but said he did have another place to store it if he had to keep it, which was a roundabout way of saying, hey, I don't really need to sell this thing.

If that were the case, I reasoned, he wouldn't have brought up selling it in the first place. What was the likely truth is that he could store it elsewhere, but there was some cost or inconvenience involved, which he hoped to avoid by selling it now. I countered by agreeing with him that there was no need for him to sell it and no real need for me to buy it because while it was a neat car, a unique car, perhaps even a valuable car, it was a niche vehicle that most car buyers could live without, especially with the right hand drive. We traded a few more assertions, and then came that moment where either you walk away, hoping he will offer a lower price to your back, or you make one more offer to see if it's his turn to walk away.

"I'll offer $6000, my friend, and that's the best that I can do." He had a pained look on his face, as he thought about it. I wondered if that was theatrics or was he really in a quandary about what to do.

"Done," he said, and I owned an Aston Martin DB-5.

Driving it home, I felt a bit self-conscious, with people staring at the Aston Martin, probably wondering why I was driving from the right side and wondering what it was. I imagine some people recognized the type from the James Bond movie and wondered what it was doing on the freeways of Detroit. I was enjoying myself, that's for sure. I loved the look of the car and the beautiful noises it made. I can still hear it, going up through the gears, blipping it for the downshift, and then back on the gas. It was intoxicating.

You have to make a choice with a car like this. Do you want to make it perfect and enter it into the Concours de Elegance that are held each year at places like Meadowbrook, the old

Dodge Brothers estate near Detroit? The Jaguar and Ferrari guys do that with some of their cars; even going so far as to trailer them there, so not to risk any road wear. Or do you want to use it as a daily driver where it would see rain and maybe road construction and possible parking lot damage? I bought this beast to drive and drive it I did.

Of course, I wouldn't drive it in the winter or during a summer heat wave, but the rest of the year I put a lot of miles on it. My sales territory at this time consisted of Ohio, a bit of western Pennsylvania, Indiana, and Michigan. I would set up a trip that was essentially a big clockwise circle. I always looked forward to getting out of the office and back out on the road.

*My father, Walter Nowak, of blessed memory,*
*daughter Jennifer, and me.*

Most of my business was in Columbus and Indianapolis. It's about 180 miles to Columbus and 260 miles from Ann Arbor to Indy. I'd head south out of Ann Arbor on US-23 toward the Ohio state line, maybe stopping to see some clients in Toledo. Normally, I was in a hurry to get to Columbus and my first pit stop would be in Bowling Green, Ohio, for a coffee refill and bladder service. Gas was usually cheaper in Ohio than in Michigan, so it was a good place to fill up. Two hours later, I would be in Columbus.

Some guys didn't like traveling. With a car like this, who could mind?

I might stay in Columbus overnight and then head southwest to Cincinnati or west to Dayton where I had a couple of large customers. Heading west out of Dayton in the Aston Martin on I-70, it was another two hours to Indianapolis, one of my favorite towns. We had a state government customer plus a big installation at a mail order music fulfillment company there that had to process more than a million documents per day. I remember that contract very well as its proceeds bought my first Jaguar, the XJ6L, back in 1974.

After Indy, I might shoot out to Terre Haute where I had another big mail order music fulfillment account. If not, it was time to head back up I-69 north through Fort Wayne, where a big insurance company had tossed out an IBM system in favor of ours. After that, it was just 150 miles back to Ann Arbor.

The point of this little travelogue is that I enjoyed driving 750 miles in three or four days, with work breaks in between the motoring segments. I was out on the open road, free as a bird, but with a purpose and a destination. You could do that in any car, and I have, but it was so much more enjoyable to do when you were piloting a unique car like the Aston Martin DB-5.

All of this driving did take its toll on the car. I noticed some rust in front of the rear-wheel wells and wondered how that could be on an aluminum-bodied car. I took it to Import West Collision over in Inkster, and my friend Steve advised me that where the aluminum met the steel frame, a type of

145

electrolysis could take place, and that it would eat away at the aluminum. He fixed it up, and it looked fine.

I found some more "rust" a bit later on, and I returned to Steve to see what it would take to fix it. I also asked what to do about the various stone chips I was getting in the front. After much discussion, we concluded it might not be a bad idea to paint the car, the whole car. We picked out a color very similar to what was on it and found out later that we really should have researched that a bit further and used an Aston Martin factory paint color, rather than one that was "close." Who knew? We weren't collectors.

I got a firm quote from Steve of something like a $1000 for the job, which seemed like a lot of money at the time. After he got into it, I got a phone call from Steve, crying the blues. He had discovered a number of additional areas on the car that needed to have the aluminum replaced. He didn't ask for more money, to his credit, and he did a fine job, but as he took my check he said, "Never again will I work on an aluminum-bodied car for a fixed price. Too many expensive surprises."

One of the characteristics of the Aston Martin that endeared me to it was the feeling of control that it imparted when you were running at high speeds. It sometimes acted a bit cranky and even noisy at normal cruising speeds but seemed to get quieter once you were moving above 75 mph. Even with the windows rolled down, which I would often have done, because of the lack of A/C, it didn't have very much in the way of wind noise.

It was so quiet at high speeds; I began to doubt the speedometer. I arranged to do a timed test, late one evening, on an isolated stretch of I-96 west of Lansing, where I would have it going as fast as I could get it to go, with the windows up, aging Avon Turbospeed tires with sidewall cracks notwithstanding, and then get my stopwatch ready, as I approached a highway mile marker. I looked at the speedometer, and it was right on 150 mph, but it didn't seem like I was really moving that fast. As I passed the marker I would start the watch and stop it when I passed the next one. I wrote the number of seconds down, reset the watch and then waited for another mile marker to start another test mile. I couldn't take too long because either the High Sheriff would appear or the tires might fail. I'm not sure which would have been worse. Either one would be expensive.

If you cover the flying mile in 60 seconds, you're going 60 mph. If you do it in 30 seconds, you are doing 120, and if you could cover that much ground in 20 seconds, you'd be doing 180. Mile after mile, the Aston Martin would take 24 seconds. How fast is that? You can do the math, or I can do it. Here we go, class, so pay attention.

D = S x T. That is, Distance traveled equals Speed x Time. Since the distance traveled is one mile, whether you're covering it in 60 seconds or 24 seconds, we could say:

The S x T at 60 mph ought to equal the S x T at the faster unknown speed. We have to get the units consistent, so I'll change the 60 mph to its equivalent in feet per second, which is 88 feet per second. Putting our known values into this Distance equals Distance equation we have:

88 feet/sec x 60 seconds equals S feet/sec x 24 seconds, or

5280 feet equals 24S feet/second, and solving for S, we have: S = 220 ft/second.

220 feet/second is our speed that we'll have to convert back to miles per hour. So, in an hour's time, we would have traveled for 3600 seconds and covered 220 feet/sec x 3600 seconds or 792,000 feet. How far did we go in miles? At 5280 feet to the mile, we get the distance covered by dividing 792,000 feet by 5280 feet/mile and the answer is 150 miles.

When you cover 150 miles in an hour, how fast did you go?

The speedometer said 150 mph. It was spot on. Not bad for a 15-year-old car. I must confess that when I first did this little equation, I somehow came up with 144 mph and that little error was pointed out by my English friend, Alan Ware, who suggested I redo the math.

After about two years of fairly heavy use, I began to tire a bit of the car. I had another domestic car at the time, probably an Olds Cutlass coupe, and I found myself driving that more and more, especially if the weather was hot.

When you decide to sell a car, you do a reverse justification. Just like when you bought it and used half-baked justifications and rationales to buy it, the same is true when you sell it. All of sudden it has faults that you didn't mind for a long time, but now are major problems. As you might expect, the right hand drive thing became the big problem. I was used to it, didn't really mind it, but it always was a physical and mental adjustment.

I put it up for sale on my little corner near our house, Cayuga Place at Stadium Boulevard in Ann Arbor, and put an ad in the paper. Now, I have sold a lot of cars off of this corner, but the Aston just didn't get much interest locally. Most Ann Arbor citizens wouldn't know Aston Martin from a Purple Martin. It is just not a car town.

There was a Ferrari dealer in Dearborn called the Sports Car Exchange, owned by a nice guy named Bob Schneider. I used to stop in there and admire the Ferraris, Alfa Romeos and the exotics he took in trade. Eddie Atkinson, my guide to all things English, had worked there as well. Bob told me he would take the car on consignment and keep it indoors. We settled on an asking price of $9000 with a small selling commission for him. Probably took two months to sell but Bob never complained, even though space was a very valuable commodity in his small dealership. A guy who worked at Ford, Bill Hallendahl, bought it and kept it for at least five years. He wished we had painted it a correct Aston Martin color but didn't feel strongly enough about it to have it repainted.

Ford Motor Company bought the Aston Martin firm from its British owners and needed to have an Aston Martin at their press conference announcing the sale. Since there were no Aston Martin dealers in Michigan at the time, and they didn't have the time to get one from somewhere else, Hallendahl's Aston Martin DB-5 was brought in for the press affair.

I understand that Bill eventually sold the car to a collector for a decent price. Good for Bill and good for that particular car. I hope it is well looked after. It never let me down, always lifted my spirits when we were hurtling down the road, occasionally at 24 seconds to the mile.

# "If It Don't Stay Together, I'll Always Have Thought It Shoulda"
## 1982 VW Scirocco Rally Car

*This was Rally Car #2, the successor to the '76 Capri. That's son Joseph posing with me just before we left for a rally up north. He and his brother Mike would often go along with the support crew.*

Prior to acquiring this car, we had been campaigning the Capri as a race car for a year and as a rally car for two years. It had taken its lumps and bumps and was still in pretty good shape, considering all the abuse it had endured. It still had the black paint job and gold pinstripes that marked it as a John Player Special, a street car that Ford had been marketing in England and elsewhere as a tie-in to the John

Player Special Formula One race cars that employed Ford Cosworth engines.

One of the reoccurring problems we had with the Capri as a rally car was getting back on the road once we went off into the tullies. Rear-wheel drive is great for getting the rear to come around when you really need it to but not much good when you're nose down in a ditch after going off. The weight of the engine is at one end of the car and the drive wheels are at the other end.

The front-wheel drive cars didn't have the ability to use the throttle to turn the car, but they managed by other means. Some used an emergency brake on the rear wheels that had its ratchet catch removed so that when you pulled it, it was momentarily on to break the rears loose and then off when you let go of the handle.

The big advantage of the front-wheel drive was slogging thru mud and snow and getting unstuck when you ran off the road. Saabs and Audis could often keep on going after an off road excursion, while we knew if we went off, particularly in the winter rallies, we were done. We suffered a real heartbreaker at the Press On Regardless rally. We had covered 700 miles in two nights of rallying, but late in the rally we went just a little way off into a shallow ditch and could not get out of there and did not finish. This happened just ten miles from the end, and we were running second in the stock class and tenth overall in a field of one hundred cars. We retrieved the car, put it on the trailer and headed back to the Detroit area, a drive of almost 600 miles. No one spoke for the first 300 miles. We all felt just awful. I felt the worst, as it was my error that put us out.

When we stopped feeling sorry for ourselves, probably around Grayling, the discussion started on what we would be doing the following season. My co-driver and navigator at the time was Bob Sharp who worked at Volkswagen of America. There weren't sponsorships available, at least not for us, but he said he might be able to assist in getting a new front-wheel drive car for me that I could purchase at an attractive discount.

After we got back, we began to look into this deal pretty seriously. One thing led to another, and pretty soon I was poring over VW brochures. The Golf was available, but I liked the look of the Scirocco better.

There was one available at a VW dealership up in Utica, and I went over to look at it. It was black with red and silver accent stripes and special edition alloy wheels. The bucket seats were just like Recaros, which were the best seats available at the time. I made the arrangements to purchase it and waited for the deal to go through the corporate approval processes. It was all on the up and up with lots of official paperwork. I think I paid something like $9700 for a new VW Scirocco.

It was a fun car to drive. Lightweight, responsive, with very little torque steer, you could really have fun on a twisty road. I wondered if I was doing the right thing, taking a neat little car and doing the things necessary to make it into a rally car.

I did that to the Capri, so taking another nice new car's virginity away was something I could live with, even though it was painful to watch.

Out came the interior, in went the custom roll cage. Large aluminum shields were bolted on the bottom to protect the engine, transmission and gas tank. We had to run the odometer cables to the rear wheels because the driven wheels in front would be spinning too much and would throw the mileage calculations way off. Big rally lights had to be attached to the front bumper. Extra wiring and switches had to be installed. All of this work was done expertly and inexpensively up at Don Ensley's English Motors in Utica.

We had a welder come in and fabricate the roll cage. In the process of welding in the roll cage, he melted a breather tube inside of a wall panel that was connected to the gas tank to allow air in to replace the fuel being pumped out. This

turned out to be a costly error that was not discovered until we were en route to our first rally.

That first rally was the 100-Acre Wood in Rolla, Missouri. Because the car had less than 500 miles on it before we started its conversion, we took it off of the trailer part way down and drove it for a while to put some miles on it, so it would be properly broken in before we drove it in competition. We planned to drive it several hundred miles, but it appeared to run out of gas after about 60 miles. This didn't seem possible, as we had filled it up just before the trip. We looked under the car to see if there was a leak in the tank. What we found was a gas tank that had shrunk to the size of about two footballs in volume. The fuel pump was so powerful that when it pumped the fuel up to the engine for the fuel injection and there was no air coming in the blocked breather tube, it collapsed the gas tank!

Having enough fuel in a normal size tank is always a concern on a rally because the service stops for refueling can sometimes be a hundred miles apart and with a lot of time spent in the lower gears, fuel goes quickly, and you might not make it. Now with our collapsed tank, we were in real trouble. We took a vote on whether to continue on to Rolla. Two guys said no, two guys said yes, so we proceeded on to the rally, hoping we might find a VW dealer in St. Louis who might have stocked a spare gas tank for the Scirocco.

There were no tanks available at dealers along the way, but we continued on, finally arriving in Rolla, Missouri, at the Holiday Inn, the rally headquarters. Looking at the overall map of the rally and the location of the service stops, it appeared that we might be able to just make it if we drove with an eye towards getting good mileage, a most unusual condition for a rally effort.

It was interesting to discover that the route book noted several underwater bridges. If you haven't ever crossed an underwater bridge, it can be pretty exciting. It seems that certain streams in Missouri are dry most of the year but are

filled with water in the spring, as you would expect. The bridge consists of a paved surface across the creek bed with markers that stick up through the water at the four outer corners of the "bridge."

We drove out to the start of the first special stage and got ready to go on the maiden voyage of our new rally car. We got through the stage quickly, as the car was a joy to flick around. Its light weight made it easy to slow down and easy to accelerate, which is what rally cars are always doing.

After the first special stage there was a service area on the transit to the next special stage, so we were able to gas up. We were on the second special stage, moving pretty well, when something happened to the shifter mechanism and it wouldn't come out of second gear. We needed to get into a higher gear for gas mileage reasons and because we were being overtaken by another rally car that had started two minutes behind us and had caught up.

There were two choices: let the other car by and limp through the stage and see if we couldn't get it sorted out after the stage was completed. Might just be a rock or a stick that had jammed the external linkage. Or I could try to get it to change gears by brute force, which is what I did. It did come out of gear, all right, but it didn't go into third, but rather into first. The motor lived, but the clutch didn't. We were done. Damn, Damn, Damn.

After all the rally cars passed through the stage, we retrieved our car and put it on the trailer for the long haul back to Michigan. We noticed that one of the trailer's steel braces had come apart, and we needed to find a welder to fix it.

The welder worked on it for about an hour and charged me $10. Fair enough. As far as guaranteeing that it would hold together for the entire trip back to Detroit, he said, "If it don't stay together, I'll always have thought it shoulda."

Back in Utica, we had a new clutch installed and got ready for the next rally. I think the next outing was in Michigan,

probably the Northern Lights Rally, normally held up in the Grayling area. This was a winter rally with lots of snow and mud. Front-wheel drive or four-wheel drive is what you want in that slop. The rally was going OK; we were still in the hunt, when the oil pressure light came on. We pulled over, and listened for a minute, noticing that the engine temp was normal, no smoke, and no knocking noise. We checked to see if there was a normal amount of oil in the crankcase, and there was. We decided that there was sufficient oil pressure and somehow the sensor had gone bad. It was tough to wail on it with that red light staring you in the face, so we covered it up with tape. Lucky for us, we were right. I believe we finished in the top third in the Production class.

The big rally event of the summer was the Sunriser 400, held in Circleville, Ohio. Southern Ohio has some great rally roads, so we were looking forward to it. Michigan rallies are usually kind of on the rough side, especially the ones in the Upper Peninsula, like the POR, but Ohio roads were smooth and fast for the most part. This particular event was going to start at 4 PM, so we would have four or five hours of daylight. Daylight can be dangerous because you can see farther ahead and therefore tend to run a lot faster. Nothing wrong with going fast, but if you're wrong and you make a mistake, it's usually a big one.

We were running along the southern slope of a river valley that ran east-west and was about a mile across from ridge to ridge. We could see a mile or two ahead, and the road we were on followed the river, running parallel to it. The road was situated above halfway up the slope between the river and the ridge. We were probably running about 100 mph on this beautiful smooth dirt road, assuming that the road we could see ahead of us was the road we were on.

All of a sudden we got the surprise of our lives. Our road took a ninety-degree turn to the right because there was another smaller river flowing into the main river from the

right. Our road would continue after that turn to a bridge that crossed the river we weren't prepared for.

There was no hope of making that corner. We were going too fast. I threw it sideways to scrub off as much speed as possible, but it was too late. We slid off of the road, out in to space, did a slow roll in the air and landed on our roof in the river. We probably fell one to two stories and found ourselves in three feet of water. Other than minor bruises, we were fine. We needed to get out of the car as quickly as possible because we knew that other rally cars would be arriving in two minutes or less and they might make the same mistake we did.

Whenever you're sitting upside down in a race car, you do want to leave your helmet on while you undo your safety harness because when you do unbuckle, you're going to fall on your head. We unhooked, got the helmets off, and rolled the windows down, so we could get the doors open. We scrambled ashore just in the nick of time, as here came a Datsun, going way too fast, and off they went, landing on top of our car. That probably hurt. Didn't do our car any good, that's for sure.

We climbed the embankment up to the road and set some flares a hundred yards up the road from the corner and that slowed the rest of the field down, so we had no more company in the water.

Our rally was over, of course. The wrecker arrived a couple hours later and brought the Scirocco ashore and set it back on its wheels. We took the spark plugs out of the VW motor and had the starter turn it over a few times to make sure there was no water inside the motor. If there had been water in the cylinders and we tried to start it with the plugs in place, then we could have grenaded the engine because fluids do not compress.

The plugs went back in, and it started right up. Amazing. It didn't steer very straight or want to stop, but we were able to

drive it slowly back to rally headquarters and put it on the trailer for the long sad tow back to the shop.

After a 48-hour mourning period, we had a meeting to see what could be done with the car. It had no glass, not a single undented panel and the roof pillars leaned about 15 degrees toward the passenger side. You would normally just total the car and that would be that. But the mechanicals seemed fine; the roll cage proved its worth and was still intact. What it needed was lots of bodywork and a new roof. I bought another Scirocco body shell for $75, and we removed what was left of the original roof and its pillars and welded the new roof on.

It must have taken about a month of evenings and weekends to get the car ready to go again. We were running behind schedule to make the POR in the Upper Peninsula and just got it done by the time we were scheduled to start our 575-mile run up to Houghton, Michigan. We finished the painting of the roof ten minutes before departure. The paint was "air dried" at 65 mph out on northbound I-75.

This was our second go at the Press On Regardless rally. It covers 600 to 750 miles of bad mining roads and takes two nights to complete. Less than half the cars would be around at the end.

We drove out to the start of the first special stage and waited for our turn to start. For a month we had worked long nights and weekends to get the car back in shape, and now we were going to be rallying again. "Three, Two, One, Go!" We were off and running hard. The car lasted about a minute before the fuel pump quit. We were done.

All those hours worked, all that money spent, and we lasted about 60 seconds. The 100-Acre Wood in Rolla was a heart breaker; the Sunriser 400 in Circleville was another heart breaker, and now this, this 600-mile trip to the POR in Houghton to run just 60 seconds. Yes, we had run other rallies successfully in the Scirocco, but these rallies were the big ones. This kind of stuff makes you want to weep.

I began to convince myself that this little car was snake bit. We had run the wheels off of the Capri with hardly a mechanical problem. Sure we crashed out a few times and had trouble getting extricated from a ditch or ravine, but the car could be trusted. I was losing trust in the VW and began to look around. I knew a guy that was interested in buying the Scirocco so that was some comfort. I just needed to find something better than what I had.

Audi and Mazda fielded factory teams for John Buffum and Rod Millen respectively. They finished first or second or crashed out in every rally from 1978 through 1982. We didn't compete against them because we ran in the Production class, which was essentially stock, while they ran in the Open class, where just about anything was permitted. Millen's RX-7 had four-wheel drive. Ever see a four-wheel drive Mazda RX-7 at a dealer? Audi had the Turbo Quattro, an awesome car with close to 400 HP distributed among all four wheels.

Another Audi was being campaigned out west in Seattle called the Audi 5 + 5. Audi only made the car in 1983, and not many of them. It was the small lightweight 4000 body with the five-cylinder engine from the larger 5000 car. It had a five-speed transmission, hence the name 5 + 5. This particular 5 + 5 being rallied out there was painted in Audi team colors. The owner worked at an Audi dealership and likely received some indirect financial help, like buying it new at a good price, free spares, and the like.

I became aware that this car was up for sale, probably through my Volkswagen of America connections as VW owned Audi. I got in touch with the guy and we talked about the particulars of the car, how he did with it, what he did to it and what he wanted to get for it. It turned out that I could sell my Scirocco for more than the Audi would cost.

The only problem was that the car was in Seattle, and I would have to take a chance that when I got there and inspected the car, it would be all that he claimed it would be. He sent some recent pictures, and I was hooked. I sold my Scirocco to some would-be rally driver and set in motion plans to acquire the Audi 5 + 5. I never did see the Scirocco at a rally after that.

Looking back on the VW Scirocco, I concluded that it might have worked for another guy, who might have been a bit more tender with it. I think the Capri spoiled me. It would take a beating and keep on going. I never put the Capri on its roof in a river, though, so maybe that's not a fair comparison. In any case, the Scirocco was gone, and I was hatching a plot to acquire the Audi 5 + 5.

# We Left Early the Next Morning
# Without Waking Her
## 1983 Audi 5 + 5 Rally Car

*This was rally car #3, the successor to the VW Scirocco.*

The more I studied the Audi's specifications and its possibilities, the more I wanted it. Here was a rally car ready to go with roll cage, odometer hookup, extra lights, extra wheels, and no apparent body damage. It had an estimated 3000 miles on the clock, of which the owner estimated about half were driven on special stages, the all-out racing part of professional rallying. He said he had laid it on its side once, but everything was repaired and working at the dealership, which provided him with the facilities to keep it well maintained.

Rallying is a tough sport, hard on cars, tough on crews and rough on the wallet. Sponsorship is nearly nonexistent, except for two or three factory teams, and even they don't seem to be rolling in money. I suppose part of the problem is that it is difficult to be a spectator at a US rally. Our rallies are almost always run at night in remote places. Who wants to sponsor a car in a sport that has virtually no spectators? It's like watching submarine races.

There is no question that the finest rally drivers in the world are Europeans, especially the Scandinavians. They are national heroes, well paid, and are sought after by manufacturers such as Subaru, Peugeot, Ford and the rest. Massive amounts of money are spent to develop rally cars that are nearly indestructible and incredibly fast. The support teams can completely rebuild a severely damaged car overnight.

When you compare that to our underfunded effort and that of most of the teams here in the States, we could hardly be called professional rally drivers. That didn't stop the Sports Car Club of America, the sanctioning body, from naming the US series, SCCA Pro Rally. Audi, Mazda, and, to a lesser extent, Dodge provided assistance at the time. Most of Dodge's help went to Doug Shepard: an engineer with Chrysler who I understand is still driving rally cars after all these years.

Audi sponsored John Buffum. The Audi Quattro team was the class of the sport. Mazda sponsored Rod Millen, the New Zealander, in his RX-7 turbo. Rod developed the four-wheel drive version of the car in order to compete with John. The fact that this other Audi out in Washington, the 5 + 5, had some slight sponsorship possibilities and was painted in Audi Team colors made it almost irresistible to me. We wouldn't be a factory team, but we would look like one and that was enough for me to take a trip out west to buy the car if it passed muster.

161

It would have been prohibitively expensive to drive out there with a trailer and haul it back, so the plan was to fly out and drive this car back to Michigan. I didn't have much time to accomplish this, so I knew I would have to drive almost straight through to get it back here in the least number of days possible. Two thousand miles is a long way to cover by myself. None of the guys on the team could afford to take that much time off from work so I began to look for a person who wasn't employed, could drive reasonably well, would be pleasant company and could be persuaded to do this against their better judgment.

There he was, sitting at the dinner table, my oldest son Mike, a senior in high school. I approached him after supper, out of earshot of his mother, with the idea of flying out there on the coming Friday, making sure the car was OK, and then starting back to Michigan all in the same day. It would then take us three more days to make it back, and if all went well, he would only miss school on Monday. He liked the idea but told me that first semester's final exams were scheduled for the middle of the following week, and he sure didn't want to be AWOL for them. He planned to study this weekend for them as well.

I persuaded him that he could bring his books along, study on the plane, study in the car when he wasn't driving, study in the motel room at night. Why, he might study more on this trip than he would at home, I contended. Being a dutiful son, he consented, but worried about things going wrong and, of course, what his mother's reaction would be when she was informed of the plan. I waited perhaps too long to tell her, saying in an offhanded manner on Thursday that I had better get to bed as Mike and I were catching an early flight to Seattle in the morning to acquire a car and we would be gone for a few days.

Poor Mike took the brunt of her anger, and I was spared for the most part. "How," she thundered, "could you keep this a secret from your own mother until the last possible moment, conspiring with your #$*&! father to fly to the west coast just before your finals and then drive some stupid rally car across the Rocky Mountains in the middle of January?" She had a point or two; I had to agree. We left early the next morning without waking her.

It was a long flight to Seattle with a change of planes in Chicago. Mike studied hard all the way. The Audi owner met our plane and took us to the dealership to see the car. It looked good and drove well, so money and paperwork changed hands. We threw our bags in the back and headed for home, getting as far as Pendleton, Oregon, the first night.

We left about 6 AM and had gone about five miles when the High Sheriff pulled us over for excessive speed. I guess we were somewhat above 80. The ticket was about $75 and fortunately was the only one. The car liked to run around 75, so we kept it there and out west you're not going to get a ticket for that. The muffler was a "competition" unit, meaning it was pretty loud. We both lost about 10% of our hearing.

Mike was driving across Nebraska, and I was catching a nap. The wind began to pick up, and I woke up to see how we were doing. We seemed to be driving straight down the highway, yet the car was kind of cocked to one side, crabbing along. I asked Mike, "How come the car is not straight?" He replied that he didn't know but that it was hard to keep it on the road. I asked him to pull over, so we could see if there was a problem with the car. We got out and both of us fell right on our butts. Black ice! He had been doing a pretty good job, balancing the car against the wind that was pushing us sideways.

We arrived home very late Monday night. We recovered and Mike did well on his exams, as I knew he would. At the time he was taking Russian, German and Chinese. When he graduated in June, he was in the top five in a class of at least a thousand kids, a triumph of environment over heredity, at least from my side of the family.

The car looked like hell with three days of road salt and grime. I ran it through the car wash, and it was as good as new. It was time to haul it over to Don Ensley's English Motors shop in Utica to get it ready for the next rally, the Northern Lights Pro Rally out of Houghton Lake, MI.

We were getting used to the car, so we weren't the fastest team in the Production (stock) class, but we were in the hunt.

On one particular stage a car ahead had crashed into a tree, somehow knocking part of the tree across the road. The road was blocked. Rally cars were coming every two minutes, so in no time we had four cars stopped ahead of us with drivers and co-drivers all trying to pull the tree out of the way. The tree was moved aside and we all jumped back in the cars for a Le Mans type start, buckling up as we ran up through the gears, not an easy thing to do. This was going to be fun. Here was a train of five rally cars, nose to tail, pushing each other hard, some trying to pass on the narrow two tracks with trees tight to the side of the road, a recipe for chaos.

All of us were affected by a phenomenon known as the "Red Mist," which I explained more fully in the chapter on the 1976 JPS Mercury Capri race car. Suffice it to say that when you see the Red Mist, you are so into the battle that nothing else matters but winning the moment.

First, the lead car went off, probably as a direct result of the pressure to stay in front of the crazed group on his tail. Then, the new leader and the car immediately behind him came together after an ill-advised pass that resulted in both of them ending up in the trees. Now, there was just one in front of us. He was clearly driving over his head, and it was just a matter of time before he made a rally ending error. He went straight on, when the road did not. We were now running alone, triumphantly. We weren't leading the rally by any means, but four close competitors had fallen by the wayside. Great fun!

We finished the rally with a good overall time. It was one of our better finishes: twenty-third overall out of seventy-one entrants, and fourteenth in class out of sixteen in our class. Not too bad. We were pleased with our new rally car and pleased with ourselves. It was a good way to start a new season.

One of the more endearing characteristics of the Audi was its ride quality. The big comfy seats absorbed a lot of the harsh ride. We would have been driving for six hours with just a short dinner break around midnight, followed by another six or seven hours before it was over, yet we wouldn't be trashed like some of the other teams. The other secret to not getting mentally and physically beat was to have as quiet a muffler as possible. Fortunately, we had changed the loud one Mike and I had listened to for three days to one that wasn't noisy but still worked fine. Nasty sounding exhaust noises may be cool, but you don't want to listen to that racket all night long. I wonder how those motorcyclists put up with their loud exhausts on a lengthy road trip.

In subsequent rallies in Ohio and Pennsylvania we did OK. The car number assigned to you at the start of every rally reflects your seeding: your year-to-date ranking in the points. If you have a number in the teens, that's a lot better than being in the thirties or forties. In a sixty-car field, we were in the high twenties or low thirties. Not bad. We were finishing. The car number in the picture above was 16. That was a big improvement over previous years.

There was a low-key rally being held in Cadillac, where you really didn't need a support crew to run it, so I entered with my son Mike as my co-driver. This deal started in the middle of the afternoon and would run into the night but be over before 11 PM.

We were doing pretty well and had just finished a special stage and were slowing down to get our official time from the scorekeeping crew that was stationed about a quarter mile past the finish. A spectator stepped out onto the road, and I had to swerve to miss him. We slid off and hit a tree at a speed estimated at 25 mph. I looked over at Mike after the impact. He was slumped forward, unconscious. He had loosened up his belts just after the finish line, so the impact threw him forward in his harness and that impact knocked him out cold. I got him out of the car, laid him down on the ground and he came to. A big relief, to be sure.

The impact had also knocked our alternator out. Everything else seemed to be OK, other than our crumpled hood and fender.

It was starting to get dark, and we didn't want to run our lights any more than we had to because the battery was only going to last so long.

We would start a special stage with the lights on, estimate how far it was to the first turn and then turn them off. About the time we guessed we would be at the turn we would turn them back on for a few seconds and then turn them off, guessing again when the next corner would need some brief illumination. Each time the lights came on, they were a bit dimmer. We knew we could not continue that much longer, so we turned the headlights off and resorted to a flashlight employed in the same way, that is, on long enough to get through a corner and then off. Mike held the light out of his window, turning it on and off as needed. Pretty soon the flashlight gave out. Another rally car passed us, so we followed his taillights awhile, but he eventually got away. We limped into a service area, and another team gave our battery a charge with their jumper cables. We were good for another stage, but that was it. We had to retire. We had gotten farther than many others would have, but we still came up short, about 25 miles from the finish. That's part of the heartbreak of rallying. If you don't finish, it's scored as if you weren't there. There is no difference between a DNS, "did not start," and a DNF, "did not finish."

Sometimes we had problems with the Audi that seemed like we were doomed, but we managed to keep it together and finish the rally. We were running an event out of Wellsboro, Pennsylvania, the Susquehanna 400, when we had a big problem with the car after hitting a boulder near the edge of the road. We broke one of the bolts that held the lower A-arm for the left front wheel in place. Upper and lower A-arms are the most significant parts of the suspension in that they are responsible for allowing the wheel to go up, down, and turn at the same time. They are really the bridge between the wheels and the chassis of the car, and they "locate," that is, fix the position of the wheel relative to the rest of the car. With one of the lower A-arm attachment bolts broken, the wheel was free to "locate" itself forward and backward in the wheel well. The other bolt was all that was keeping the lower A-arm on the car.

We were in real trouble because the car could barely be steered. Our solution was to tie a long canvas towing strap around the lower A-arm and attach the strap to the front bumper. Another towing strap was tied around the A-arm and run back about 15 feet to be tied around the rear bumper. With these two straps more or less holding the A-arm in place, our wheel was "located" again, sort of. We found that the car could now be steered, but another factor was present. The wheel still had a lot of fore and aft movement, so when you stepped on the gas, the wheel moved forward and turned the car to the right. When you let off or touched the brakes, the wheel moved rearward and the car turned left.

It was soon apparent that the easiest way to steer the car was to give it more gas when you wanted to go right and to let off when you wanted to go left. There were difficulties of course if you were going too fast into a right hand turn. To let off would turn the car in the wrong direction. Similarly, you wanted to carry excess speed into left-handers so that letting off and braking would get you around the bend quickly. Got that? No braking, lots of gas for right turns; no gas, lots of braking for left turns. My brave co-driver was Clark Bond. What a great name, eh?

Every chance we had we would stop, leap out and tighten the canvas tow straps, which were stretching with every turn. We drove that beast that way for the last third of the rally, a distance of more than a hundred miles, but we made it and had one of our highest finishes. I think we were fifteenth over all and sixth in the Production class. We actually got a check for a few hundred dollars. Talk about pressing on regardless.

We took the car up to Sudbury, Ontario, for a winter rally. That was a great time. There was a huge lumbering operation up there owned by the E.D. Eddy Company, who own a parcel of land equal to three of our larger counties, probably bigger than Rhode Island. They keep the roads plowed all winter, but there was almost no traffic on them. The Canadian organizers had the good sense to hold this rally in the daylight, so we could be done by dark and party till dawn, rather than drive until dawn.

These rally roads were wide, smooth, and had snowbanks that were at least eight feet high. It was like driving on a super wide toboggan run with soft walls. You couldn't slide off the road. You couldn't crash. Well, you could, but you really had to work at it. How fast do you think you can drive on a snow-packed road? We were running over a hundred and the four-wheel drive Quattros were up around 130. Great fun. We did pretty well, finishing in the upper fourth of the field.

I was beginning to tire of rallying; the crew was getting tired of the travel as well, and there was a lot of pressure at home to hang it up. We had been doing this rally stuff for about three years, and the season seemed to be about eleven months long. Reluctantly, I decided to sell the car. Maybe I would get another rally car later on, maybe not.

There are lots of foreign students at the University of Michigan and one of them—a would-be rally driver from Greece—saw his opportunity to own an Audi Team rally car.

Maybe I forgot to explain that cars painted in Audi team colors weren't necessarily official team cars.

I hated to see that car go. It ran hard without complaint. It never developed even the first rattle. I found that amazing, given all the washboard roads, rocks, and general bad terrain it had been driven over.

The car was gone for a couple of months, and my resistance to automotive temptation was waning. One of the other teams on the tour used a late model Mustang equipped with about 300 horsepower, and they were always putting up twin rooster tails of gravel, making great American V-8 basso profundo sounds and having a hoot. They had very little money tied up in the car, and it seldom broke. They knew when to go fast and when to cool it, so they almost never went off. They knew, like us, that if you leave the road in a rear-wheel drive car, you're probably not coming back.

All of a sudden, rear-wheel drive didn't seem like such a bad idea. I saw an ad for a '69 Camaro with a built 327, and I had to go have a look. A '69 wasn't quite historic in 1983, so what the hell. For $2500, why not? I was off to see the car. My wife has often remarked that I was off.

# This Car Was No Virgin

## 1969 Chevrolet Camaro Rally Car

*This was the fourth rally car, the successor to the Audi 5 + 5.*

The delightful Audi 5+5 was gone, never to be seen again at any US rally. Several months went by, and I was having second and third thoughts. I had quit because it was beginning to get expensive, the crew was getting tired of the travel and prep time, and mama-san was unhappy at home. There had been fatalities recently when a rally car traveling at high speed collided with a car load of rally workers who had gotten lost and inadvertently drove in the wrong direction on an active special stage road.

I decided that if I just ran the regional and national rallies held only in Michigan with maybe one excursion per year to Ohio, the travel and expense burden would be significantly reduced. The other change would be to acquire an inexpensive but reliable car to rally that might not be the most competitive configuration but would still be a lot of fun.

A guy up in Pentwater was rallying an old Dodge police car with 400 cubic inches of unlimited rear-wheel power, and another guy had a Mustang with a built 302 that we saw do reasonably well over the last couple of years. Both of these teams had concluded that they were not going to be able to compete with the factory sponsored teams or even those with modest sponsorship, so why not just go have a great time sliding their cars around, *Dukes of Hazzard* style, and be done with it? They usually avoided winter rallies for obvious reasons.

I first saw the '69 Camaro sitting out in front of some guy's house up near Novi. Interesting story about how the town of Novi got its name: There used to be a stagecoach line that ran between Detroit and Lansing, and this was the number six stop, with the six written in Roman numerals. The descendents of the early settlers probably attended public schools, where Latin could no longer be taught and the "VI" became vi, and the No. VI stop became Novi.

This Camaro has been "restored" a few years before, that is, repainted and its chrome spruced up. The seats and interior were in good shape, probably original. No apparent rust on the body, a healthy sounding motor, an asking price of $2300, what's not to like?

Purists might be alarmed to learn that I was contemplating using this potential collectable as a rally car, putting a cage in it, taking much of the interior out and subjecting it to all that can happen to a car sliding sideways at night on a gravel road. What the hell, these were pretty common cars around Detroit as reflected in the price, so I wasn't risking a national treasure. I had done this to brand-new cars, real virgins you might say. This car was no virgin. It probably spent quite a few evenings away from home out on Woodward Avenue near 14 Mile Road, having a go against Pontiac GTOs, Mopars, and fast Fords.

I was impressed with the motor. It was a 327 cubic-inch small block with a big four barrel carburetor. It didn't have headers or a nasty lumpy cam. It might even been stock, but you could toast the rear tires in the first two gears without any effort, just what you needed to get the rear end to come around in a tight corner at night on a rally road that tightened further halfway through it.

When we finally arrived at a price of $2000, I bought it and trailered it home. I didn't convert it to a race car right away. It was a lot of fun to drive around town, getting a stoplight challenge every so often. I would usually win unless the other guy was a serious street racer. I defined serious street racers as guys who beat me.

After a few weeks of playing outlaw with the car, it began to show a bit of smoke out of the pipes, so I took it down Weaver's Arco where they know about such things as small block Chevys. The diagnosis was that it needed a valve job, some seals, some carburetor work and a tune-up. After that it went over to Stu's Welding in Westland for the roll cage. Cages were getting more expensive every year. They used to be $500, and now they were at least $1000. Then it was hauled up to Don Ensley's English Motors for bottom shields, rally lights and a front-wheel odometer setup.

We entered a summertime regional SCCA Pro Rally held in the Alma-St. Johns, Michigan, area, and it was a lot of fun just standing on the gas and moving dirt. We could make twin rooster tails of gravel just like those Mustang guys, maybe better. At the top of the rally pecking order, the difference between the first and second place finishers might be a matter of less than a minute after ten hours of driving. Where we were finishing in the standings, it might be five or ten minutes separating places. With attrition rates of 50% or greater, just finishing was an accomplishment. We knew we weren't really competitive anymore, but we had good times, big grins, and relatively small expenses.

After a few of these relatively low-key events, we decided to make one more trip to the Upper Peninsula, to the Press On Regardless in Houghton, Michigan. The POR, as it was called, had a well-deserved reputation as a real car buster.

We managed to persuade a local Chevrolet dealer in Hancock, across the river from Houghton, to give us a hundred dollars to have his name on the car. We were headed down the first special stage when the car began to overheat. We made it to the end of the stage, pulled over to see what the problem was, and found that we had multiple leaks in the radiator. It must have been that the pounding dislodged some of the cooling tubes or cracked them. In retrospect, a new radiator would have been an inexpensive upgrade. We added water and stopped the leak and proceeded through another stage or two, but it was clear we weren't going to keep this engine alive for 650 more miles, so we had to withdraw.

We had entered four PORs. We did not finish any of them. The first year we entered the '76 Capri, crashing just ten miles from the finish while in tenth place overall and second in the Production (stock) class. The second year our VW Scirocco ran for about sixty seconds before the fuel pump gave out. The Audi 5 + 5 crashed out early in the third year, and now this old Camaro packed it in due to radiator problems.

We fixed the radiator, ran another rally with the car and decided it was time to hang it up for good. If there was any latent longing to return again, my wife was making one of those offers one could not refuse. No, it wasn't the usual threat of divorce, but rather the offer to buy any new car I might like, within reason, no Ferrari I'm afraid, but just about any other new car out there could be mine if I would promise to sell the Camaro, the spares, the trailer, and anything else associated with racing.

This was late in 1982, and the enthusiast press was all agog about a new Corvette arriving in the spring of 1983 as a 1984 model. "How about it, your sweetness? Does that offer you made include a new 'Vette? How much, you ask? Oh, I think we could get one for about twenty-five large ones."

She consented to the deal. It was time to dust off the old For Sale sign and roll that '69 Camaro out to the corner of Cayuga Place and Stadium Boulevard, from where many cars had departed. I pulled the roll cage out, put the interior back in, and had a buyer shortly. This was the end of rallying, the end of racing for the foreseeable future, and the end of a period in which I had bought, raced, fixed, raced, wrecked, fixed, wrecked again, fixed again, then finally sold, a total of five cars in seven years: a '60 Austin Healey Sprite, '76 Mercury Capri, '82 VW Scirocco, '83 Audi 5 + 5, and the '69 Camaro.

"Nancy, where did I put that Corvette brochure?"

# I Think I Done Good, Momma

## 1984 Chevrolet Corvette Coupe

*This is a picture of me, son Joe, and my mom
in Grayling showing off the new car.*

This was the payoff. I was awarded this car by agreeing to give up driving rally cars and retiring from racing in general.

My wife had been after me to hang up the rally driving, and this new Corvette was as pleasant a bribe as we could come with.

Corvettes have been a big part of the American automotive scene for more than 30 years. It could be argued that the Corvette was and is America's only sports car. Carroll Shelby might disagree, as would a number of the German and Japanese manufacturers that have sold cars either built here or built almost exclusively for the US market.

The Corvette evolved from its introduction in 1953 as a small two-seater with a straight six-cylinder engine and automatic transmission to a fire-breathing V-8 with styling that reminded one of a shark or jet fighter. By the late '70s and early '80s, the styling had become dated. The car still offered mind-blowing acceleration, but the handling, build quality, and ride were hardly on a par with BMW, Mercedes, Jaguar, and Acura.

GM wanted to use the next generation of Corvettes to showcase its technological advances such as sequential fuel injection, new composite materials, extensive use of aluminum in the suspension components and increased horsepower while still meeting emissions and fuel economy targets.

The car magazines like *Car & Driver*, *Road & Track* and *Motor Trend* would often write glowing articles about imports, and by comparison, American offerings almost always appeared to be a year or two behind. Yet the American companies spent enormously on advertising in these same magazines, and the magazines were always looking down the road for an American car that was praiseworthy, so they could talk about it in glowing terms.

Some wags liked to say that some of the magazines' Car of The Year awards should really be called The Advertiser of The Year awards, but that's a little unfair.

The new Corvette certainly looked like a strong Car of The Year candidate. The spy photos showed a much cleaner look than previous Corvettes, and the cars were designed to be world class in handling as well. *Car & Driver* was able to get a road test done before the first car was delivered, and they claimed it would corner like no other production sports car available in the market, with a skid pad rating of more than 1 G.

The Chevrolet dealers were smacking their lips. Here was a car that people would pay more than sticker price for. Some dealers were getting premiums of $2000 over the normal retail price, "sticker," as it is often referred to. I visited Rampy Chevrolet in Ann Arbor, where I had purchased several cars in the last ten years. They treated me as a valued customer, and as such I was able to order one at the straight retail window sticker price. Other guys were paying more than sticker, but I was in at sticker, and I was informed that I should feel grateful. I parted with a deposit of $500, which was required to order the car.

I had to go up to Alma, Michigan, for some business at Total Petroleum. I drove up US-27 and stopped in at a small Chevrolet dealer just south of Lansing to pick up another Corvette brochure to look over while I ate lunch. The dealer said he would be happy to order one for me at "$500 over." I declined, letting him know that I was one of the favored ones at Rampy and didn't pay anything "over," as I was paying straight sticker, as a member of the privileged class. He replied, "Well, I don't think you understand what I'm saying. What I'm offering is not $500 over sticker but $500 over my invoice."

"That's sounds great, but why would you offer that when everyone else is at sticker and above? In Detroit, big dealers are actually buying future Corvette deliveries from small dealers and paying the small dealer a premium over their cost."

His response was diplomatic, and I can't remember the exact words, but the meaning was clear. His message, again paraphrased, went something like this:

"I know that, and I want no part of it. These cars are a pain to service, and, frankly, the Corvette customer thinks pretty highly of himself, if you get my drift. We're out in the country, farm country. I sell mostly pickups with snowplows on them and four-door sedans to go to church in. If you want to have one of the two I'm allotted this year, you can have it for $500 over, but take it to Rampy or someplace else for service, OK?"

"How much down?"

"Two hundred dollars, three hundred dollars—whatever you got."

"Jeez, I'll have to cancel that car I have on order downstate at Rampy, but I imagine they'll still bring the car in as I ordered it because they won't have any trouble selling it."

"One more thing, mister. I'd be obliged if you didn't run around and tell other folks about our deal, especially other dealers. I don't need the aggravation."

"OK. No problem with that. They wouldn't believe me anyway. I'm going out to the car to get my checkbook for the deposit to cement the deal. I'm running behind schedule now, so how about I come back tomorrow and we'll put the order together?"

"That's fine. You don't really need to give me a check today. Tomorrow's OK. You're probably going to ask me this, so I can tell you right now. The difference between the window sticker price and invoice is $3800. You're buying it for $3300 less than you would have paid in Ann Arbor, plus tax and license, of course. Better get going or you'll be late for that appointment."

I think I done good, momma.

I checked off the stuff I wanted, going over the details with my boys that evening, sprawled out on the living room rug. Joe, our middle kid, sat next to me on the floor while we went up through the gears in our imaginary car. He said he liked the way the engine sounded with me verbally "blipping" the throttle before each downshift. The long-term effects of being raised that way are still evident in that guy's behavior yet today, as I often get emails about what he's thinking about buying next. I think the current flame consuming him is one of those Honda Ridgeline pickups.

I called the home office and told them I'd be taking the day off to buy a car but would be calling in. The weather was nice and warm that morning, so I decided to ride my Harley Davidson Sturgis up to Mason by the back roads. Riding a Harley to a Chevy dealer to order a new 'Vette, I should have had an American flag on my back. I stopped once just north of Chelsea on M-52 to look at a small herd of whitetail deer in the middle of a field. It was a fine day for a bike ride and a fine day to order a new car.

The owner of the Chevrolet dealership was a nice guy. Like a lot of small-town businessmen, he was polite but busy. I imagined he did most of the selling, paperwork, and general administration. There were a couple of mechanics out back and one other person in the building. This was a low overhead operation. I suspect he made good money and had a loyal following. You can't screw people around in a small town. They never forgive, and they never forget.

We got the car ordered, some money changed hands, and he would let me know when it was scheduled to be built, and when I might be able to take delivery. I got back on the Harley, taking a different way back. I headed for Rampy Chevrolet to go through the sure to be unpleasant process of getting my deposit back.

The Rampy people were not amused by my decision to cancel my order. Did I have one on order elsewhere, they wondered. "Yes," I said, "I did."

Their initial position was that other dealers would not be able to keep their promises to deliver a car that was going to be in very short supply, and therefore they would protect me from my foolishness by keeping my car on order and hanging on to the deposit too. "The deposit check, please," I insisted.

They demanded to know the name of the other dealer. I refused to say. I did say that I would be getting in touch with the Chevrolet Zone Sales office to report their refusal to refund my deposit and would likely not buy any other cars here in the future if I did not leave with that check. The check appeared in about ten minutes. The sales manager's scowl followed me out the door, and I never did buy another car there.

I hated to have such hard feelings because I would like to bring it there for service. I learned long ago that while the sales department might be miffed if you bought their brand elsewhere, the service department couldn't care less where you bought the car if they could make some warranty dollars off of it.

About two months later, I got the call from the dealer that the car would be delivered to him in about two weeks. He would call me when it arrived. He did have the Vehicle Identification Number, the "VIN," for me, so I could get the insurance certificate.

The big day arrived, and I had one of our systems guys drop me off to take delivery of the car. The car looked beautiful. It was a medium bronze color with light tan leather seats. When you lifted up the hood, you could not see the engine. This was the first "styled" engine bay. You knew there was an engine in there somewhere, but you certainly couldn't touch anything but the dipstick for checking the oil.

We took it out for a test ride. This was the first time I had sat in one because none were available at the time of order. If you waited until they had them in the show room, yours wouldn't be delivered for another three or four months.

It was a bit cramped, frankly. Not as much headroom as I would like to have. If I leaned the seat back some, it was OK. Not great, but OK. I couldn't hear any rattles, but we were just on fairly smooth city streets. It had major league acceleration. There is nothing like a small block Chevy 327/350, or a Ford 302/351 for that matter, when it comes to acceleration. The steering was quick, and the brakes were strong.

We finished up the transaction, and I headed for home, taking the back roads again. There were some twisty sections that I had enjoyed on the motorbike. It took some getting used to in the 'Vette because the steering was so quick. I found myself turning in too early and too much. This car behaved like a race car. I'm sure I would get it figured out.

One thing I did not care for was the discovery that the suspension was rock hard, race car hard, and that was hard on the butt. There was no give at all. Chevrolet wanted to have great skid pad numbers for the auto enthusiast press, and they got them, but at the expense of riding comfort. I always liked a firm ride. The Jaguars in particular had a firm ride, but they could dampen the bumps.

I made it home OK, and everybody who stopped by wanted a ride or at least a peek at the engine room. It made a strong impression on everyone. I liked the way the engine sounded and the Bose audio system as well.

It was time to take the first business trip down to Ohio and Indiana. It was good to get out of Michigan because the highways were in such bad shape. They had been neglected for years because there wasn't enough money or it got spent on something else. Driving the Corvette on US-23 towards Toledo, for instance, was a real torture test. The suspension was so stiff that even with the seat belts on tightly, I would be bounced toward the ceiling, bumping my head, hard. I sent a letter of complaint into Chevrolet headquarters in Detroit, but received no reply.

Down in Ohio, the roads were pretty good, and it was fun to tool along, returning waves of admiration from envious drivers. Occasionally, I would drive down to a customer in London, Kentucky, where we had a big installation. Kentucky had, and probably still has, the best roads in the middle of the country, smooth and serpentine.

I was beginning to have some electrical problems, and strange stuff happened, like not being able to get my key out of the ignition, so I had to carry another set to lock the doors when I left it. The other problem was that cracks were beginning to appear in the fiberglass in the rear quarter panel. I think the rough ride contributed to this.

I took it back to the selling dealer for its first checkup with a list of problems. To their credit, they fixed everything the first time, including repairing the fiberglass.

I made a few more trips out of state and enjoyed the car. The big problem was that I spent at least 50% of my travel time in Michigan.

I made a resolution that I haven't broken since. I would never consider another car without test driving it before I ordered it or bought it, if for no other reason than driver's headroom. Years later, I had an opportunity to buy a new Jaguar XK8 convertible at a very good price. I had the money and had the hots for the car. I remembered this Corvette and took the Jaguar out for a ride. It was a great car with the top down, but when we put the top up, I didn't fit. Damn, I wanted that car, but now I know better.

Coming back from Detroit one day on the Jeffries Freeway, I-96, I came upon a particularly rough stretch of road and hit my noggin so hard on the Corvette's headliner, I was momentarily stunned. That really hurt. I had a splitting headache too.

That was the beginning of the end. I wouldn't own a car that I was getting hurt in on a regular basis. Just after that hard knock, I happened to be driving through Plymouth and decided to stop at Don Massey's Cadillac dealership. Maybe I was getting too old for this hard-ass suspension and needed something a little kinder to my anatomy. They had the usual mix of big cushy sedans and Eldorado coupes that I always like the styling of. There was a dark blue Eldorado convertible sitting on the show-room floor that appealed to me.

Whatever I bought next, I was in pretty good shape on the trade-in. I only had the Corvette five months, so the mileage was low and the car was still in great demand. Somewhere earlier in this book, I said that you make your money on a car, if money can be made, when you buy it, rather than when you sell it. These 'Vettes were still selling at "sticker," or higher, and I had bought it for $3300 under sticker, so I wasn't going to lose money, maybe even make a little.

I didn't want to sell the car. It was a beautiful car that offered outstanding performance but was just the wrong car for a 6'2" guy. From the heights of anticipation, I journeyed to the depths of despair in just five months. I had sold my racing interests to buy a car I was now getting ready to sell. I was leaving the 'Vette. The only thing to be determined was what car was I leaving it for.

I traded it in on that dark blue Cadillac Eldorado convertible. They gave me $24,000 for the 'Vette. I put another $4000 with it, and I was driving a beautiful blue car with a tan canvas top and a butterscotch leather interior. It had a nice soft ride.

I was like the guy who left one beautiful wife for another. Makes you wonder why. I'd like to say that my Cadillac Eldorado and I lived happily ever after. It was a beautiful car. Unfortunately, it didn't work out that way.

# I Was Getting Older and Dumber

## 1983 Cadillac Eldorado Convertible

*One of the prettiest cars ever to grace our driveway.*

This was a truly beautiful car. Dark blue body, tan colored top, butterscotch leather interior, all complementing the dramatic sharp-edged styling of the early eighties Eldorado. There was nothing else available at the time that looked quite like this car. It looked as good with the top up as it did with the top tucked away under its tonneau cover.

Cadillac has built convertibles in the past but announced in 1976, somewhat prematurely, that the 1976 model would be the last one. They did build convertibles again but not until the mid-eighties. How could there be a 1983 Cadillac convertible?

There exists a cottage industry of relatively small companies that build custom convertibles out of stock sedans. These same specialty firms build presidential limousines that have bulletproof glass and other security features. My first rally car co-driver, John Erickson, worked briefly for a firm in Mt.

Clemens, Michigan, that built Mercedes Benz station wagons out of Mercedes Benz sedans for years before Mercedes offered their own wagon.

This particular Cadillac convertible was built by Hess & Eisenhardt, one of the oldest of these firms, founded in 1876 in Cincinnati, Ohio. They built many of the limousines for presidents of the United States and as well as kings and highly ranked potentates from other countries. The limo that John Kennedy was riding in Dallas was a Hess & Eisenhardt vehicle. They also had a thriving business building convertibles. Cadillac, Jaguar, Lincoln, and other luxury coupes were converted into open cars.

The trick in making a convertible out of a coupe is to stiffen the chassis to make up for the fact that there is no firm roof. Most cars built today are unibodies, that is, they have no underlying frame. They get their overall strength by carefully engineering the sides and top to close the box so to speak. If you remove the steel roof and replace it with struts and canvas, you better beef up the underlying car by adding cross members underneath the basic chassis.

This H & E conversion had about three thousand miles on it. It was used as a demonstrator and looked like a brand-new car. Working at Don Massey Cadillac at the time was a personable young guy by the name of John Rogin, who would later get his own dealership, which, I believe, is still in operation as John Rogin Buick in Wayne, Michigan. I expressed some interest in the dark blue convertible, and John suggested driving it home to show to the wife, leaving my Corvette there overnight.

I brought it home, and we went out for a short drive in the evening on the tree-lined residential streets near our house in Ann Arbor. What a pleasant experience, gliding along in this very comfortable open car, looking up at the leaves turning red and gold, as this was early fall, one of the nicest times of the year in the Midwest. She knew I was unhappy with the Corvette and liked the Cadillac, in part because you could put four people in it fairly comfortably, which was out of the question in the 'Vette.

"If you really have grown to dislike the 'Vette's harsh ride and its tendency to make you a bit shorter, then you might as well trade it in on this one." That was enough consent for me to take it back and begin serious negotiations with John Rogin.

One of the things I was concerned about was service after the sale. Don Massey Cadillac, a classy dealership that also offered Rolls Royces, is in Plymouth, fifteen or twenty miles from Ann Arbor, and while that isn't as bad as going to Troy or Detroit, it takes 45 minutes of somebody's time if you have to have someone go with you to drop your car off. John assured me that he would provide a loaner, usually a late-model used Cadillac when I dropped mine off for service. With a loaner, you really don't need someone to bring you there, and not having your car isn't so bad if you're driving one that's about as nice that belongs to the dealership.

As far as price was concerned, it was difficult to get him to budge because of the relative rarity of Cadillac convertibles. He claimed that if it were new, the price would be $32,000, so offering it for $28,000 with so few miles was about as good as he could do. The value of my trade was not much of an issue. They were willing to pay close to sticker for it. I think we ended up at $27,000 for theirs, $24,000 for mine. Michigan's sales tax law required that I pay 4% on the $27,000 rather than on the difference. This law remains in effect today, at a current rate of 6%, a great boon to the state treasury and a bad deal for the car buyer.

The Cadillac was a great road car and a good all-season car with its front-wheel drive. GM had been building front-wheel drive cars with big V-8 engines since the Olds Toronado was introduced a dozen years earlier. Eldorados, Toronados and Rivieras are essentially the same car and were all built in the same plant in New Jersey.

My peers asked why the 'Vette had been sold, and I had to tell that bruised noggin story a few dozen times. More than a few opined that trading a Corvette in on an Eldorado was a sign of advancing age and pending senility.

One of the biggest attractions that the Cadillac had was room, lots of it. You could have long-legged, tall people in the front and not worry about headroom or hip room or legroom. The back seat was for kids and packages, like most convertibles. It didn't accelerate like a 'Vette, but the Cadillac's 350 cubic-inch engine was no slouch either.

The other big attraction of GM luxury cars is that in matters like air conditioning, automatic transmissions, power windows, power steering, power seats and power whatever, they had that down cold. GM invented most of that stuff a long time ago. My 1962 Cadillac Fleetwood offered all those features as standard equipment. They have been refining and defining luxury for decades.

Not to take anything away from Lexus, Infiniti, and Acura, who have taken these features to an even higher level of luxury and reliability, but it was GM, and Ford to a lesser extent, who developed our appetite for automotive comfort and convenience. Where the Japanese succeeded was in bringing these features into their lower-end and mid-priced cars like the Honda Accord and not charging extra for them. The Japanese certainly built those extra things in their cost model but making them standard on mid-market cars to be sold in the US convinced the buying public that you got more for your money when you bought their cars.

The other two big features of Japanese cars were good fuel economy and reliability. These were the two areas where GM, Ford, and especially Chrysler had not kept up. The US could build an economical car. The problem with the US-built economy offerings was that they were cheaply built, not particularly reliable and no less expensive than the more reliable Japanese cars. The US could build solid reliable luxury cars, but they didn't offer good fuel economy and they were rather expensive, relatively speaking. Is it any wonder that Lexus and the more expensive European marques, like Mercedes and BMW, have made giant inroads into Cadillac's traditional markets while Toyota and Honda dominate the low and middle end of the automotive spectrum?

The Cadillac part of this car was good, but I was beginning to have some problems with the Hess & Eisenhardt part of the car. I began to hear some strange sounds from the rear of the car, coming from just behind the rear seat. The sounds would be there one day but not the next.

One particular day, the sounds, squeaks actually, were louder than they had been. I looked in the trunk and under the rear seat but couldn't find anything out of the ordinary. Sound can carry a long way in a car. Where you seem to hear them is not necessarily where they originate. I crawled under the car to see if maybe the exhaust pipe was rubbing against the bottom or if anything else was amiss. Again, nothing was obviously wrong, but the sound remained. I put up with it for another day before making an appointment to bring it in.

Rogin had arranged for the loaner, a three-year-old Cadillac Sedan de Ville, so I didn't have to worry about transportation. The service guys at the big successful dealerships have bedside manners that the medical profession would be well served to copy.

I explained the situation to the service writer, who took extensive notes, with much head nodding and a furrowed brow. He said he would call me later in the day, which he did.

They didn't find anything unusual, but went to the trouble of greasing every lube point they could find in the area of the rear axle and in the top raising mechanism in the trunk. This seemed to make the problem diminish but not go away entirely as the test driver dutifully reported. The service guy suggested I pick it up, drive it and predicted it would either get better or worse with use. If it were the latter case, he and his men would be delighted to have another go at it.

The squeaking seemed to diminish with use, but not go away altogether. However, another convertible problem arose. It seemed that the top would not stay tightly clamped to the top of the windshield. It doesn't have to open more than a fraction of an inch for wind noise and rainwater to enter and cause considerable dissatisfaction with the car.

I brought it back and was treated to another late model Cadillac as a loaner. I explained the new problem to the kind and gentle service writer and brought up the old squeaking problem under unfinished business. He suggested that I should leave it for the balance of the week, so they could do a thorough job working on both problems.

When I picked it up the following week, it didn't squeak and it didn't leak air or water. Oh, happy day. Looks like Massey's merry men had taken care of things.

About a week passed before the top came loose again. I lived with it until a new noise, similar to the old noise, was emanating from somewhere in the rear of the car. Back I went, a little hot under the collar, to return the car to the most sincere and ineffective repair people I had dealt with to date.

We were all scratching our heads. They weren't sure what to do next. Someone suggested, perhaps Rogin, perhaps me, that we get Hess & Eisenhardt involved. They made arrangements for H & E to send somebody up to try and figure these problems out. It was determined that I should leave the car again, grab another loaner, and light a candle at Our Lady of Perpetual Maintenance.

The Hess & Eisenhardt guy did come up and make some tweaks that helped a great deal. The same problems would return, however, after a month or so. I was getting a bit tired of explaining why I always seemed to be in a different Cadillac.

During that first year of ownership, the car spent 45 days in the Massey Cadillac service department. I was always pleasant to John Rogin and he to me. Neither of us built the car, and he always came through with another Cadillac to drive. In retrospect, I should have taken the car back to Hess in Cincinnati and left it for a time. They might have found what was missing or poorly fabricated. Lemon laws just apply to new cars, so I had no out there.

I decided the car had to go. It was driving me nuts. It always looked good and had no engine, transmission, or electrical problems, but the convertible component problems were getting to me.

I put it up for sale, but there were no takers. It must have taken three or four months to sell that car, and then I had to just about give it away. I had paid about $28,000 for it, and a year later I couldn't get $20,000 for it. Nor could I get eighteen or seventeen. I finally parted with it for sixteen, a loss of $12,000 in twelve months. It was the worst bath I had ever taken on a car.

My confidence in my judgment was badly shaken. The Cadillac Eldorado was a mistake. The Chevrolet Corvette was a mistake. My last everyday street car before the Corvette was a 1984 Olds Cutlass Supreme that I had ordered with a very small V-8 engine and a stick shift, over the impassioned pleas of almost all of the employees of John Lee Oldsmobile in Ann Arbor. I was getting older and dumber. The trend was not good.

After that buying binge of semi-exotic cars, I needed to make a safe choice, a conservative choice. I needed a glass of milk after all that strong drink. Which car would you say is the absolute safest choice of all the cars built in America, a car with a great reputation, a car known to have good resale, a car known for its economy of operation and low maintenance costs? Which car would that be?

Right you are, if you thought of a Honda Accord. I drove past Sunshine Honda in Plymouth many times on my way to Don Massey Cadillac. It was time to stop in.

# Young Bones Were Probably Breaking

## Old Bones

### 1984 Honda Accord Sedan

The safest car choice of any car built in America, from a dependability/resale perspective, is the Honda Accord. These cars have a reputation for rock-solid mechanical reliability. Honda cars have historically retained more of their original value than almost any other car. The 1984 Honda Prelude, for example, retained 55% of its original purchase price when it was five years old. Only one other car manufacturer could say that, and that was Mercedes Benz.

To put that retained value in practical terms, it meant that a $12,000 1984 Honda Accord, which had a retained value of 50%, was worth about $6000 after sixty months of use. Most domestic brands retained only about 30% of their original value. A $12,000 Dodge would be worth about $4000 after five years, $2000 less than the Honda. Even though most cars are rapidly depreciating assets, the ones that depreciate the least are the ones with the best reputations for quality.

My confidence in my car selection abilities was badly shaken. I had recently sold an '83 Cadillac Eldorado convertible at a huge loss. It had replaced a new '84 Chevrolet Corvette that was put up for sale just ninety days after I had taken delivery because of quality problems and a general dissatisfaction with the car. Any time you sell a car within the first year or two of ownership, you're going to take a stiff financial beating, and I did lose big time, especially on the Cadillac.

I made a stop at Sunshine Honda in Plymouth to inspect the latest Honda Accords, Civics and Preludes. The dealer's personnel were kind, informative and in a wonderful negotiating position, at least from the dealer's perspective.

Accords in particular were in short supply. Sunshine Honda had a bigger allotment than Howard Cooper Honda, the dealer in Ann Arbor, so you could get your car sooner, but you had to pay sticker or awfully close to it. Howard Cooper, on the other hand, would cut you a slightly better deal, but you might have to wait two or three months. "What'll it be, pal? Pay more and have it this week, or pay less, have it next quarter?" I needed a car now.

I took an Accord out for a test drive at Sunshine and thought it was an adequate car. Quiet, competent and kind of boring is the impression I had. Then I took a Prelude, Honda's "sporty" model out. This was more like it. It looked sharp, moved out nicely, had better seats and a better stereo system. It cost a little more too, but it had, as noted above, the best residual value of any car at that time.

As I got more serious about a new Honda, I thought it would be prudent to involve my long-suffering wife Nancy in the process for a change. I needed a brave vice president to tell me I was being an idiot, if I was, because I had convincingly demonstrated a capacity for doing dumb things when it came to buying cars.

She liked the Prelude but had one question. "Where would the kids sit? This model has almost no back seat. It's essentially a two-seater, and at last count we're a family of five." I said that I was aware of that. I reminded her that we still had her Subaru wagon that held four people, and we also had a motor home, so we would either take two economical cars on a short trip or the motor home on long trips. She said that sounded kind of dumb to her and what didn't I like about the roomier Accord? To say that it wasn't quite as sporty or too plain Jane for my tastes was pretty weak. The fact that the Prelude cost another $2500 more than the Accord didn't help either.

I had to make a choice between doing what I planned to do in the first place, disregarding her valid objections, or face the facts that buying a practical car like a Honda Accord was a safe buy both politically and economically. I knew she wouldn't lie down in front of the bus and say I couldn't have the Prelude. She did know that, more than anything else, I didn't want to make another mistake. As I recall, she used the argument that if you just couldn't bear to drive this car after a year or two, and its resale was as good as they say it was, you could unload this car without taking the huge financial bath you took on the Cadillac. That was the clincher. The only decision left to be made was color.

We decided on a charcoal-grey Accord with a light-grey interior. So did 50,000 other people. I'm not sure which color of the limited number offered was the most popular, but I'll bet it was charcoal grey. Any parking lot in Ann Arbor, which was kind of a ground zero for imported cars, that had a hundred cars parked there, would have twenty-five Honda Accords and more than half would be charcoal grey.

Maybe that's how bumper stickers got started, so you could identify your car. My favorite, sure to offend everyone, was "Nuke The Unborn Gay Whales." Speaking of Ann Arbor's typical foreign car, it was probably a dark-blue clapped-out '72 Volvo wagon with a McGovern sticker.

I liked the Honda. It was the poster child for Soichiro Honda's design philosophy. His credo was balance. By that he meant a car had to have just enough motor to move it along at a reasonable rate. If the motor was too small, performance would suffer, but what he worried about mostly was that the motor might be too powerful. If it was, it would take more braking power to slow it down; it would burn more fuel requiring a larger gas tank; and, if he succumbed to the marketing department and elected to make it faster than it needed to be, a bigger, heavier motor would be needed to provide this added power, requiring a heavier subframe as well as a stronger, heavier transmission, and all of these excesses added to its cost which meant he would either have to charge more for it or accept a lower profit.

If he charged more for it, it could mean he would sell fewer of them. If he sold fewer of them, his fixed costs like plants and administrative personnel would have to be spread over fewer units produced, raising his costs and further reducing his profits.

Honda was a brilliant engineer. He knew that achieving this balance was a difficult and never-ending task, but it was the key to making the car profitable for his company and a good value for the consumer. Toyota and Subaru endeavored to do the same thing and have generally succeeded. These companies would provide just enough capability and not more, because that upsets the "balance" of the components. This is one of the primary reasons why there haven't been any V-8 engines in Honda Accords, and it was a good long time before we saw any V-6 engines. Mr. Honda believed that they were not needed and would only unbalance his flagship car. This particular Honda was the LX with a 1.8 liter four-cylinder and a manual transmission. Just right.

No one had any problems with Honda Accords. That was gospel. I began to wonder if I was snake bit, as I had a problem after just two weeks. The clutch went out. How can this be? I'm fairly gentle on clutches and transmissions.

The dealer cheerfully replaced the clutch and sent me on my way. One month later I was back with the same problem. Two clutches were burned up in six weeks! What is going on here? But that was the last of it. No more clutch problems, ever.

Unfortunately, there were other unusual problems. After another month, the dash came loose. The entire dash came undone. It was quickly made right by the dealer, but I had never heard of such a thing, even on a Yugo. One other bit of weirdness that happened a month or so later was that the gas tank filler tube, the one you see when you're filling up, fell off. It came undone at the filling port. Again, the dealer made it right, but I began to wonder if there were gods of automotive affairs whom I had offended. No one else had these kinds of problems with a Honda, the gold standard of automotive excellence. But that was the end of it. There were no more problems.

These Honda Accords were pretty good in the handling department. You could fling them around, and they would go around the corner almost as if they had rear-wheel drive. Mr. Honda knew that the biggest enemy of any car is weight. The less it weighs, given adequate component strength, the less power it needs. If you can get by with a smaller engine, then the smaller engine will in turn weigh less, reducing overall weight. Handling is all about weight and where the weight is. If you can get to a 50/50 front/rear weight distribution, the car will handle much better than if the weight is 65/35 front to rear.

I had a chance to enjoy the benefits of the Honda's handling when my son Joe and I decided to attend a SCCA Pro Rally in southern Ohio as spectators, and we took the Accord down to Circleville to see the Sunriser 400.

Watching a SCCA Pro Rally out in the woods takes a bit of planning. You need to get into the woods ahead of the competitors because the road they would be using is the same one that you used to get to your viewing location. If you were going to watch Special Stage #6, you had to get out there in position almost before the rally cars left the headquarters hotel. Once they all flew past your position, your next opportunity to see them would be Special Stage #12 or later, so you needed to hustle to get into position.

We had seen them flying through SS #6 and it was time to jump into the Honda and head for SS #12. As spectators, we were given maps that provided the most direct route to subsequent stages. These routes usually involved gravel country roads, so there was an opportunity to drive your own little rally to get where you needed to be. In this particular event, SS #12 was at least 25 miles away, and we would have to drive rather fast to get there in time. We had to leave right then and keep our foot in it if we were to get there before the rally cars did.

A young guy with his wife and kids and some older people were standing near us on SS #6 and were wondering how they might find another location to watch these rally cars do another stage. I suggested that they follow us, cautioning them that we would need to be scooting right along, and it might be difficult to keep up. The young guy said he would try. I watched him herd his kids, his wife, who was holding a newborn child, and the old folks into a weather-beaten 1969 Chevrolet Impala. I could see that the tires were almost without treads. I don't know where all the kids came from, other than from the mother, but I counted six kids, the newborn baby, the guy and his wife, and somebody's parents who had been cashing Social Security checks for a long time. No exaggeration, eleven people got into that old car.

We got out to the main road, which was smooth gravel, and I booted that Accord right along. The old Impala stayed right with us. I raised the ante a bit, and my boy's eyebrows began to rise as well. He cleared his throat, and said, "Mom would really be honked off if you loaded this almost new car into the trees." I looked back and that old car was sliding around the corners, *Dukes of Hazzard* style, and he was having as good a time as I was. I might have held 15% back because we didn't have a competition roll cage or seat belt harnesses or really good headlights, but I was moving. Might have been seeing the Red Mist, but having my son in the car was probably the main thing holding me back. The guy behind me in the Chevy Impala was still keeping up.

I could just imagine the scene in that big old Chevrolet. Eleven people were compressed against one side of the car, and then the centrifugal force of the corner threw that mass of humanity over to the other side of the car to be compressed again. Somewhere in the middle of this pile of bodies was a very small baby, held tightly by a frightened mother, ignored by a lunatic father. In the back seat, young bones were probably breaking old bones as bodies flew back and forth.

We drove like this for almost 25 miles. While it was great fun, I imagined there was a fair amount of suffering going on behind us. As we neared our destination, the Chevrolet Impala dropped off and soon disappeared from my rear-view mirror. I pulled in to a parking area near the beginning of the stage, and we walked the rest of the way in. About twenty minutes later the young guy and his tribe walked up to where we were waiting for the first rally car to come through.

Being a natural prick, I asked if he was having car trouble, perhaps an overheated engine or failing brakes, both very real possibilities. "No," he said, "the car wasn't the problem. My wife was nursing the baby. The baby got sick and made a mess on my wife's new outfit. She got real mad, even cussed me some in front of the kids. I had to slow down then." I had to walk away. I didn't know whether to laugh or apologize.

Can you imagine a nursing mother trying to feed that baby under those conditions? I'll bet I've told this story a hundred times, but it was really pretty stupid on my part, all things considered. I came away impressed with this guy's driving skills and the Honda's handling. And I have to admit, mea culpa recited, it was a hell of a lot of fun.

I drove the car occasionally on business trips but found that I was using the Dodge van for everything else. Our daughter Jennifer had gone through several Pintos and needed a car to go to school, so we let her drive the Honda. Nancy seemed to prefer the Subaru, so Jenny drove the Honda until she moved to Los Angeles for graduate school at USC. The Honda became the house car again when I picked up a 1986

Lincoln Town Car, and Jenny was given a 1985 Audi 5000 wagon, all at about the same time in 1992. Nancy drove it again until she was given a 1994 Mustang GT as a Valentine's Day present in February of 1994.

Jenny's Audi gave up the ghost in California, so the Honda was given to her again, and we got a drive-away company to find someone to drive it out to California. Jenny used it for several years. It finally met its demise on a California freeway when our daughter fell asleep at the wheel. She didn't get seriously hurt, but the car was totaled, and that was the end of a very useful car.

Mr. Honda, may he rest in peace, built a car with just the right balance of power, room and economy. Dollar for dollar, I believe Honda is as good a car as you can buy. That was true in 1984 and is still true today.

# "Son, It's Not How You Play the Game But How You Choose Up Sides"
## 1965 Austin Healey Sprite Race Car, Act II

*Here is Don Ensley, the best English car guy in the USA, carrying the checkered flag on one of many of our victory laps.*

I had been out of racing for several years now. I had sold the last rally car, a 1969 Camaro, and had more or less resigned myself to growing up.

As chance would have it, I ran into Virgil Darga one day coming out of Meijer's. After a few pleasantries, I asked him what he had done with the race car I had sold him about eight years ago. This was the Austin Healey Sprite, my first race car.

"Well, I still have it. I have done quite a bit of work on it over the years. How many has it been? I thought I would like racing, but after I went through the Waterford Hills Drivers' School, I began to have second thoughts."

"Really? What happened? Did you have an accident?"

"No, nothing like that. Not even a close call. It was a bit intimidating, but a lot of guys told me that Drivers' School might be. I was just uptight all of the time. Maybe I would wreck somebody else, and they might have gotten badly hurt. I just didn't think it was worth the risk, you know? I ride motorbikes, so I'm not completely risk adverse."

Virgil went on to say that he had kept the car, working on it, hoping the day might come when he would give it another go, but thus far, now seven years after he bought it, the day hadn't yet arrived. I knew what his problem was. He was too intelligent to do this.

He asked me if I wanted to see it. He would like to show me all the work he had done. "Sure, why not?"

He really had it looking good. It looked like a restoration project, well done. He lifted the hood, and I could see everything was new under there. There was a new generator, new battery, and new radiator—all shiny and black. "I put new brake lines on, with new brake assemblies all around. I rewired it too."

"Wow. Virgil, you have done a lot of work here. I'm impressed. Think you'll ever get the urge to go racing again?"

"I kind of doubt it. I just haven't sold it because I haven't made that decision yet, and I guess I don't want to have to decide one way or the other. On the other hand, I certainly could use the space in here for other projects. My wife is not going to have her car outside in the winter, so you can guess where my regular ride has to sit in the wintertime. Maybe if this race car was going to a good home, I wouldn't feel so bad about giving it up."

"Have you tried to sell it? The way you got it looking, it shouldn't be too tough to sell."

"I always think about selling it this time of year with winter coming on. It's become kind of a friend, you know? We have spent a lot of time together in here. Maybe if I knew it was going to a good home, I wouldn't feel so bad about giving it up. I would want to sell to a guy who would do more with it than I did—a guy who would race it, and maybe even win a race in it."

"Virgil, this may sound a little crazy, but I might be interested in buying it back from you. I would have to think about it some 'cause I did leave racing a couple of years back, actually it was Pro Rally racing, but you know what I mean, and I know Nancy would be less than thrilled if I took it up again."

"Well, if you did want to buy it, I would sell it, 'cause I know you wouldn't just polish it and look at it. How much did I pay you for it?"

"I can't quite remember, but I can look it up. I think it was around $2000, maybe a few hundred more."

"Tell you what. I'll sell it back to you for whatever I paid for it. I'll get some of my money out of it, and you'll get your car back considerably improved."

"Virgil, let me go home and contemplate my navel for a day or two and make sure I really want to do this. But don't sell it to anyone else in the meantime. I got the right of first refusal, right?"

"You do, man. Let me give you some phone numbers, so you can get a hold of me here or at work."

I knew when I got back in my car that I was going to buy this old race car back. It looked so good. The price of these kinds of cars had gone up considerably. There were fewer of them every year, and the alternative, Showroom Stock, involved getting a nearly new car and making a race car out of it. New cars were getting more expensive every year. I knew that if I bought Virgil's car for $2000, or something like that, I could sell it over the winter for $3000.

It was clear he had upgraded all the ancillary systems, but he must not have done anything to update the motor. If he had, he would have told me. That meant it still had the motor I sold it with. That was a better-than-average motor, but it wasn't a monster motor either. I better include a new motor in the budget if I planned on winning. I knew a guy in Plymouth, Don Cameron, who specialized in these small 1100 cc (68 cubic inches displacement) engines, and who might have one available or who would build one to order.

The next day, I brought the subject up to the wife, a radical departure from the way I handled things like this in the past. As I expected, she was not crazy about the idea. She said she liked having me around on the weekends, and wasn't I getting a little old for a young man's sport?

She had a point on the age, that's for sure. I didn't start racing until 1976, the age of 37. That's kind of when a lot of guys who started in their twenties get out of the game. It's now the mid-eighties, and I'm in my late forties. So? Some guys just take longer to grow up.

Virgil was happy to hear from me, glad that I wanted the car. We made some arrangements for the monetary transfer at the same time he would deliver the car. It was good to have the old car back in my possession.

I wanted to take what Virgil had done with the car as a base and build from there. I had been down to the SCCA Runoffs at Road Atlanta recently as a spectator and saw how the winners in this class configured their cars. The Runoffs are the national amateur road racing championships held each year in the fall. You had to be a regional champion in your class to be invited. These drivers were the top road racers in the country.

The guy who won in G Production, our class, had a fully adjustable front sway bar, a monster motor if 1100 cc's can be made into a monster, and a side-mounted exhaust for lower ground clearance.

I would do all of that and more. I knew that the service manager, Barry Hartzel at Bob Owens Jaguar/MG/Subaru, had raced Austin Healeys for years and was a specialist in suspensions. He held the track record in F Production in an MG Midget. I hope I have pointed out by now that there was no difference between an Austin Healey Sprite and an MG Midget. They were exactly the same cars except for the name. Barry's F Production car had a slightly bigger motor of 1250 cc. He could duplicate what I saw and probably improve upon it. I called him, and he said to drop the car off and he would go through all the suspension pieces, make sure they were OK, and make up a fully adjustable heim-jointed front sway bar for me.

The engine would come from Don Cameron, over in Plymouth. He had built a 975 cc MG Midget engine for his brother Paul last year, and Paul held the track record in H Production. Don said a motor like Paul's in the 1100 cc size would set me back about $1500.

I wanted the car to look jazzy too. It would get a fresh coat of black paint and fiberglass extensions at the upper edge of the wheel wells. The rules allow you to run a wider tire, but it must be contained within the fender. Therefore, you needed to extend the fender outward. Steve, the Russian over at Import West Collision, would do that for me. I got a better bucket seat for it, more wheels and eight new Goodyear slicks, plus four new rain tires.

My initial $2000 investment would grow to about $6000 before the season started. I had been around Waterford Hills long enough to know that you have to spend a fair amount of money to be competitive, and you have to spend it intelligently. You also have to drive well. That's what it took to win. The car was a dream to drive. It handled superbly. I avoided major dustups with other drivers. The years of driving at Waterford Hills and the years as a Pro Rally driver had honed my skills. I was smooth; the car was bulletproof, and we won.

There are two big reasons to race: to win the race and in so doing to gain the respect of those other drivers that you respect because they're strong competitors. That's why you plan and prepare and spend and solve the problems that arise—to win the race and to win the respect of those you respect.

We won more than half the races and we were the 1985 Waterford Hills G Production Class Champions. I say "we" because as usual I had a lot of quality help. I remember my father saying, "Son, it's not how you play the game but how you choose up sides." You could take that two ways, but what he was telling me was to always play as hard as I could; but in a team sport, you need to have the best teammates in order to have the best team.

My old friend, Don Ensley of English Motors in Utica, kept the Don Cameron engine in fine tune. Steve Steeb, an original member of my Waterford crew from back in 1976, was now racing his own H Production Austin Healey Sprite, but he would help out between race weekends with oil changes, tire work and general maintenance. I let Steve use my car for his Drivers' School. My car number has always been #9. Steve's car numbers have always been #91, reflecting our long relationship.

We campaigned that car one more year, coming close but not winning the championship again. Then, for reasons that are unclear to me now, I put the car up for sale. I think I was beginning to have some financial problems. There was a period in the mid-eighties where I had left Scan-Optics for another employer, Spectrascan. I was not selling as much, therefore not earning as much, and I extended myself beyond my ability to pay my bills in a timely matter. In fact, I found myself about $20,000 in debt. I finally worked that off, but that was the year I had what could be called a hard candy Christmas.

I sold the car to a young guy who, like Virgil Darga, was buying the car to start racing next season. Unfortunately, he was offered some serious money for the motor, and he sold that to somebody, and then parted out the rest of the car to various people. That really honked me off. A race car is always more than the sum of its parts. It gets its value when all these parts work in harmony, and the result is a winning car. All the development and experience with that car is tossed away, like last year's decals.

Well, no matter. I had a great time with the car as my original race car, and as a championship winner. This one owned me twice.

# I Didn't Care; I Wasn't In It For Love

## Three 1989 Ford Thunderbirds

*This 1989 Thunderbird is for sale at John Ryan's Glenbard Auto Sales in Lombard, IL for $2,595.*

I bought three of these Ford Thunderbirds while working as a new car salesman at Briarwood Ford in Saline, Michigan.

These were my demos. You would "buy" a car at close to dealer cost, make a token payment each month, and were required to sell it as a demonstrator before it got 5000 miles on the odometer. Generally, the salesman made a few hundred dollars on selling his demo, and as soon as that was done, he picked out a new one. Of course, you could always keep it if you wanted to buy it outright.

The first of these was a burgundy Thunderbird LX with a 3.8 liter V-6, and I was taken with the styling. I like slab-sided cars like this. It reminded me slightly of the '49 Ford. The

2005 Ford Mustang and 2006 Ford Fusion/Ford 500 are from the slab-sided school.

I had just taken delivery of this new 1989 T-Bird in early January, and we drove it to Detroit to the North American Auto Show at Cobo Hall. It was slushy on I-94 and icy in spots. I thought the car really handled well. Everyone was driving 40-50 mph, but this car was easily driven, at 65-70 mph. It may have been the relatively skinny tires or the suspension components, but either way, this rear-wheel drive car was quite controllable in sloppy conditions.

This car was based on a new platform, which would also be used for the Lincoln Mark VIII. It seemed like the base price was around $17,000, and no one else offered a full-size two-door with a decent back seat and rear-wheel drive. After I ran up 5000 miles on this T-Bird, I sold it to a customer, made a hundred or so on it, and promptly bought another one, this time dark blue.

Thunderbird! What a great name for a car. These 1989 Ford Thunderbirds were good cars but a long way in design and size from the originals. A little history, if you please...

The first T-Birds produced by Ford back in 1955 were visually stunning. Nothing quite like the Thunderbird had existed up to that point. You might counter that the Corvette was of the same genre, but the 'Vette soon evolved into a sports car with a four-speed manual transmission as an option, and people began to race them.

Not so the T-bird. It was meant to be a car for the boulevard, a car to arrive at the country club in or to make a grand entrance driving up to the yacht club for the Commodore's Ball. Ford marketed it as a "personal" car and never called it a "sports" car. It had a V-8 of course, but the motor was not a big part of its appeal. It sold on its looks. The straight crisp exterior lines, the cushy interior with bucket seats and a dashboard out of a spaceship, the long hood and short rear deck, dual exhausts, and the porthole windows in the removable hardtop were just too much to resist. The 1955 Thunderbird had the "secret sauce." It possessed style plus substance.

Over time, the Thunderbird began to resemble its middle-aged customers. It began to put on weight and became longer, wider, slower and lost a great deal of its original appeal. There was even a four-door version at one point.

The 1989 Ford Thunderbird was a pretty car, not beautiful, but pretty. It was not seen as a classic in styling by the automotive press but still nice looking. The hardware underneath the skin was decent, and that was improved in subsequent years with the choice of a supercharged 3.8 liter V-6 or a 5.0 liter V-8 engine. So, yes, the styling was good, not great, but the substance was there, particularly the high tech suspension.

I drove the blue T-Bird for about 5000 miles and sold it easily to a customer who wanted a "new" car without the new car price. If the salesman didn't abuse the car, these were good deals. The people who bought them preferred demos driven by the older salesmen for obvious reasons. I replaced the blue one with another burgundy Thunderbird, identical in every other respect.

If there is a kernel of curiosity about why I was working at a Ford dealership in the first place, permit me to elaborate.

Most of my adult life has been spent selling high-end technical products like optical recognition systems, medical devices, etc., that sold for $125,000 to over $1,000,000. I had crisscrossed the Midwest since 1965, usually covering four or five states, driving 30,000 or more miles per year. I really wanted to get off the road. Other than computers, cars were about the only thing I knew something about.

We have all endured bad car salesmen, and I figured I could do a better job of it than any I had dealt with, with the exception of Eddie Atkinson, a wonderful Englishman, who I met at a Ferrari dealership, and who helped me buy my first

Jaguar and was last employed as the sales manager at a BMW store in Ann Arbor.

I interviewed at a few car dealerships and decided to take a job at Briarwood Ford in Saline, Michigan, a small farming town outside of Ann Arbor that had a big Ford Motor plant.

The job was offered under unusual circumstances. They had just hired about ten guys and expected half of them to quit in a month or two, as selling cars is tougher than it looks. The sales manager said he would take me on, but there wasn't a desk available right now; however there would be, hopefully, in a month. "Two or three guys are off almost every day, so just use their desks," he said, "and when no desks are available, just stand outdoors. If it's raining or you have a customer you found outside, you may come in. Otherwise, stay outside." I couldn't believe what I was hearing and couldn't believe I accepted those working conditions. I guess it was just the matter-of-fact manner in which I was told made it seem like it was perfectly normal. Talk about "outside sales"!

I soon realized I had been inadvertently provided with a big advantage. If I saw someone drive onto our lot and park by the pickup trucks, I would saunter over there and strike up a conversation while the other salesmen looked out the window. Being outside, I already had a 50-yard head start on anyone else. Customers generally don't care who sells them the car. The first sales guy who contacts them owns them unless they ask for another guy. Some dealerships have an "up" system where you take turns meeting someone who walks into the dealership. If they ask for a particular salesman, you have to take them over to that guy's desk, but other than that, they're yours. Being outdoors gave me most of the drive-in "ups."

The only problem with "outside sales" was the heat. This was the summer of 1988, a period of record heat in Michigan. There was no shade, just the hot sun beating down on that black asphalt. Damn, it was hot.

Sometimes, I would think about my prior sales jobs involving big system sales where the commission check might be $25,000 to $50,000. Here I was, indistinguishable from a thousand other car salesmen, sweat showing through my white shirt and loose tie, working my tail off for $150 per car. Maybe I would have to get back on the road again. This was hard on my dignity, not to mention my income. I looked at it as a challenge. I learned everything I could about the cars and trucks we offered. Later on, the dealership would hold product knowledge contests, and I usually won or placed high among the finalists.

Working at the dealership was a mixed bag. I liked the action of selling something in a rather short time frame, like a day or two, as opposed to selling a computer system that could take six months to a year. I think the big difference between myself and the other guys was that I liked cars, and I liked the customers. They were just like you and me, looking for a deal, hoping not to make a mistake, and hoping not to take a big hit on their trade-in.

Some were "dirt bags," people you couldn't get accepted by Ford Motor Credit if you cosigned for them. The "dirt bags" and "near dirt bags" were usually "upside down" on the value of their trade-in. That is, they owed more on it than it was worth. If they bought another car on credit, the old debt had to be paid off and added to the debt on the new note. Now, they were even worse off when it came to replace that car. Still, they were usually nice people, just not very good at managing money in particular, or life in general. Those who worked for Ford at one of the nearby plants could have their car payments taken right out of their paycheck. This plan was called "payroll deduct" or "payroll destruct," depending on how much was left.

Other customers were "bricks" with great credit. They often paid cash. Some folks leased, which made sense to me only if it was a company car, provided as an employee benefit, and expensed by the employer against taxable profits.

Individuals who leased never seemed to pay attention to the details, like the capitalized cost (purchase price) and the residual value, which had a lot to do with what you could buy the car for at the end of the lease.

The lease customer, like the conventional auto loan customer, focused only on the monthly payment. That's a bad idea. If you waltz into a dealership and tell them you need a car and can afford a monthly payment of $275, you'll be offered a car that is just a little more than that, say $300/month (What's another $25/month to you? Less than a dollar a day!), and you won't know until the paperwork is presented that you're going to be on the hook for 48 or 60 months, instead of the 36 months you thought you specified, but the sales guy seemed to forget about. Now, you have to start over or take the deal out of embarrassment. Start over, friend, with a different salesman and probably a different dealer.

Some of us tried hard to put the customer in a car he/she could afford and still make a little for the dealership and myself. I usually made a hundred or two on the car. You had to start at sticker price and come down slowly so that the customer earned his price. Then, I took the deal up to the Tower to get it approved by the sales manager. This was a real tower, elevated about five feet above the sales floor where management could see and probably hear everything that was happening.

On a new Taurus that posted a window sticker price of $18,000, the dealer invoice figure was about $16,000, which didn't include the holdback (money that the manufacturer sends to the dealer later and usually amounted to about 3% of the window sticker at that time), I would normally take $1000 off of the sticker to be competitive. If the customer was satisfied with that, I would march up to the tower to hear the usual refrain, "Nowak, you're weak. Weak as water. Tell them that this car is high demand and we can't sell it for that. Take $500 back."

My counter was always the same, "They are "shopping" this deal and there is an identical car over at Varsity Ford which they may buy. They just want to see if we can do a better deal for them. That's why they're here. Should I send them back over there?" That would usually settle the argument, but not always.

It is an article of faith among new car dealers that any individual who enters a dealership to seriously discuss the purchase of a new car is aware of the hassle he has to endure to get a decent price, and 90% of these people will buy a car somewhere in the next ten days, so you better take your best shot. If they leave without buying or ordering, the likelihood of them returning is slim because another dealer can always beat your price by a hundred dollars. Always.

Some dealerships are run like feudal kingdoms, where the king or kings, the owners, treat most of their employees badly. Not at every dealership, but many of them. New-car sales managers and used-car sales managers are subjected to a lot of verbal abuse, pressure and disrespect. This load of ill feelings is quickly passed along to the salesmen. There was an underground civil war going on between most departments most of the time. You just had to stay focused on your job and ignore all the other crap. Some of the sales personnel kissed a lot of fanny in order to get deals handed to them by the owners whose friends would call directly in hopes of a special price. The recipients were known as "house mouses" and were scorned by the regular troops.

A friend of mine owned a Ford dealership up North and sold it several years ago, and when I asked him why, he explained it this way. "You might think dealing with Ford is a big problem. They're not easy to work with, but that's not the reason. You might think it's the competition, but they're really not a factor. Maybe you think it's the customer who hits you over the head with *Consumer Reports* and who knows all about dealer invoice pricing and holdbacks. No, it's the people working at the dealership that are too much to take. That's why I'm out of there."

Every month at our store there was the competition for "Salesman of the Month." A huge scoreboard covering one whole wall of the lunchroom had everyone's name and their sales for each day of the month. The average car salesman sells ten cars per month. Old-timers tell me that has been true for sixty years and will probably always be true. This dealership had to sell about 220 new and used cars per month. They hired about 20 to 25 salesmen, and generally hit their target, although some months were 32 to 34 days.

Car salesmen at the time made between $50 and $500 per car. The usual commission was around $200, maybe a little less. Used cars paid considerably higher than new cars. At ten cars per month, the new car salesman would net $2000 before taxes, and that would amount to $24,000 per year. Not too great, considering we worked every day from 8 AM to 5 PM, plus two nights per week, plus every other Saturday. This usually totaled up to around 50 to 60 hours per week. A lot of these guys had just squeaked thru high school, and had few options. They all smoked, to the man, and put away serious quantities of alcohol. Turnover was high, and there was a fair amount of movement from one dealership to another. One guy I knew worked at a Lincoln store in Ann Arbor and then moved a half block down the street to a Chrysler/Plymouth dealer. He went back and forth between these two dealers four times in a ten-year period.

If I may brag a bit, I was good at this. I made "Salesman of the Month" three or four times in 18 months. My best month was 31 cars, a record that stood for twelve years. Like all top salesmen, I was hated for it because it showed the other guys up. I didn't care; I wasn't in it for love.

One of my techniques for getting new business was to go out there occasionally on a Sunday afternoon with a case of cold Cokes and some paper cups and approach browsers who liked to come around when the store was closed, so they wouldn't be hassled by salespeople. I would tell them that I worked there but really couldn't sell them a car because we were closed, but I did have some refreshments if they were interested. They took the cold Cokes and also received two business cards. The guy would put his in his shirt pocket where it might be laundered with the shirt, but the woman would put hers in her purse and she would be the one to ask for me the following week.

This really set some of the other sales guys off. I was marched to the back lot by the sales manager who said he didn't like to see trouble among the sales guys, and while he couldn't stop me, some of the boys might start to play rough. I told him that I didn't see anyone there I couldn't handle, so I would take my chances. He countered with "Just don't do this every weekend. You have to get away from here or you'll burn out." Fair enough. If management had thought about it for ten seconds, they would have seen the merit of having a company-sponsored refreshment wagon out there on Sundays. Only in Michigan, home of the automotive industry, are dealerships not open seven days a week. Madness. Or stupidity.

The other thing I did was install my own computer at the dealership, using one of my phone lines to tie it in to Ford's new car inventory database. One might think that management would object, but you can pretty much do what you want if you're a producer. This was useful when somebody needed a car we didn't have, but was available 75 miles away at another Ford store. I tried to sell what we had in stock, but if we were going to lose the sale over color or options, I was into that database and on the phone. Our big competition was Varsity Ford in Ann Arbor, who had four times the inventory we had. There was no love lost between these two stores and no dealer trades either.

If you want to sell cars, then you have to get people in the car so it can work its charms, especially if these folks were husband and wife. I would work hard to persuade them to do

so, telling the customer, "Let's see if this car is worth haggling over." You didn't want it to be a commodity because then price is the only differentiator, and you sure didn't want that.

If I got my way, I would put the guy in the back seat, put the lady in front because if she was pampered a bit and catered to, she liked that. She was the primary decision maker 90% of the time. That's a fact, mister.

I would drive the car off of the lot, explaining "Insurance regulations, ma'am," and continue to drive for another couple of miles, allowing them to see the interior, and listen to me talk about some new features before I would pull over in a parking lot to let one of them drive. I drove a known route of very smooth pavement with some twists in it plus a railroad crossing, commenting on how quiet it was, how smartly it cornered and how smoothly it crossed the tracks.

You know who I offered the first chance to drive it: the woman, of course. She would usually take me up on it, feeling quite gleeful that her husband was still riding Coach while she had been upgraded to First Class. I never kept exact numbers, but I would estimate that 75% of those who went on the demo drive bought a car from us, and of those who declined to go, only about 10% went ahead with the purchase at our store.

One fine day, an old friend from Connecticut, Dick Coburn, called to say he was starting a new company that would be manufacturing a new type of computer printer using an ion deposition process he had developed. Would I accept a salary of $75,000 plus commission to join his new firm, KCR Technology? I was making maybe $45,000 at the time and working 55 to 60 hours per week. I would have to travel a bit, but I was ready to get back on the road and sell these new systems, which would sell for $150,000 and put $10,000 in my pocket for every one I placed.

If you're going to get into sales, always sell something expensive. Most systems sales where the product or service costs more than $100,000 usually pay 5% to 10% commission plus a base salary. You'll get annual W-2 statements with five zeros on them if you sell the big ticket items. I wonder what a sales guy for Boeing makes when he gets an order for a new plane. Must be a big number.

So, I was on my way out of the car business. I decided I would buy the last Thunderbird that I had been driving. It was burgundy with the usual grey-cloth interior. I was now traveling across three states, and it was a great highway car. Got decent mileage, drove comfortably, and had timeless good looks. I call that the "blue blazer" look because even though it isn't the latest style, it never goes out of style.

Three 1989 Thunderbirds, good cars all. Perhaps Ford was doing so well with other cars and trucks, they didn't sell the Thunderbird on its styling and technical merits. Too bad.

I wonder how many guys owned three of the same car in one year. I don't know how many 1989 Ford Thunderbirds were sold, but you would have to agree, I did my part.

# He Was a Dancer, a Fighter, a Wild Bull Rider, and a Pretty Good Ladies Man

## 1986 Lincoln Town Car

*King of the road.*

Budget Rental Cars first introduced me to these big cars. They always seem to have a special deal going where you could rent Lincoln Town Cars for about the same rate as smaller cars.

I often flew into Louisville or Indianapolis on business and would reserve a car with Budget because they had fairly low rates. If they had a deal on the big Lincoln, that was a bonus. I would leave the airport driving a big comfy car, feeling upbeat and ready to tackle the world. I hated to think I needed a car to bolster self-confidence, but driving this big car helped mine.

Customers liked to go to lunch in them too. If I were hauling my boss around to meet clients, he would like the fact that I thought enough of the occasion to get a nicer car. I would be remiss not to point out that there was no increase in expense because management could get confused. The other benefit was that these huge cars got pretty decent gas mileage, usually 20 to 22 mpg, which was very good, considering that we were usually running late so the car was being hustled right along.

Styling wise, they were outrageous. They had a hood the size of a small imported car, a trunk large enough to hold a golf cart, and a back seat suitable for group procreation. The mid-eighties design had very distinct edges and creases that proclaimed strength and substance. The car has had two styling changes since then where the body has been rounded to make it more aerodynamic. Frankly, I preferred the older version with all the straight lines.

In one sense, the Lincoln Town Car was quite old-fashioned. It had a V-8 engine in the front, a proper ladder frame underneath the body, an interior that would easily hold six adults, and rear-wheel drive. Detroit had been building cars with this configuration since the late fifties, actually much earlier than that. V-8 engines were introduced in the fifties, but frames and rear-wheel drive go back to the beginning of the Twentieth Century. Now, in 2006, only Ford and Chrysler of the domestic manufacturers still build cars with a body on frame construction, and these are the current models of the Lincoln Town Car, the Mercury Marquis, and the Ford Crown Victoria. Higher-priced European cars, such as BMW, Mercedes, and Jaguar have always had rear-wheel drive, although the construction was usually a unibody with subframes. The significant exception to that is the 2005-2007 Jaguar XJ, which has a space frame, made of aluminum.

If you have the misfortune to get into a wreck, the unibodied cars are harder to put back together, whereas framed cars are inherently stronger and heavier. The other nice feature of framed cars is that you can tow things with them. You can do some light towing with a unibody but nothing substantial. This requirement to tow is the principal reason why all trucks, be they full-size, mid-size or mini-trucks, are all built with proper frames. Just about all SUVs have frames too.

I was driving through Lansing one fine day in my '89 Ford Thunderbird and had to stop at a Ford dealership there to talk with a mechanic who raced Ford Mustangs. My interest in Mustangs had begun about a year or two earlier when I acquired one for the purpose of racing it in a stock class at the Waterford Hills Racecourse near Clarkston. I wanted to pick this guy's brain, as he had been doing that kind of racing for several years.

The mechanic was sort of helpful, in a general way, but didn't want to give away any hard won knowledge or demon tweaks. Couldn't blame him, really. I decided I had gotten about as much as I could from him, so it was time to leave. On the way out to my T-Bird, I passed by a white Lincoln Town Car with a sign in the window offering the car for $5995. That seemed pretty low for a Lincoln just five years old that must have cost $20,000 new, probably more. Usually that's a sign of high miles or a rough condition. Intrigued, I opened the door and looked in. The car had a blue velvet cloth interior that gave it kind of an upper-class bordello look. How would I know what an upper-class bordello looked like?

I looked at the miles on the odometer that indicated something like 35,000 miles. Maybe it was 135,000 and the odo had rolled over to show just 35,000. If that were the case, the interior would have shown more wear. The thing to look for is the condition of the pedals: brake and gas. If they have rounded edges and a worn appearance, beware. People will re-carpet, re-upholster, even put a new headliner in, but nobody changes the pedals out. These pedals looked normal for the claimed mileage.

The big white car interested me. The T-Bird I was driving was OK, but it had begun to develop some problems, and I was thinking about making a change. The Bird seemed to just eat the front brake rotors and pads. It had a few squeaks and rattles too. And the tires would need replacement in a couple of months. It was a good handling car with independent rear suspension, and the tire wear had to be attributed in part to enthusiastic cornering on my part. Old rally car drivers steer with both ends of the car.

The truth is that I was getting a bit bored with the car. I had worked previously as a salesman at Briarwood Ford, and this was the demo that I was driving when I left about a year before. I was able to buy it at a good price, and I liked the car's looks and handling. It had the 3.8-liter V-6, so it would move along, although the 5.0-liter V-8 was the right motor for the car. My two previous demo cars with Briarwood Ford were also Thunderbirds. Part of the reason why I chose Thunderbirds for demos was that they were fairly easy to dispose of.

This particular Thunderbird now had about 50,000 miles on the clock and still had decent resale potential. It was probably worth more or less what the Lincoln was worth.

I went back in and had a sales guy get the keys to the Lincoln, so I might take it out for a test drive. It drove pretty well, especially out on the highway where it just floated along. There was no wind noise, no motor noise, and no tire noise. Talk about splendid isolation.

The handling wasn't bad for a big car. You would never mistake it for a sports car, but it would turn quickly and accelerate decently, just like the Budget Rental cars I used to rent and, mea culpa, occasionally flogged pretty hard.

I returned to the dealership and had the used-car manager appraise my car. He said it was worth about $5500, more or less. Now I knew we were in the ballpark because the price on the Lincoln was a bit more, but every dealer has his used-car prices somewhat inflated, so he can come down a bit and still come out OK. The old adage, "It's not what you spend, but what you save," gets a real workout in car dealing. The long and the short of it was we agreed to a trade. His '86 car for my '89 car and the sales tax melded in, so there was no cash out of pocket.

I didn't have the title to mine with me, but I promised to mail it in right away, so the deal was done in about an hour.

One of the benefits of a big car is that everything on it has to be pretty strong. Big wheels, big brakes, big shocks and big springs are all part of the package. A stout V-8 sending power back through a decent automatic transmission to a differential designed for all this weight and power is a good package. My "new" Lincoln had that indestructible atmosphere about it.

I had recently sold a Dodge van that was getting a bit long in the tooth and needed to replace it with something that could tow my race car and its trailer around. I was scrambling around looking for a truck when I happened to secure some sponsorship from a local moving company. They would lend me an old diesel pickup with a flaky clutch, bad brakes and a short semi-trailer that hooked to the fifth wheel plate in the bed of the pickup. I would use it primarily to haul the car and race equipment to the track for a race weekend. That was nice, but I often needed to haul the race car short distances for some engine work or the like, and the "big rig" wasn't available. I thought, what the hell, the Lincoln could pull an open car trailer if I had one. So that was the solution, occasionally renting a tandem axle trailer and pulling it behind the Lincoln Town Car. Might be a little out of character, but the car didn't seem to mind.

Speaking of that diesel pickup from the moving company, the clutch failed in the middle of the rush hour while going through Detroit pulling that semitrailer with the race car in it. When traffic stopped in front of me, I had to yank hard to get it out of gear. When it was time to move, I had to jam it into first gear, which it didn't like at all, and then go up through the gears a crunch at a time. The brakes on the pickup truck were marginal, at best, without the semitrailer hooked up. With it on there, it was a frightening experience to go any place, as the semitrailer brakes were not functional either. I really couldn't downshift for braking because it was always so hard to get it back out of gear. Here I was with no clutch, almost no brakes on the pickup, and lots of weight to contend with, and a transmission that was not going to last very long. This is when you ask yourself if you are stupid or really stupid.

I managed to get to my destination and drop the car off. Magically, the clutch came back, and I was able to get this old rig back to the moving company in Ann Arbor. After that bit of trauma, the Lincoln did a lot more of the towing.

Nancy, my dear wife, had been working on adopting a retired Greyhound dog as a pet, and when the big day arrived to get the dog, we threw a blanket in the back seat of the Lincoln and went into Royal Oak to a pet adoption agency to pick him up. I wasn't sure what to expect but was pleased to find out that we were getting a nice-looking male that was the color of a deer.

Greyhounds normally range in size from fifty to eighty pounds with the males naturally being larger. This guy was the largest greyhound I had ever seen, tipping the scales at about ninety-five pounds without an ounce of fat on him.

My wife sat in the back with this giant of a dog, looking beneath him in my direction. "Nancy," said I, "what have we done? Not only is he the color of a deer, he is the size of a big fawn or a young doe!" He really didn't have room to lie down with her sitting back there, so he stood all the way home. He was about three when we got him, and he lived with us until he was about fourteen.

When that sad day arrived about three years ago, we had to take him to the vet to be put down, so he rode in the back of my 2000 Lincoln LS and contentedly slept all the way to the vet's. What a great dog he was. What a sad day. The wife and I cried for several days, often just spontaneously breaking into tears when we thought of him. Still do, as I'm writing this.

Greyhounds were part of the royal court in Egypt as far back as 5000 years ago. It seemed appropriate that this prince of a dog would occupy the back seat of a fine car, as he came into and left our lives.

Somewhere I've read that when your pets die they go to a place just outside of heaven and wait there by the Rainbow Bridge for you to arrive. When you finally show up, you all enter heaven together. I don't know if that's true, but I hope it is. Might be a good reason to behave yourself.

Do you ever wonder why seeing someone special or going somewhere interesting or eating at a nice place had the effect of transforming your mood from sour to great? I suppose that's because you get out of "yourself" and participate in the special thing that was going on.

Certain cars, like this Lincoln, would do that for me. I would admire the car, as I was approaching it, hurry a bit to get in and get ready to go, and then get underway, as this transformation took place. In the space of thirty seconds, my outlook had brightened, and while this didn't solve any of the problems or make any of the worries go away, I felt better. It's one of those things that could be construed as a weakness, I suppose, but I preferred to consider it relatively inexpensive but effective therapy.

One of the inherent problems of being a salesman is that most of the time business is tough to come by. You want an appointment, but the prospect has other things he would rather spend his time on. You finally get the appointment, and now you need to persuade the guy to consider your system as a better one than the one he has. He doesn't want to hear that because everyone resists change. In time, you get your chance, but he invites others to compete for the business. You work like a dog on the proposal, enter your bid, and after an evaluation process that takes months, you win or you don't.

If you win, you're on top of the world. If you lose, you're in the depths of a bitter depression. Might even think about having a drink or a dozen. In between the winning and the losing is the struggle. It's the struggle that really wears on you, and that is where the special car comes in. It seemed to heal my mental bruises, restored my self-confidence, and massaged away the hurt feelings. The struggle is every day, and the car's therapy works every day. I don't think special cars are going to put psychiatrists out of business, but they do the trick for me.

It is interesting, even funny, how cars affect others' perceptions of you. If you're driving a fancy import or an expensive domestic car, you're given the benefit of the doubt. You are treated better, have more credibility, and have that "winners" aura. Some folks don't like to see that you're doing so well. Envy and jealousy will always be part of the human condition.

In California's image-conscious culture, many people attach considerable importance to the brand of car being driven, at least as far as first impressions go. But first impressions only go so far. The car may get you in the door, but in the final analysis it has as much to do with winning the day as the band does at a high school football game.

It has always seemed to me that the car ought to get the credit, not the owner. If not the car, then the designers and builders should receive the accolades.

The Lincoln was no Jaguar or high-end Mercedes in terms of exclusivity, but it did work its charm, especially on folks who hadn't ridden in one before. I have often heard my customers and friends say, on the way to lunch in the Lincoln, "So this is what a Town Car is like. Not bad. Lots of room, nice ride. Not bad at all." When I would tell them you could get a used one with lots of life left in it for under $6000, you could hear the wheels start to turn. The next question was always the same question, every time. "I'll bet she really drinks the gas, eh?" They wouldn't believe me when I said that the highway mileage was in the low- to mid-twenties, and you could burn the cheapest gas available in its relatively low compression engine.

I guess what folks may not realize, and this is heresy to the auto companies, is that Lincolns are big Fords, Lexuses are big Camrys, Cadillacs are big Chevys. The difference between a Lincoln Town Car and a Ford Crown Victoria, for instance, was mostly in refinements like a nicer interior, a smoother ride, and more standard features, especially high-end sound systems and climate control systems. But underneath the radically different exterior shapes, both the Lincoln Town Car and the Ford Crown Victoria use the same motor, the same transmission, the same full frame, and the same rear end. The refinements and added standard features do add to the cost of the Lincoln Town Car, but when you realize that at least 60% to 70% of a car's cost is direct labor and employee costs such as health care and retirement benefits, and that the labor hours to build both cars are essentially the same, and that Ford Motor Company does make a profit on the Ford Crown Victoria, selling for $29,000 in 2006, how much more profit is there in the Lincoln Town Car currently selling for around $43,000? You get the picture.

The Town Car and the Crown Victoria are said to share the same platform. Car companies often use the same basic floor pan and the same suspension pickup points and use these on a variety of cars. If they can share the platform, obviously they can share many of the same mechanicals.

Remember the Ford Fairmont? This nice low-priced family sedan was the basis for the '79 Ford Mustang, which revived the Mustang "brand" and started Mustang on the way back to decent sales figures. Well, that Fairmont/Mustang platform was also shared with the Ford Thunderbird and the Mercury Cougar. Then, it wasn't too much of a stretch to make a Lincoln Mark VII out of a Thunderbird. You could say, without exaggeration, that the lowly Fairmont begat the Lincoln Mark VII, selling for four or five times the price of the Fairmont.

Speaking of shared platforms, the first Jaguar S-Type and the current Thunderbird Convertible were on the same Lincoln LS platform, although I'm told that in subsequent model years, the Jaguar S-Type and the Lincoln LS had little in common.

The bottom line with this Lincoln, and the two Lincolns I've owned since, is that they were and are as reliable as a hammer. Nothing, at least in my experience, has ever broken or failed. There have been no engine, transmission and other drive train problems. No interior pieces or exterior trim pieces came loose. No paint problems were observed. The Lincoln dealers have been competent, and of course any Ford dealer can fix the car as well.

I don't have any stock in the Ford Motor Company, but it appears that of the forty or so cars in this book, about eighteen have been Fords. If we add in the three Jaguars and the Aston Martin, both brands now owned by Ford, I must confess that more than half are cars built by Ford or by companies they now own. Oh dear, there goes my objectivity. Not really, though, as this is more of a history book than a brand preference market survey.

If I had to be nailed down on the topic of best brand, I think there is a particular brand of Japanese car, built in the USA, that demonstrates its quality by having three or four of its cars and trucks in *Car & Driver's* "Top Ten" every year for the last ten years. Your guess?

Then what became of the Townie? It was replaced, surprise, by a Lincoln Mark VII that I bought from my good friend,

Craig Weidner of Weidner Ford in Cadillac, Michigan. The Town Car went out on the street corner, off of Stadium Boulevard, where many of its predecessors once sat, and was sold to a guy who wanted a big car for his large family. I hope it served him as well as it did me. It was a great business car, a sturdy tow vehicle for my race car's tandem axle trailer, and a fine family car.

That summary kind of reminds me of the description of an all-around guy I once heard about in a country & western bar. "He was a dancer, a fighter, a wild bull rider, and a pretty good ladies man." The big Lincoln was all of that.

# I Could Have Kissed Her

## 1988 Lincoln Mark VII Coupe

*Still handsome after all these years, an '88 at the Elks Lodge in Holland, MI.*

Let me begin at the end of my ownership of this car. I sold it to a nurse who worked at St. Joe's, a local hospital. She answered my ad in the paper and came over to see the car. I had put the price in the paper, my regular practice, and provided the usual elements in the description of the car, like mileage, color, major options and the model year.

She looked the car over, asked again about the price, and said she would like to take it for a drive. I went with her, of course, because I think the seller misses out if he doesn't. When you're along, you provide a narrative on how long you've had the car, why you're selling it, and have a chance to demonstrate some of the features, like the sound system and the climate control system.

This lady aroused my curiosity too. Not for the usual reasons, but for the fact that she didn't seem the type for the car or vice versa. I had always thought of the Lincoln Mark VII as a man's car. Sure, you saw the occasional lady behind the wheel of this particular Lincoln, but not often. This car was meant to be driven at relatively high speeds for trips of several hundred miles at a clip. It didn't seem, at least to me, like the kind of car a lady would drive around town, running errands.

Here was a nice lady, a registered nurse no less, who wanted to own this executive muscle car. It's none of my business who drives what, but I was sure she would conclude that it just wasn't for her. I even went so far as to mention at least one thing that might make the car unsuitable for her, namely rear-wheel drive, which can be a handful in the wintertime, especially in a powerful car like this that had most of its weight in the front where it did no good tractionwise.

She said she really liked the car and would like to buy it. She made an offer that was about 10% less than what I had priced it at, and when I offered to split the difference, she said she would take it. "Lady," I said, "I know you're going to enjoy the car, but I must admit I'm a little surprised that, of all the used cars available today in Ann Arbor, you prefer this one to a front-wheel drive import that would get better mileage and might be a better car in the winter for you."

"I realize," she replied, "that I don't seem like the typical Lincoln Mark VII driver, but I'm pretty sure this is a good car. I don't make a lot of money, so if the engine gave out, I would have to get into my savings to get it repaired, but I don't think that's going to happen.

"You want to know the real reason why I'm going to buy your car? It's really very simple. I love the way it looks."

I could have kissed her. She loved the way it looks! Here was a kindred soul. That's as good of a reason as I can think of to buy a car. Oh sure, the car has to be solid and have decent resale and all of that, but looks are important, more important than almost anything else on a car.

Consider the successor to the Mark VII, the Lincoln Mark VIII. The newer car was mechanically superior, had the latest in engine technology, a very good suspension, a nice interior, a superior sound system, as well as better fit and finish. Was it a big seller? No. Why not? Well, it was kind of homely. The side profile of the car was weak. The front was so-so. The rear was awful. It seemed to be designed by a committee. Any time you have the trunk falling downward in the side profile, it looks weak.

About the same time the new Mark VIII hit the market, the Lexus SC was being sold. It was about the same size and general side profile as the Lincoln, but its trunk carried a rising line upward, providing a styling continuity with the rest of the car. It was, and is, a handsome car. It sold well, at a premium price. Styling plus substance.

I don't pretend to be a stylist or automotive designer, but, like everybody else, I know what I like. This lady knew what she liked, what looked good to her, what pleased her, what seemed to her like a beautiful piece of machinery. She bought it because she "loved the way it looks."

I always liked this car, for no other reason than it seemed to me like a powerful executive coupe. If the Ford Mustang could be considered a halfback in football parlance, then the Lincoln Mark VII was a fullback. The same mechanicals were in both cars, with the bigger car weighing a bit more.

It shared its platform with the '79-'93 Mustang and the mid-eighties Ford Thunderbird. When the T-Bird got its new platform in '89, the Mark VIII, the successor Lincoln to the '88, was built off of it.

I had driven one of these Mark VII cars several years before, and it made a favorable impression. There was a black one sitting on a used-car lot in Ann Arbor, and I took it out for a test drive.

At any rate, I had it doing about 75, heading south on US-23, and noticed that the tachometer was showing a mere 2200 rpms. The 5.0 liter engine was just loafing along, no big deal. The solidness of the car, the quiet, the sweet interior, all combined to provide a great ride. It reminded me of how a professional weightlifter, capable of lifting 400 pounds, would hardly have to exert himself when lifting 200 pounds, yet that weight would be a big, perhaps insurmountable challenge to the average guy. I didn't buy that car but was sorely tempted.

I got a call one day from Craig Weidner, a Ford/Lincoln dealer up in Cadillac, Michigan, who occasionally raced Ford Mustangs and had become a good friend. He had helped me get support from Goodyear Tire and always had time to kibitz about racing. He called to tell me that he had just taken a cream puff of a Lincoln Mark VII in on trade. He must have remembered me verbally lusting about Mark VIIs during one of our trackside conversations. If I were interested, he would send it down to Ann Arbor, and if I liked it, I would give his man a check and that would be that.

The car arrived a couple of days later at a mutual friend's warehouse, and I went to look it over. There was a very subtle dimple in the hood that you could only see in a certain light that I thought I could live with. The rest of the car was fine, white exterior with a blue leather interior. I wasn't crazy about blue interiors, usually specifying tan or black in cars I have ordered. I took it out for a short spin and was reminded of the black Mark VII I had taken out several years earlier. The car had good acceleration, made very little noise, and felt as solid as a branch bank. All the systems worked, so I bought it. It seemed like the price was around $8000.

This car was indeed a body builder in an executive suit. It had the looks, the muscle that a 225 horsepower V-8 provided, and the kind of ride that was somewhere between firm and comfortable. I always liked a firm ride but frankly have never been crazy about bucket seats. They hold you in place all right, but you can't move around, so the numb butt that is caused by circulation problems is hard to alleviate. On long runs, like Ann Arbor to Indianapolis, I would move the seat up and down, change the tilt, harden and soften the lumbar support just to change the contact points between my anatomy and the seat. I wouldn't have wanted to spend much time in the back seat either, but that's true of almost any two-door "sports" car.

To return to a familiar theme, weight is the enemy of all cars. Weight hurts handling, acceleration and gas mileage. Weight comes from using relatively cheap materials such as steel or iron when aluminum or titanium would be stronger and lighter, yet obviously more expensive.

The Mark VII was designed and built at a time when the cost of lightweight suspension pieces was ruled out by the time-worn consideration popular with the bean counters at Ford and elsewhere that said if they could save $5 per car, Ford would save millions each year. True enough. In the end, it is still a value proposition, namely, how much car are you getting for YOUR beans, not the manufacturer's.

The problem with the Mark VII, its cousin, the Ford Thunderbird, and its father, the Ford Mustang GT, is that these all had heavy cast-iron V-8 engines in the front under long hoods with only the rear suspension, the gas tank and some of the body providing rearward weight. Sixty-five percent of the weight was biased toward the front. This hurts handling and tire wear, not to mention braking performance in that the lightly loaded rear tires will break traction if the brakes are applied hard when the car is turning.

Contrast that with the enlightened thinking at Ford that went into the design and manufacture of the 2000 Lincoln LS. The LS has all aluminum double A-arms in its front suspension, aluminum double A-arms in its rear suspension, aluminum hood, aluminum head and block, and an aluminum case for the transmission. All this aluminum plus placing the battery in the trunk provided a 51/49 front/rear weight distribution before the driver got in and skewed the weight a bit more forward again. Having the weight more equally distributed to all four tires improves handling and improves tire life.

If I were Lincoln (Ford), I would have been pushing the engineering quality of their more advanced cars like the Lincoln LS a lot harder. But perhaps Ford has concluded that engineering excellence is on a par with safety, which has never sold very well, except to the Volvo/Mercedes crowd. Not to beat this to death, but the LS weighs about as much as the Mark VII, yet gets better mileage, has more top speed, and handles better. This four-door sedan outperforms the "sports car" Mark VII in part because of its weight distribution.

We have to remember that the Mark VII was designed in the early eighties and its long manufacturing run is a tribute to its good looks as much as it is to its acceleration and solid ride. That's what sold my buyer, the nurse, who always wanted to have one, just for its handsome profile.

You will occasionally see well-preserved Lincoln Mark VIIs tooling around today. I did run into my nurse friend several years after she bought it, and she was proudly driving her Mark VII, then at least ten years old.

It is a driver's car, still handsome after all these years.

# A Firm Believer in Managing the News

## 1988 Ford Mustang 5.0

*This one will own me forever.*

A black, 5-liter V-8 Mustang LX, 5-speed, no air, no radio. This was a basic street rod, and one of the more significant cars in this collection. It was kind of an illegitimate car, with a checkered past.

What were we doing with such a stripped no-nonsense car like this at Briarwood Ford? We would have never ordered one like this. It must have come from another dealer in an ill-advised trade.

Not a good car to steal with its bare-bones interior, lack of a sound system and no air-conditioning, but stolen it was. Apparently, several guys were able to drive it off our lot, drove it around for 30 miles, missed a curve, and ended up buried up to its axles in a farmer's field.

The car was found the next day, battered and bruised, with most of the windows broken, about ten miles away from the dealership. It looked like they took out their anger on the car for not having been born with the right equipment.

The dealership sent the car over to its body shop as a low priority project because they knew it was going to be tough to sell it after it was repaired, given its vandalized past.

A month or two later, the car reappeared out in our back lot, repaired and looking as new as a dealer's body shop can make it.

About this time a germ of an idea began to appear in that part of my brain that has been responsible in the past for making some questionable choices. Wouldn't this make a nice race car? Racers often look for stolen and recovered vehicles because they're cheap to buy, and a trashed interior is not a problem because the interiors are generally removed to save weight. This car had its interior intact, but it was bare bones, as a Mustang LX interior can be. If I could buy this car at the right price, it would make a fine Showroom Stock race car. It would need a roll cage, competition seat belts, a fire extinguisher, lettering, and maybe a spare set of wheels and tires, and it would be race ready. Showroom Stock classes permitted very few modifications in an attempt to keep the class cars equal and lower the cost of preparation. I wonder what the dealership would take for it…

The other problem was that I promised my wife I would get out of racing, and while I didn't say out forever, I certainly implied it.

So here I was, facing great temptation, yet did not see this as a moral issue but rather as an economic one. So much for twelve years in a small-town Catholic school system.

Owning a race car is a bit like having a pet horse. It's not the initial cost; it's the care and upkeep, especially when you think that a better transmission or a new set of cylinder heads is all that it needs to get into the winner's circle. Of course, the appeal of Showroom Stock was that you couldn't do this legally and therefore wouldn't spend the money, in theory.

Temptation won out, and I purchased the car for about $8000, which I think was about $4000 under sticker or $2500 under the net dealer cost. Not a great bargain but not bad for a car with thirty miles on it and just cosmetic damage, as far as anyone could tell.

The other side of my brain where my conscience lives kept whispering that this was a naughty thing to have done, and while I don't think one should ever lie to one's wife, I'm a firm believer in managing the news. If you've gotten the impression that my wife Nancy is a long-suffering saint and I have always been a naughty boy, you're pretty close. My major in college was Mathematics, but my major in life has always been Guilt Management.

To keep all this under wraps for the time being, I had the bank loan payment book and the insurance paperwork sent to the dealership. I overlooked the fact that the State of Michigan Secretary of State's office, which handles motor vehicle licensing, sends the title and registration to the owner's home.

I was talking with a young couple at the dealership about a new car when the phone rang, and the girl on the switchboard said, "It's your wife, and I think she is mad about something, something she got in the mail."

I barely recognized the wife's voice. She sounded like a hanging judge or the principal at St. Anne's Grade School summoning me to the office.

I still remember the chill in her voice as well as the words...

"You bought a car a month ago that I haven't seen, and I just know it's being built somewhere to be a rally car or a dragster or some damn thing. You are done. You are out of here."

It was not a good idea to leave my wife in an agitated state for long. She was a good argument for gun control. I know she would be loading it right now if she had one in her possession.

I told the young couple I had an emergency at home and would have to let another sales guy take over. They probably bought a car from him that morning; I just can't remember and didn't want to.

Driving in lunatic mode, I drove the ten miles from the dealership to my home in about eight minutes. She saw me coming and set off on a dog walk at a furious pace, almost faster than the dogs could walk. They were sort of trotting. I could barely keep up, and I asked, rather lamely, "What's the problem with me buying a car?"

"The problem is that since I have not seen it, I'll bet you're making a race car out of it, and you said you were done with racing."

"I didn't say I would never, ever, race again."

"You're despicable, no, worse than despicable. Get away from me. Where is that car right now?"

"It's up in Cadillac at Weidner Ford."

"Are they putting a roll cage in it?"

"Probably."

After awhile, she cooled off and life went on. They never really forgive you. Or forget. I suspect that if she outlives me, a statistical likelihood, she will put one word on my gravestone, and it will be: UNFORGIVEN.

It was the 55th or 155th application of the strategy that it's easier to get forgiveness than permission.

About a month later, the car arrived back in Ann Arbor, and I introduced my sweet bride to the car, now equipped with competition seat belts, window net, fire suppression system and a stout roll cage.

"This is a cute little car," she observed. "Too bad you're messing it up."

In defense of Nancy, she always fought hard but fair when it came to objecting to my buying expensive cars, motorcycles, sailboats or race cars. She would voice her reasonable objections emphatically; I would offer what I thought was a good defense, not great but good, of what I had in mind. The subject would lay dormant for a week or a month, and then I would go ahead with the deal. I knew where she stood, that she wouldn't like it. My internal justification was that she shouldn't like it; her position was logical, and I would have been surprised, almost suspicious, if she had said, "Good idea."

On the other hand, if husbands listened to every caution expressed by their wives, even if well founded, we would all still be living in England, or wherever our grandparents came from. So, aside from some casual grumbling along the lines of "Why couldn't you be a bit more like the other guys in the neighborhood?" the issue of race cars and weekends spent at racetracks and dollars spent on engines, not much was said. Sometimes it's tough, but you can't let your marriage interfere with your life.

There were two circumstances that made this potential domestic dispute less of problem than other guys had. First, she worked almost every weekend of the year as the Choir Director, Organist and Soloist at St. Thomas Church in Ann Arbor. She participated at Saturday afternoon and Sunday morning masses for twenty-some years, about the same period as I was involved in competitive motor sports. Thus she was occupied, and we couldn't have done much together anyway. The other favorable factor was that I didn't have much in the way of tire expenses from about 1990 through 1999 because of support, that is, free tires from Goodyear Tire. A simple little two-page proposal written to a fellow in their competition department for six sets of tires each year resulted in getting tire sponsorship, almost unheard of at the grass-roots level of racing we participated in.

My contemporaries usually addressed the domestic objection problem by bringing wife, children, and dog to the track from Friday night through Sunday night and selling the deal as "camping out and watching Daddy race." Grim-faced and justifiably worried wives, unruly and unhappy kids, thirsty and overheated dogs, plus all the work and worry that goes along with racing, made for an unhappy bunch.

I really think the guy should go to the track with two or three buddies, leaving mom and the kids and dogs at home. He does this one weekend a month. They'll probably work on the car some and have a few beers Friday and Saturday night, but he's not going to be fooling around chasing skirts or spending big bucks like he might if he was a spectator at a NASCAR race. When he comes home Sunday night with a trophy and maybe a dent or two in the car, give your warrior a warm welcome and a decent meal.

One of the beauties of Showroom Stock racing was that you could drive the car to the track, and if you could stuff spare tires and tools into the car, you arrived with everything you needed. Once there, you jacked the car up, put the "racing" tires on, set the tire pressures, put the magnetic car numbers on, checked the lug nuts and the engine oil, and drove the thing onto the track for Saturday morning's practice session.

As this tale unfolds, it will become apparent that this simple approach gave way to a much more complicated setup.

Showroom Stock racing hadn't changed all that much since I tried it in a '76 Capri fifteen years earlier. Back then, it was apparent that some guys were breaking the rules in subtle ways that made a difference and improved their lap times. This continued to the point that, almost without exception, the engines were breathed on to some extent. No one admitted to these little felonies, but sometimes a few beers loosened tongues and confessions were heard. "I just cleaned up the heads," or "My steel flywheel was out of balance, so I replaced it with a balanced aluminum one that weighed almost the same." Right.

A typical lap at Waterford Hills in a Showroom Stock V-8 Mustang or Camaro could be done at that time in about 1:20 to 1:25, that is, between 80 and 85 seconds. If you could gain just a mere half-second per lap, you'll enjoy a five second lead in a ten-lap race. It's about 1.5 miles around with speeds ranging from 30 mph in the tightest corner to 110 mph down the short back straight. If you cover a mile and a half in just under a minute and a half, you're averaging just over 60 miles per hour. A five-second lead at 60 miles per hour (88 feet per second) provides a lead of about 440 feet. That's big. You wouldn't want to overdo it.

If you thought somebody was seriously breaking the rules, you could file a protest with Tech Inspection, but it had to be about a specific mechanical component. You couldn't just say, "He has an illegal engine." You had to state it was the heads or over-bored cylinders, or whatever, and you had to post a $50 or $100 protest fee. If the engine was torn down and found to be legal, you paid for the teardown and reassembly, usually costing at least $500 and forfeited your protest fee. Five hundred dollars is a big price to pay when you're really not sure what was done. Since we were just racing for trophies and plaques, it was hardly worth it, especially if Tech Inspection didn't find the naughty thing that had been done. Cars were weighed, but it was so difficult to get weight out of a truly stock car, no one was below the minimums.

The upshot of all of this was that we were all a bit naughty. The truly felonious had very aggressive valve jobs or engines bored out 40 thousandths over. One guy ran a Chevy 350 cubic inch in a Camaro that was only supposed to have a 305. Funny, he didn't do all that well.

The first year with the Mustang was a bit frustrating in that while there were plenty of Camaros and Mustangs battling it out, we were all racing for second place. The Competition Committee had allowed a Corvette into our class, and guess what, he won every race that first year, and every race the second year. I think by the third year the guy was doing something else, so we didn't have to deal with him.

My primary competitor was a guy name Jeff Nowicki, driving a Pontiac Firebird. His car was always well prepared, and he had a full crew, team uniforms, corporate sponsorship, the big trailer—the works. We looked like poor relations compared to that deal, but our car was always sharp looking, and we had all those free Goodyear tires in our arsenal. And we were focused. That made a huge difference in concentrating on racing and making sure the car was ready and I was ready.

Nowicki and I were often battling for the lead in that third season. I think he won about half the time, and I won about half. The track announcer complained to me during one of the breaks that Nowak and Nowicki were hard to keep straight in the heat of battle. These Polish guys were ruining the neighborhood.

In any case, Ford Mustangs, Chevrolet Camaros and Pontiac Firebirds are front-end heavy cars. They were designed to accelerate quickly in a straight line. They can be made to corner and slow down, but they do neither without protest.

You really have to be smooth, so as not to slide either end of the car. If you slide the rears, the tires spin and you lose time. If you slide the fronts, the car won't turn until you slow down some, losing more time.

You arrive at some empirical value for what the tires like, say 40 psi, and then set them about eight pounds below that, so they build up to what you hope is ideal. I think we would set them at around 30 to 32 pounds cold. We would get about a weekend out of a set. That included a practice session, qualifying, and three races. They still had plenty of rubber left, but their virginity was gone, and the car was at least a second per lap slower.

Tires were about $800 to $1000 per set, but for us, no charge. Thank you, Goodyear Tire and Rubber Company. Thank you very much. I have bought Goodyear tires ever since for my street cars and always will.

Brakes were another asset to be conserved. Because the cars were more or less the same in weight and power, there were only slight differences in acceleration and top speed. We often arrived at the corner at the same time. He who brakes first loses. He who braked last had better be smooth because he had to slow down almost two tons of car, driver and fuel in a shorter distance because he waited a half second longer.

What worked for me was trail braking. I waited until the last possible second, braking hard while still going straight, yet still carrying a bit more speed than might be prudent and then finishing the braking in the first third of the corner. The braking that you left to the corner transfers weight forward, pressing the front tires down, improving their ability to stick, helping the car turn. Once the car was turning decently, you needed to gently squeeze the gas back on, beginning at the apex. Give it too much power too soon and it would want to go straight before you're on the "straight." And we wanted to hit a late apex, that is, hit the inside edge of the corner as far into the corner as possible. This had the effect of lengthening the next straight; because once you hit the apex, the turning phase was effectively over.

This was tricky stuff in overweight, overpowered cars on a twisty course. You had to keep reminding yourself that these weren't really purpose-built race cars, but street cars modified to be on a racetrack. That didn't make them race cars, just safer cars for this purpose. Tires, transmissions, engines and once-a-month race car drivers often broke or suffered damage because they were being run at the limit.

In the early '90s, the SCCA had organized a race at Michigan International Speedway (MIS) in Brooklyn, Michigan, that interested us. We usually avoided SCCA competitions, even those held at Waterford Hills because they seemed too populated with wealthy dentists or radiologists who were "doing racing" for a couple of years before they went on to ballooning or whitewater rafting. These guys would tear up their equipment, and yours, until they finally tired of it and moved on.

The MIS race provided that rare opportunity to run on a track where NASCAR ran, and you could just hold your foot down forever. All NASCAR oval or tri-oval courses are run counterclockwise. We ran the track clockwise, getting off the high banks in what would have been Turn Three, and entered a twisty infield course before rejoining the main speedway in what was normally Turn One and heading backwards up the main straightaway. We would be running about 140 to 145 mph before we had to get it down to about 50 mph at the exit to the twisty bits.

We qualified in mid-pack and realized after qualifying that we had been slightly naughty in that we forgot to roll the right side window down. The decreased drag was good for at least five mph. The race began, and we were doing OK, having passed a couple of cars. What I found interesting is that we were generally keeping up with the Corvettes who I would have thought would have a big aerodynamic advantage. Our little brick of a Mustang was doing all right.

When you're running 145 and you're on the high line up near the retaining wall, which seemed to work best for us, you realize, again, that you're not in a purpose-built race car, like the NASCAR guys have, but in a unibodied economy car with a V-8 engine and a cage that met the minimum SCCA safety specs but little more than that.

I had another Mustang on my tail driven by Bob Reid, who was slowly catching me. He was making his gains on the high banks, and I noticed my rpms were not as high as they were earlier in the race. Pretty soon, I developed a miss, and Bob blew by. We struggled on and finished near the back of the field. After the race we concluded we were having fuel delivery problems and replaced the fuel pump before the next event and didn't have that problem again.

After three years as racing in the SSGT Class, the powers at Waterford Hills Race Course decided to do something about the level of cheating going on. They reasoned that if there were fewer rules, we would break fewer of them. The new ITGT Class was created, and it was almost a "run what ya brung" deal. If you had a Mustang, you had to have a Ford motor in it, and that could be almost any Ford motor that had ever been in a Mustang. If it originally had fuel injection, you had to have some kind of fuel injection system. There was a weight lower limit, and you couldn't run racing slicks. That was the essence of the rules. It was like having the Ten Commandments reduced to three: no murder, no theft, and no slicks.

I had the car brought over to a guy in the Clarkston area that did race car prep to install a fuel cell and a better cage and take advantage of the loosened rules in the suspension area. Big mistake. This guy had no project management skills. I finally woke up and yanked the car out of there and had it finished elsewhere.

About this time, I met Gary Butzke, who would help me race this car and its successor over the next six or seven years. Gary was an engineer at Magneti Marelli USA, an Italian firm that operated plants in the US and had a development lab in Farmington Hills, Michigan.

Magneti Marelli had developed an aftermarket fuel injection system that they hoped to sell to Edelbrock and others in the small block V-8 street/drag racing market. They had put the first unit on another manager's 5-liter Mustang, taken it to the drag strip, and found considerable performance improvement. My car provided a platform to test its applicability in a road racing situation. They replaced the

Ford EMS (Engine Management System) with their own and installed a control interface in the cockpit. This system could have resident in its memory three different fuel maps and three different spark maps. All the maps could be modified on the fly by up to 15% through the control interface keypad that was plugged into a phone jack in the dash, which was connected in turn to the EMS. Gary could also burn completely new chips at the track if needed.

After we installed this highly flexible system, we began to have serious overheating problems. Obviously, one's first reaction was that the new EMS was the culprit. The engine builder was sure it was some kind of software gremlin that was leaning the fuel mixture excessively. So many variables are present in a stressed motor running up and down through the gears; it was difficult to draw any conclusions.

We grenaded a motor and switched engine builders. The new builder's motor also detonated. We finally figured out that we had radiator pressure problems caused by faulty radiator caps. These cooling systems will not flow properly if they lose pressure. Magneti's EMS was not the problem.

I was desperate to find a new engine that would provide the kind of power we needed to compete and be reliable. I called my friend Craig Weidner at Weidner Ford up in Cadillac, Michigan, for some advice. He suggested calling a guy at AER out in Denver, a firm that had a good reputation as an engine re-manufacturer and who had helped him out with sponsorship when he was racing Ford mini-trucks nationally. Craig called him first to introduce me, and then I got in touch with him.

This guy agreed, with almost no persuasion on my part, to provide a remanufactured 5-liter Ford V-8 at no charge, other than freight. "And about the freight," he continued, "we can ship under a contract we have with a common carrier, so if you're out there in Michigan, it will be under $100." Unbelievable. About five days later, this crated motor was delivered to Magneti Marelli with a freight bill of

$68. Total cost of this new motor: sixty-eight United States dollars. I'll never know for sure why the man was so generous. I think he thought highly of Craig Weidner and wanted to help Craig's friend.

The motor was installed, and the Magneti system wired into it and we had a winner. That AER motor would just wind and wind with never a complaint from it. No overheating, no problems, just horsepower. Now we added a better flowing intake manifold, better headers, higher volume injectors, a fully flowing exhaust system with three-inch pipes in and out of Flowmaster mufflers, as we had to stay under some decibel limit, and then Gary tweaked the EMS until the thing reminded me of a small-scale version of a NASCAR stocker.

*Gary Butzke, Crew Chief, looks after his baby.*

What a sound! I've been a fan of engine/exhaust systems sounds since the days of my English TR-3B sports car that I liked to wind up in first gear in the tunnel that went under the Detroit River over to Windsor, Ontario. The Mustang wasn't loud, wasn't quiet, it was just the right blend of engine sounds. I can still hear it.

Now that we had some wins and Goodyear Tire with us, I developed other sponsorship deals. Griggs Racing Products,

Avis Ford, Godfrey Moving & Storage, Florida 5.0, the Heidelberg Restaurant in Ann Arbor, and ABC Storage—all contributed dollars or parts or both. Over these last years, I estimate that sponsors picked up about 50% of the costs of racing, and I paid the rest.

I have always believed that race cars should be prepared by professionals. All of the engine work, chassis setup, and bodywork were done by individuals who did that for a living. It costs more to do it that way, but you were reasonably sure of getting through the weekend without spinning a main bearing in the motor or having a clutch go away. My job was to raise the money, drive the thing, and keep it clean. As a result of this logical division of labor, the car seldom failed and always looked good. Sure, we had a year of serious engine problems around 1990 but that was a freak deal involving radiator failures due to faulty caps, as strange a failure as I have ever heard of. Generally speaking, the car ran well, so my job at the track was simply to concentrate on driving it to the best of my ability.

On the subject of ability, I was far from a "natural." I hadn't started racing until my late thirties, and other than the required drivers' schools that you had to attend to get licensed to drive race cars, I had no formal training. I did start in underpowered English cars, which did teach one smoothness—as the last thing you wanted to do was slow down any more than you had to, because those old cars provided very little in the way of acceleration. You learned to carry the right amount of speed into a corner and carefully maintain that speed if at all possible. A three-day course at the Bondurant Driving School in Phoenix was money well spent. The older I got, the better I performed. In the early '90s I was in my early fifties and had been at it for about 15 years with a few timeouts.

I had learned five things at Bondurant and from all those years at Waterford that made me faster than most. The first is confidence, gained from having gone through a corner at speed and knowing you could do it, lap after lap, hitting the same apex, remaining on the same line, knocking a tenth of a second off when everything came together. The second was patience. If you're around at the end, you'll be in the top half of the field. The third was accident avoidance. You learned who the nutcases were and whose ability could be trusted. The fourth was a thing I'll call focused intensity. You had to push yourself mentally and physically pretty hard to keep focused on the task at hand, especially when you were running alone and the pack was somewhere else on the track. And the last thing was to baby the car whenever possible.

In SSGT we were always a contender with the '88 Mustang, but in ITGT we generally had a third or fourth place car. The Corvettes had reestablished themselves as the cars to beat. Danny Kellermeyer, an engineer with Chevrolet, had built several cars that were dominant. He sold or rented a fleet of yellow Corvettes that always qualified at the front of the pack. We were not going to win in ITGT unless we changed cars, and it never occurred to me to acquire a Corvette. We were beating some of the 'Vettes and gave away only about a second a lap to the Kellermeyer fleet, so I felt we just needed a little bit more car.

The '94 Mustang would be available soon, and it promised better aerodynamics and better handling, both of which would make us more competitive. I began to look around a bit, hoping to find a source for a stolen and recovered car. The local junkyards, car dealers and classified ads yielded nothing.

I did locate a '94 Mustang Cobra that I did buy with the idea of taking it apart and making a race car out of it. The problem was that the one I bought was too nice. It had but 1900 miles on it, perfect paint and interior, and had a softer suspension than the stock '94 Mustang GT. I drove it as a street car and eventually traded it in on a Dodge pickup.

With the considerable assistance of Larry Shinoda, the famous automotive designer, I was finally able to locate a 1994 Mustang body shell in a Ford salvage yard that we were able to purchase for $500, signing papers stipulating that this would be an off-road race car and it would never see a public roadway.

I got to work on selling the '88. It had a reasonably good track record and still looked great.

I shot a video of the car, crawling underneath the car, sitting in the driver's seat, starting it up, showing the gauges, especially the oil pressure, blipping the throttle a few times, so the great sounds were evident. I then included on the same tape in-car camera footage from a recent race.

Bob Bossche became aware of the car's availability through Craig Weidner and requested a tape. He was pretty excited. The racing footage really sold him on the car. We agreed on a price and a time payment plan. When he made the final payment, I delivered the car to his home in Door, Michigan.

It was my strong suggestion that he tear that wonderful AER motor down, as it had a season and a half of hard racing on it and was overdue for a rebuild, although it didn't smoke or give any outward signs of battle fatigue, which of course he ignored, probably for budgetary reasons.

Bob beat me in several races during those first two years that I had the new car, a fact that he will never let me forget.

That 1988 Ford Mustang did me proud. When I look at the pictures in the scrapbook, I can still hear that 5-liter motor feed those big Flowmasters, making beautiful music. I owned it for five years, and it will own me forever.

*The proud owner of a great car.*

# Honor, You Say? Whose Honor?

## His Honor

## 1994 Ford Mustang Cobra Street Car

*Three Ford Mustangs. The Cobra is in the middle.*

I bought this car to convert to a race car, but it was so nice I couldn't do it.

The plan was to acquire a '94 Mustang to replace my '88 Mustang race car. The '88 had served me well, won its share of races but wasn't competitive, at least in my hands, against the late model Corvettes at Waterford Hills, the road racing course located 35 miles northwest of Detroit in Clarkston.

I had been scouring the junkyards looking for a wrecked yet not too badly hurt '94 Mustang. I found several, but the prices were out of sight, like $8000 to $10,000 for real basket cases. I talked to several guys who seemed to have knowledge of stolen and recovered cars but nothing came of that.

In desperation, I started buying copies of what I always called the "pulps," those $1.50 weekly magazines you find at gas stations that had pictures and descriptions of hundreds of cars and trucks available in the Detroit metropolitan area.

The car I was looking for could have been just about any '94 Mustang GT with a manual transmission, yet I knew that the Cobra version came equipped with a nicer interior, white gauges that changed to green at night, leather upholstery, larger tires and wheels, bigger brakes, a softer suspension, a better exhaust system, and better looks. Mustang Cobras were a bit more expensive than GTs, and far fewer were built. The bigger tires/wheels and brakes were what I was really after.

Once you focus in on a particular model, like the Mustang Cobra, your search narrows down to one or two cars available at any given time. I looked in the *Detroit News* each weekend and bought every new pulp that came out. I called on each one and finally found one up in Roseville that was available for about $20,000 and had less than 2000 miles on it. These cars sold new for around $24,000, about $3000 more than the Mustang GT.

The seller, a young guy, lived in a new house in a new subdivision and said he was kind of up against it, in that he recently had to take a new job that paid less than his old one and the payments on this car were getting to be a real load. Like a lot of guys who bought special editions of Mustangs, he hoped to drive it very little, and some day have a valuable collector's car.

This is not a good idea from a financial standpoint because almost every car is a depreciating asset for most of its first fifteen years and only begins to appreciate gradually after that. It might take at least another five years, maybe ten, if it's rare and in very good condition to get back to its original purchase price. So after twenty to twenty-five years, you're back to square one, if you haven't used the car much and you picked a model with collector appeal, one with the "secret sauce." That's a long time just to break even, much less get any profit out of a car. That doesn't stop people from trying it, but most get tired of the wait and the car goes on the market.

The worst time to make that decision, that is, to sell it, is in the first year or two of ownership. Why? Because a buyer can get a new one, with a full warranty for just about what you paid and not much more than you're asking for your used one. Yours is a year or two old, and has taken a depreciation hit of at least 20%, even if you didn't drive it at all.

And that's the situation this fellow found himself in. He kept the car garaged while his regular ride sat outside. The car had less than 2000 miles on it and was as close to perfect as any used car I've ever seen. It was black on black with 17-inch brushed aluminum wheels with low profile Goodyear Eagles. It was flawless. In the course of the conversation, he indicated he owed about $19,000 on the car, having paid about $23,500 for it less than nine months earlier.

He was asking about twenty large for the Cobra and said even if he got that, he was losing his butt on the car. I have always found it a good strategy to agree with the seller on the difficulty of his position. What's to be gained by debating it?

My response was that I sympathized with him, but all I had to spend was $19,000, and I was willing to part with that much. He seemed to be heartbroken. He said he had to go inside and talk with his wife. She came out and repeated his tale of loving care and financial desperation and opined that I was trying to take advantage of the situation. One thing I had to admire about her, she spoke the truth and didn't care if it queered the deal or not.

I didn't care either. My response was I felt badly that they were in those circumstances, and if they didn't want to sell the car for $19,000 that was fine with me and I would go look for another one. I suggested they talk it over, and I would call them tomorrow.

He took the initiative and called me the next day and said they would be willing to come down to $19,750 but that was it. You know that's not "it." So my response was "$19,250 and that's it." We both knew that the next one to speak loses. That's how the game is played. The natural next price is a compromise at $19,500. Neither one of us said anything for 30 seconds. Finally, I spoke. "Listen, I'm a cash buyer. I'm here now. You're going to lose me over $250. You tell your wife its $19,250, or nothing, because we both know there are more of these Cobras for sale every week. I can wait. I would like to buy yours because you've been so nice to it. I'll call you back in 15 minutes, and you can tell me to take a hike or tell me when I can pick it up."

I called back in 15 minutes and got an answering machine. They must have been engaged in hot debate. I left a message, and he called back an hour later. "I got to have $19,400. I just have to." I could guess what had happened. They must have called Ford Motor Credit to get the exact loan payoff amount, and that was it: $19,400. And I could sense that honor was beginning to be involved. When that happens, you know a guy is really dug in.

Honor, you say? Whose honor? His honor. His wife was really beating him up. He was being taken advantage of by another guy, and she was telling him he wasn't fighting hard enough. I was beginning to feel a little sorry for him, but not much. I have been there myself, and sometimes a bad deal is the only deal you can get. I knew I could find another Cobra, but probably not one with low miles like this one, and I really could not find anything wrong with the paint or the interior or anything else. It was the most unused used car I had ever encountered.

Maybe I'm getting soft because I heard myself say, "Done."

I picked the car up the next day from a young couple that probably got over this deal but not right away. They were out of debt, at least this debt, and I had a nice car. Who won, who lost, who cares?

I loaded the car into my race car trailer, and they asked if I planned to race it. I think I told a fib at that point. As it turned out, I never did race it, so maybe it wasn't a fib, but it felt like one at the time because I most certainly planned to.

This all took place in the fall of the year. I had sold the '88, and I had the winter to convert this car into next year's race car. My main ride at the time was a Ford F-150 pickup that I used both for business travels and to tow the big trailer and its contents to the track. The truck came in handy for business because I was selling a computer system for processing health claims that consisted of four PCs and an optical recognition system. These computers were networked together and were set up in a prospect's office to demonstrate how our larger systems processed health claims. They were housed in big shipping containers that required a pickup truck to transport them around.

I didn't always have to use the pickup, so when I didn't, I drove the Mustang Cobra. What a lovely ride it was. It looked good, sounded good, had a much more comfortable ride than a stock Mustang GT, and it really moved. The motor was the same 5-liter V-8 found in regular Mustang GTs, as Ford would be unlikely to go through all the EPA hassle to certify another version of the engine for that car line. It might have made a bit more power due to a lower rear gear or due to the exhaust system that seemed to be a bit different than the stock one. It certainly sounded better.

When I had the car at home, I parked it on the right side of our rather narrow two-car garage because I didn't want my wife opening her car door into it. Therefore, when I wanted to get mine out, I moved her car out first, so I wouldn't hit hers with my door. At the same time, my pickup was sitting out on the street ready to go. As a result of the requirement to move hers to get to mine, I generally took the pickup to run errands around town.

It occurred to me that I was using the pickup about 95% of the time and that the truck, a '92 Ford F-150 that I bought used, was going to need replacement in the near future. After it developed a cracked exhaust manifold, a $300 repair, I became convinced that the 3/4-ton Dodge Ram 2500 with the 360 engine was the best deal out there.

I think the one I had my heart set on was about $24,000 out the door. At about this time, I found the '94 Mustang hulk at a Ford junkyard that would become the new race car over the winter. I decided, after considerable mental anguish, to trade both my old pickup and the Ford Mustang Cobra in on the new truck. It seems like they gave me about $18,000 for the Cobra and $8000 for the Ford F-150 as trade-ins, so I got the new truck and a check for $2000.

I really hated to see that pretty black car go. It was what all Mustang GTs should have been. Maybe I'll buy one like this one in about 20 years. It was worth the $1000 it cost me to own it for nine months.

If you're in the market for a used Mustang in the 1994 to 1997 year range, I highly recommend you consider the Mustang Cobra, perhaps one of the best Ford Mustangs ever built.

# The Thirteen-Year Valentine

## 1994 Ford Mustang GT for Nancy

*Here's a car I bought for Nancy about thirteen years ago. It was a bit of a gamble that paid off. We still have it. She loves this car. I think it will go another twelve years, maybe more.*

She needed a new car, as her '79 Subaru was getting very tired. It still ran strong, but the rust had gotten out of hand, particularly in the area of the floor pan where the driver's feet would rest. I had a welding shop repair that area to get a bit more life out of it.

I would never consider keeping a car so long that you would have to add metal to it. This car was going on 15 years old.

Nancy had a different perspective. She didn't like to have a new car. They made her nervous because she knew that one day it would get a scratch or a dent or worse. She lived in fear of that day.

On the other hand, she wouldn't accept a used car under the premise that she had had only three cars thus far in more than 30 years of marriage, so when it was time for another car, it had better be a new one. These two conflicting opinions resulted in her just soldiering on with what she had until it could go no further.

There was another factor in this "New Car for Nancy" project. We were kind of getting on each other's nerves a little. You know how it goes in a marriage. A little kindness here and there mends a lot of little things while criticism and taking somebody for granted could eventually fray the fabric of marriage to where repairs are difficult and may not be possible. We were a couple who had very little in common, but I always thought we managed to find enough things to talk about and do together, so the differences were more or less neutralized.

She was the best-looking woman ever seriously interested in me, and she liked to tell me that she married me mostly for my looks and that I was her "trophy husband." Nonetheless, we were quarreling more, laughing less, and doing fewer things together.

I had been thinking about what to get her for some time. I sent a few trial balloons her way to see if there was interest in any particular model or brand. Her response was basically that she didn't like big cars; she didn't want a minivan, and she didn't want a cute little convertible. She liked the color red better than any other, and she mentioned that Mustangs were "kind of cute," but she thought they were too big. She did say a good quality radio and CD player would be pleasant to listen to her highbrow music on short trips about town.

She drove to church three times per week and occasionally to the supermarket. She would have to deal with winter driving, but Ann Arbor is pretty flat. This didn't give me much to go on. She could drive a stick shift. In fact, she had never owned a car with an automatic transmission. And she liked the color red. She also liked "sharp looking" cars, meaning pretty or stylish or neat or whatever you think it means. You know "sharp looking" when you see it.

Clearly, we needed to find a car that looked sharp, had a manual tranny, plus a decent radio/CD sound system, didn't cost a great deal, and was red. I figured twenty grand would be the upper limit, costwise.

In my convoluted method of analysis, I needed to have an exit plan in case she didn't like the new car after she drove it for a while. Back in the early '70s I bought her a Mercury Capri that she endured rather than enjoyed. That was the car the Subaru replaced. I figured that if I had to sell her new car early on, in its first year, because she didn't like it, I would take a serious financial bath. Therefore, the car would not be disposed of. Rather, I would drive it and buy her something else. This disposability requirement shed a whole new light on things.

Now, the question distilled itself into a new, more exciting question, namely, what car should I buy for Nancy that, in the event she didn't like it after a bit, would I like to have as my own ride?

So, which car can you think of, that costs less than twenty large, looks sharp, has a decent sound system, has a manual tranny, comes in red, and I would be pleased to have for my own personal ride if this car didn't work out for the bride?

You guessed it, pilgrim. I wouldn't mind having a bright red 1994 Mustang GT with a lusty 5-liter V-8 up front, a five-speed manual tranny, and a Mach 460 Sound System. I thought she would like it too, but I knew I had to test the waters, so I showed her some press on the car, pointed a few out on the road, and suggested a possible visit to a local dealer. The car passed the "sharp looking" test, but she didn't really want to test drive one. She just wanted to keep the ancient Subaru going.

I got in touch with Craig Weidner up at Weidner Ford in Cadillac, Michigan, to see if I could buy one at a decent price. He sent me some numbers that were a little under twenty grand, and I pretty much made up my mind that this car would fit the bill. It didn't seem like a good idea to order the car and then give it to her as a surprise. I must confess that I did order it, but decided it wouldn't be a good thing to surprise her right out of the blue. That just seemed too dangerous emotionally, politically and financially. I told her what I wanted to do, not having the gonadials to tell her I had already done it, and she said that twenty grand was a lot of money, but she wouldn't fight it.

The order that was placed with Craig had the proviso that he would have the car available before February 14, Valentine's Day. He said he could do that. The plan was to go up to Cadillac and pick it up with my race-car trailer, so that when I brought it to Ann Arbor, there would only be five miles or less on the odometer. I expected she would go up to Cadillac with me, but she had some last-minute work commitments at the church that morning and couldn't go.

As we were handling the paperwork, Craig said that in order for the car to be in her name, she would have to sign the papers. I said I would sign for her, but Craig, being the straight shooter that he was, said that was a no-no. So I put the car in my name to get the deal done and planned to fix that detail later.

One other thing about Craig Weidner I found commendable was that he eventually sold the Ford dealership and went to work at Eagle Village in Hersey, MI. This organization takes in kids from rough situations and helps them get their lives straightened out. If a former car dealer and race car driver can become fully committed to good works like this, maybe there's hope for the rest of us. If you want to help

Craig help these kids out, check out www.EagleVillage.org. Good for you, Craig, you're a credit to the human race.

We loaded that pretty red car into my 26-foot race-car trailer and headed for home. I found a red bow to put on the windshield. The weather had turned nasty with snow and lots of salt on the roads. I was glad her little virgin Mustang was strapped down safely inside.

It was late afternoon, starting to get dark and snowing a little when I got back to Ann Arbor. I pulled into our cul-de-sac off of Stadium Boulevard and parked my rig next to the curb.

Alas, she wasn't home. The note on the kitchen counter said she had gone to Kroger's to get some groceries. About a half hour later, she returned from the store and we went out to look at the car, still in the trailer. The narrowness of the trailer was such that you really couldn't open the Mustang's doors. You had to keep the driver's window open and climb in through the window. I would have to do that and get it outside for her to sit in it. It was starting to snow harder. She said, "It's so clean and so pretty, I don't want you to take it out of the trailer, even to put it in the garage."

"Don't you want me to get it out so you can sit in it, maybe drive it around the block? I can easily get the snow off of it, and we can move the old Subie out of the garage and put this one inside where you can get a better look at it. What do you say?"

"That can wait until tomorrow. I can see it's a beautiful car. I think it was very nice of you to do this. I hope it's not too much car for me. Leave it here. Besides, it wouldn't be fair to that old Subie wagon, my sweet little car for so long, to be booted outside on a night like this."

This was pretty hard for a motor head to comprehend, but I've never pretended to understand grownup women.

She drove the new car here and there, nervous as hell, but liking it. She enjoyed the power and the sound of power. V-8 Mustangs have kind of a distinctive airy sound to the exhaust with some deeper undertones. Camaros and Corvettes sound similar but not quite the same.

Exhaust sounds give you an idea of the engine's potential and that's what sells cars and generates grins. The British understood this very well when they built TR3s and Austin Healey 3000s. These two in particular sounded pretty strong, and I have always loved these cars because of their siren song.

Have you ever heard a Ferrari accelerating? Not to smile is an indication that you may be comatose, perhaps dead. How about 43 NASCAR race cars, each one bringing more than 800 horsepower to the party, moving slowly around a track on their warm-up laps? If you're next to the fence along the back straight, you can feel the ground vibrate beneath your feet. What a beautiful, savage chorus of mechanical perfection.

So, the Mustang GT was going over pretty good. The only problem, not a serious problem, was that she was only using it about 25 miles per week. When she went shopping, she dutifully parked it at the far end of parking lots, probably the one woman in 100,000 who could be trained to do that. I kept it clean and pretty for her. I'd check the oil and other fluids and kept the tires up. I think it had only 1500 miles on it after the first year. She drove it in the winter and got around pretty well despite the rear-wheel drive and front heavy weight distribution. The trick was to put skinny all-weather tires on it in the winter and 150 to 200 pounds of sand in the trunk.

She let me take it on a daytrip to Columbus, Ohio, one spring day to put a few highway miles on it and kind of blow out the cobwebs so to speak. The trip down was uneventful, but the trip back had an episode caused by stupidity and resolved quite possibly by divine providence.

I was northbound on US 23 between Upper Sandusky and Findley when a series of intense snow squalls blew in. There would be a mile or two of whiteout conditions followed by five miles of bright sunshine and then another series of whiteouts. I was tooling along in an area where it had just snowed and was passing a relatively slow moving semi truck when I felt the rear end of the car break loose. I lifted abruptly, a mistake, as you never want to do anything abrupt in a car. It upsets the balance and, in this case, aggravated the skid. The rear of the car began to pass me on the left. I corrected in the usual manner, turning in the direction of the skid and the car straightened out, only to begin to rotate such that the back of the car began to pass me on the right. This began a series of oscillations that were momentarily corrected, yet the car continued to swing back and forth like a horizontal pendulum.

I just about had it under control when it made one more wild counterclockwise rotation. I could see I was going to slide off the freeway on the right hand side. The crash looked inevitable.

Whenever I have been faced with this situation in the past where I've run out of tricks and things don't look good, my brain automatically does two things. First, it clears memory on my mental calculator, so I can began totaling up the damage as the fenders get dented, glass breaks, tires squeal, and you wait for the car to stop moving. The second thing is to start working on my story. What could I have done to save it? How do I let the bride know that her fine ride has lost its virginity? What the hell was I thinking passing that truck in the snow?

The car was now sliding sideways from the center lane to the right-side lane, soon to go over the shoulder down into what could be a water-filled ditch. Just then, a right side "on ramp" appeared, making the road one lane wider. That was just barely enough additional room for the car to catch itself and stop sliding. It finally stopped on the far edge of the shoulder, just a foot from too far.

You don't believe in God?   If I didn't, I had just found another reason to.

We were visiting Nancy's mom in Holland, MI in the summer of 1999, and while out for a Sunday drive, we found a nice Victorian-style house for sale on the north shore of Lake Macatawa.  One thing led to another, and by November of the year, we had sold our Ann Arbor house and moved to that big house in Holland.

Few cars make it all the way to retirement without a mechanical crisis or some kind of dustup with another car. Nancy's car met its Waterloo one December day about three years ago.  She was headed over to the south side to cut her mom's hair when she encountered black ice on Ottawa Beach Road.  There is a subtle kink in the road by Van Wierans' Hardware, and that's where the trouble began.  As the road turned slightly left, she followed it and the rear end came around on her right side.  She turned the wheel back to the right, probably not from some latent instruction from me, but to avoid oncoming westbound traffic on this four-lane undivided road.

The car responded, and she found herself rotating clockwise toward the curb.  The car hit the curb, rose up over it, and slid sideways into a chain-link fence that bordered some industrial property.  Both airbags deployed with the one in front of her burning a small hole in her coat sleeve.  The alarm horn went off and continued to make itself heard.  She was shaken but otherwise unhurt.  A Good Samaritan from Bosgraff Builders came by, disconnected the battery to still the horn, and called me.

The wrecker guys arrived before I did and had the Mustang on their truck.  I gave it a quick glance and could see that it would need front bumper work, a new fender, a new hood, air bags, and considerable paintwork on the driver's side. Not too bad, but not too pretty either.  I told them to take it to Zeeland Collision, as I had them do work for me previously and they did a good job.

Nancy was sitting in Bosgraff's truck, and I could see she was distraught. She called her mother on my cell phone to say that she had had an accident, and there would be no haircut today. Her mother inquired about Nancy's condition, and satisfied that her daughter was OK, wondered when the haircut was going to be rescheduled. Nancy said we would come over now so that she could have her haircut. Duty called, accident or not.

I went over the next day to Zeeland Collision to get the bad news. I had done some rough arithmetic on the way over and was prepared to hear a number like $3000 for the repairs. The estimator assumed his most gentle bedside manner and said that my estimate was a long way from what they had arrived at, which was a little over $6000.

Whoa! How could it cost so much? The airbags were a big part of it, costing more than $1600 for the two of them. And all the rest, including a new exhaust system, just added up to a big number. And that big number was approximately the wholesale value of the car. The collision shop guys said that when my insurance adjuster reviewed the claim, he would probably recommend totaling the car because the insurance companies didn't like to pay to fix cars where the damage was more than 80% of the wholesale value, and in this case the damage was about 100% of wholesale.

The insurance guy turned up and confirmed their suspicions. The company would prefer to pay us about $6000, sell the car for salvage to a firm that bought these cars for a few hundred dollars and who would fix it up and then retail it, making a pretty good profit in doing so.

I knew that while the average '94 Mustang, now a ten-year-old car with more than 120,000 miles, assuming annual mileage of 12,000 miles, was probably worth no more than $6000, our former automotive beauty queen was barely broken in with less than 23,000 miles on the odometer.

We contacted the insurance company and moved a few levels up the food chain and pleaded our case. We wanted this car fixed, not $6000. I was getting a little sympathy but nothing in the way of firm assurances that they would do what we wanted. It was still under review.

I sat down and wrote a letter to our agent at Hub International Insurance about the history of the car. Reading it now, I see where I might have added a dramatic flourish or two, but the essence of the letter was true. The entire letter goes on for a bit, so I'll just give you the highlights.

Here is the essence of what I had to say to the insurance company:

December 15, 2003

Dear Sirs:

I am writing to you concerning our Ford Mustang that was involved in an accident on Thursday, December 11, 2003.

We would like very much to have the car repaired. While the estimated expense of repair received from Zeeland Collision is substantial, there are more than just dollars and cents involved in this case.

Please permit me to tell you a short story about how this car came to be, what it means to us, and hopefully you will agree that it should be repaired.

About ten years ago, my wife and I had hit a rough patch, as they say, in our marriage. At that point we had been married thirty years and were starting to take each other for granted and we began to drift apart.

I realized that if we didn't turn this relationship around, we might be calling the divorce lawyers. I got the idea to surprise my wife Nancy with a new car, as a sign that I still wanted us to stay together. She always had rather plain economy cars such as a VW, Subaru and Honda. Nancy worked as a church organist and choir director, so those kinds of cars kind of went with that image.

I wanted to change that image from plain to vibrant, just as I wanted to change our marriage from plain to vibrant. Without her knowledge, I ordered a new 1994 fire-engine-red Mustang GT with all the available options from Weidner Ford in Cadillac, Michigan, and placed the order, so the new car would arrive just before Valentine's Day on February 14, 1994.

When it came in, I arranged for an enclosed trailer to transport it down to Ann Arbor where we lived at that time. That way it would have no miles on it, no road dirt, and would look like it had just come right from the show room when it was unloaded in our driveway as a Valentine's Day present.

She was pleased. She liked the way it looked, how it sounded, how it made her feel when she drove it. Over the years she has repeatedly remarked how that car always made her feel special. Three years ago she was diagnosed with cancer, from which she has thankfully recovered. During the long months of chemotherapy and radiation treatments, her little red Mustang helped keep her spirits up when things looked pretty bad.

If she took it shopping, she would always park it at the far end of the parking lot so as not to get a door ding. The car had no nicks, no dings, and no scratches and looked like it just had come off the show-room floor.

The car is currently at Zeeland Collision, a repair shop that enjoys an excellent reputation for quality work. We want to discuss this case with your adjuster today, if possible, so we can talk about the costs involved in the repair, prior insurance costs and insurability.

Please share this letter with him, so he understands just how important this car is to Nancy and me.

Sincerely,

Pat Nowak

Holland, Michigan

The letter must have had an impact. The Zeeland Collision guys called to say they had been authorized to repair the car for us, and they were on the case, expecting to have it done in about ten days.

One little detail that I had put off for ten years was finally taken care of when we went down to the Secretary of State's office and put the car in her name.

Now, three years later, the car is still going strong. Sounds good, looks good. Almost every time she stops to put gas in it, some guy will tell her how sharp her car looks.

That red Mustang GT has done an awful lot for both of us. I hope we have it, and each other, for a long time to come.

*Pretty lady, pretty car.*

# "This Thing Is Just Like Building a Model Car, Only Bigger"

## 1994 Ford Mustang Cobra Race Car, Part 1

*Larry Shinoda supplied the graphics package and custom rear spoiler.*

I've broken this up into two parts because we had this car for five years, and there are lots of stories to be told.

This was a significant car. We built it from scratch, developed it into a champion, and eventually sold it to a fellow who still campaigns it.

I had been trying to find a 1994 Ford Mustang for some time to become the basis for a road racing car that could compete with the Chevrolet Corvettes at Waterford Hills, the track near Clarkston, Michigan, where I had raced on and off, mostly on, for twenty years.

I had been racing a 1988 Mustang, highly modified, that was almost competitive with the 'Vettes. We had nearly equal engines, around 300 HP, and ran similar tires and brakes. The 'Vettes weighed a little less than the '88 and had two other significant advantages. One, they were obviously more aerodynamic and could get more speed out of the same level of engine power. Our '88 Mustang was a real brick, aerodynamically speaking. The other advantage was weight distribution. The 'Vette had more weight in the rear, where it did some good, than we had. Ideally, you would like to have a 50/50 weight distribution so that all the tires shared the work. The 'Vettes also had a slightly longer wheelbase, and a more sophisticated suspension, both of which contributed to its excellent handling.

Additionally, the 'Vettes were developed and raced by Danny Kellermeyer, a Chevrolet engineer at the GM Tech Center in Warren, Michigan. Danny built six or seven of these cars, which he sold or leased to other drivers. Danny was and is a gifted driver and was champion of the ITE Class year after year.

You might ask why I didn't get a 'Vette if they had all the mechanical advantages plus the development that is so critical to taking the car to the next level. Well, two reasons I guess. We were beating half of the 'Vettes with our '88 Mustang, and I'm a hardhead. My wife came to the track once in 23 years and asked me if I had the best car in my class. I had to say no. She asked if I was the best driver. I answered, "Probably not." She just shook her head and asked, "So what's your strategy for winning, other than depending on Divine Providence?"

I thought the big difference between the competitors was in their driving skills. We felt that while we hadn't won any championships yet in ITE, we were coming. I was getting better with age. A three-day course I had taken at the Bob Bondurant Racing School in Phoenix in January of 1994 was beginning to pay dividends.

We knew that a '94 Mustang would not solve all our problems, but it could bring us up into the top three and maybe higher than that. Waterford Hills is a short twisty track with eleven turns and several elevation changes. You didn't need top speed as much as you need the ability to accelerate from 40 to 100 mph, and to decelerate from 100 to

40 mph, faster than the other guy, and you needed a car that handled good enough so that you didn't eat your tires going through all those corners.

Even though the Mustang's suspension components are far less sophisticated than the 'Vette's, we had arrived at a combination on the '88 that worked pretty well. The 'Vettes had independent suspensions at all four corners. We had modified McPherson struts in the front and a live rear axle in the rear with a big old Panhard rod helping to keep the rear axle located. Yet, we made it work by fiddling and adjusting, moving weight around, finding the right tire pressures, and driving smoothly.

The '94 Mustang Cobra would also have a McPherson strut setup in the front and a live rear axle, but we were pretty confident we could make it work as well as it did on the '88. If you were to fast-forward to the 2005-2006 Mustang GT, they use an independent suspension up front like the 'Vettes, but stayed with the live rear axle, and early tests say that the car really handles and has a pleasant street ride as well.

The '94 would give us better aerodynamics, better weight distribution, although not as good as the 'Vette's. We planned on spending some serious money in the engine room. Our '88 had about 300 HP from its 302 cubic-inch engine. We were hoping to develop 375-400 HP from the 351 cubic-inch motor we expected to build with better cylinder heads, a more aggressive cam, a larger intake manifold, and a more efficient exhaust system.

It was difficult to find a decent '94 car that could be made over into a race car without throwing much of it away. I had purchased a nearly new '94 Mustang Cobra with just 1900 miles on it, but it was too nice. I just couldn't do it.

One evening, I met Larry Shinoda, a famous engineer who worked for both GM and Ford, at a meeting of Ford enthusiasts.

One of his more interesting stories that night was about a presentation his group had to make to GM brass about the Mako Shark design for a Corvette concept car. They were down in Florida and were using a Mako shark as a prop that had been caught the previous day. They had the Corvette painted the same color as the shark the night before but discovered, to their dismay, that the shark had aged a bit overnight, and the fish and the car were no longer the same color. It was too late to catch another Mako shark, so their only recourse was to paint the big fish the same color as the car. They carried it off and the GM brass approved the design.

After his talk, I approached him to ask if he had any sources at Ford that he might be able to put us in touch with. Larry was very gracious and liked the sound of the idea that we would be racing the latest Ford Mustang at a Detroit area track. He would see what he could do. He called back to say he had come up dry but would keep us in mind.

Two months later, he called to say he had learned that several hundred '94 Mustang bodies had been over painted by a few mils, and it wasn't economical for Ford to salvage the bodies. Ford had shipped them to a disposal yard they owned in Mount Clemons, Michigan, and they were available for $500 if you signed a pile of papers stating that you would only use it as an off-road competition vehicle.

*Not much to start with.*

Gary Butzke and I drove up there one snowy Saturday and found a red body that was the least damaged of the cars that were left. We horsed it onto the trailer, signed the papers, and brought it home. It was rough, real rough.

The first stop was at a body shop at a vocational school in Ypsilanti for hard cases from the local high school. I had a relationship with the manager because he repaired the monthly body damage to the '88 during the racing season at his own body shop on his farm in Saline, Michigan. When I approached him about making this shell look decent before we started on the mechanical stuff, he suggested having his students do it. They would get a big kick out of building a race car, rather than just working on somebody's beater. I would have to pay for the materials, of course. So we gave him the shell on a dolly, and they set to work on it. It took about a month of hard work to get it done. I think the materials cost was around $650. It looked pretty good. Thanks, guys. Thanks, Bill.

*The young men of Ypsilanti Vocational and Instructor Bill attending a race at Waterford Hills, watching "their" 1994 Ford Mustang Cobra.*

Now, the car went back to Gary who agreed to build it for me.

I had Avis Ford in Southfield, Michigan, as a sponsor, and they agreed to provide the parts at close to their cost. That was a big savings over retail. They also provided $1000 in cash each year with which to buy the parts. Thanks, Avis Ford.

Four months later, we had a race car, thanks to the lads in the body shop and long, long hours by Mr. Butzke.

*Two 1994 Ford Mustang Cobras:*
*race car foreground, street car in the background*

I must take a moment and say that this guy Butzke was a real find. He had been my crew chief in the latter years of the campaigning of the '88. He worked at Magneti Marelli USA as a manager in their engineering lab in Farmington Hills, Michigan. It was Magneti's Engine Management System (EMS) that we had installed on the '88. We had some serious initial problems with engines in the '88, but they turned out to be cooling-related failures and not the fault of their EMS.

Gary's task was to acquire and install all the suspension components, brakes, wiring, motor, windows, the EMS, transmission, dashboard, cooling system, instrumentation, graphics, fire suppression system, driver's seat, drive train, and exhaust system. He basically built this car from scratch. We did send it out to get a roll cage welded in.

One day he remarked, "You know, this thing is just like building a model car, only bigger." I gave him the freshly painted body in early January. We had a running race car by mid-April. He did this after working eight to ten hours each day on his regular job and put in a lot of weekends too. An amazing guy, Mr. Butzke.

We needed a motor and shopped around for an engine builder who had a good reputation but wasn't too expensive. Most of the builders in the Detroit area seemed to be in the drag racing motor business. We wanted a motor that would live under road-racing conditions. I had heard some good things about an outfit down south that built stock-car engines for circle track racing, and their prices were supposed to be pretty fair. This was an outfit called Kuntz and Company, down in Arkadelphia, AR. They would build us a decent 351 for around $4000, as I recall, that was good for 350 HP, maybe a bit more.

We couldn't find anybody else that offered a better deal, so we ordered the Kuntz 351 that was really a 355 or 360. The engine was installed, and Gary calibrated the EMS for the new engine on the chassis dyno at Magneti Marelli USA. A chassis dyno consists of a set of rollers that the driven tires turn under varying loads. The car must be strapped down hard on the rollers to keep the tires from spinning. A huge fan is positioned in front of the car to attempt to cool the motor. When the unmuffled motor is running at full song, it is a very noisy place. Instrumentation tells the operator how many foot-pounds of torque are being developed at the rear wheels at different RPMs. Gary would do a "pull" at a particular rpm with a certain fuel map and spark map and look at the results on the printer. He would then vary the fuel map and/or the spark map and see if torque increased or not. He would wear acoustic earmuffs to save his hearing, and I would look on through a window. This went on for three or four long evenings before he was satisfied.

I asked him at some point if we needed to break the engine in on the track. He assured me that with all that time on the chassis dyno, that engine was well broken in.

Once we had the car altogether, there were a few banzai runs through a nearby industrial park, usually around midnight just to check things out. The car sounded awesome. It's a wonder we didn't get caught, the way that beast thundered through the still night air.

Not many guys could build a car from scratch in three and a half months. Butzke was that rare exception who could engineer, fabricate, and manage a project. On the subject of fast fabrication, Robert Cumberford, the famous automotive designer, told me that while he was working at Holman & Moody, they built a 1963 Ford in three days that led the Daytona 500.

We brought the car to the track for a shakedown on the Wednesday before the first race. It was important to take it easy in order to bed the brakes, scuff the tires, listen for problems, and look for leaks every time I returned to the pits. Everything looked good. It was an easy car to drive. I didn't have to muscle it around.

After a couple of gentle sessions, I turned up the wick to see how it would handle at 9/10's. It turned in nicely, accelerated strongly and stopped as if we had dropped a tail hook on the deck of an aircraft carrier. Gary took his stopwatch out and recorded a few lap times. We were turning 1:18's and 1:19's. This wasn't bad, but our best time the previous season in the '88 was a lap of 1 minute, 16 seconds. We consoled ourselves by agreeing that the '88's 1:16 was the best time it ever turned, after four or five years of development. We had only an hour of track time on this car, and we were doing just fine.

One last thing we had to do to the car before the first race was to get the graphics and numbers on it. Larry Shinoda, who had been responsible for the graphics on the Ford Boss Mustangs in the late '60s and early '70s, had come up with his own Boss Shinoda graphics package. I had a professional put his silver vinyl on. It looked quite dramatic.

Gary didn't care too much for it, preferring the simple black color scheme, accented by sponsor's names that we had on the '88. After awhile I had to agree with him. Guys like Gary who work on cars have their opinions. They'll express them once or twice and then drop it. I don't think I heard about it again until the next year when we didn't use the

Boss Shinoda graphics and he simply said, "I like this better."

*A beautiful car, a serious contender.*

Shinoda also provided a rear spoiler of his own design that was larger, flatter and more effective, we liked to think, than the stock one. I told Larry we really liked it, and when the car was resting in our pit between races, pop cans and water bottles were often resting on this big "shelf." I told Larry if he designed another iteration he ought to make a couple of depressions in it about the diameter of pop cans and be darned if he didn't do that.

We raced the car that first weekend with high hopes. We didn't win, but we moved up the food chain. Now we had a third place car with just two 'Vettes in front of us. It had a lot more power and much better brakes than the '88, so it was easy to overdrive it, using up the tires if I wasn't smooth.

Our races were all short sprints, usually ten or 15 laps. One might wonder how I could abuse my tires in such a short race. Well, imagine racing for a bit, and now there are just a few laps left. I would use everything I had left. Our races were quite intense from the get-go because we were in the last ten to 15 laps when we started. There were no pit stops. I drove my heart out for 20 to 25 minutes. Each lap had eleven corners. I was hard on the gas or hard on the brakes. There were always people around me. Our starts were rolling starts of two lines of cars. If my line was the slower one because somebody up front missed a shift or hit the guy in front of him, I could lose a lot of ground in just that first lap. I had to go pretty hard to make that up. Obviously, it was important to qualify well, so I would start near the front.

We assessed our weekend and were pretty pleased. If memory serves me right, we had two third places and a fourth place finish in a class of ten to eleven cars. There were usually 25 to 30 cars in the race, as they ran several classes together. Getting around some of the lapped cars that were wheezing down the back straightaway side by side was always a problem that you had to solve. The car held up fine, and we had only minor dents and scratches on our new paint job. Nothing broke or leaked. Gary was the man.

The first season was pretty uneventful in that we had no major crashes and generally placed in the top three or four positions. The motor did its part, but we didn't have the horsepower advantage I hoped for. The 'Vettes still had their handling advantage, and Kellermeyer won the championship again.

Danny Kellermeyer was an awesome competitor. He spent a lot of Wednesdays at the track testing. He would occasionally rent the track for additional testing. He had a large shop up in Ortonville equipped with an engine dyno.

He raced at other tracks and cultivated well-heeled sponsors. He was the closest thing to a true professional at our track, and the results proved that he went about it the right way. Being a Chevrolet engineer provided the opportunity to have access to parts that might not have been assigned part numbers yet. Good for him. We all envied Danny.

I was having troubles one day, and he lent me a part or a wrench to get me going. I asked him if there was anything I could do for him, and he said he always liked to use Ford's brake fluid, as he found it worked better than anything else. The next time I was at Avis Ford, I bought a few extra quarts for his use.

At the end of the season, we sent the motor back down to Kuntz in Arkadelphia for a rebuild. They gave it new main bearings, a valve job, and some kind of new valve train deal that had roller rockers to reduce friction. When we reinstalled it for the second season, Gary was having some problems, as I recall, with the recalibration of the EMS on the chassis dyno. The engine wasn't any better, just different.

About halfway through the second season, we started having trouble with that motor. The distributor shaft failed and knocked us out of the races for that weekend. Then a connecting rod failed and we grenaded it, resulting in a big hole in the side of the block. At that point we gave up on it although they did eventually send us a replacement motor. Unfortunately, that engine had a small defect in the block that ruled it out as a race motor, although it was OK for a street motor.

We bought a new 351 crate motor from a Ford distributor, Performance Marketing in Plymouth, Michigan. Crate motors are a heck of a deal. A new 351 cost about $2700 back then, and these were complete motors. You did have to add the service systems like the alternator, power steering pump, fuel pump, exhaust system, etc., but the rest of it is there, brand new, and painted Ford blue. They're called crate motors because they're delivered on a pallet with a wooden frame around the motor. A crate, in other words.

This engine had the GT 40 heads that flowed more air than a stock engine and therefore made more power than a stock crate motor would. The motor worked fine, never giving any problem, but didn't give us any big horsepower advantage either. Now, we had a solid third-place car, with the occasional second. We did find a West Coast outfit to hog out our intake manifold to flow more air and produce a bit more power.

Airflow is the secret to power. For any amount of fuel injected into a cylinder, you need about thirteen times as much air to have the proper mixture for efficient combustion. The engine needs so much air because air is 80% nitrogen, which is an inert gas that does not support combustion. The 20% that is oxygen is what we needed lots of.

So, the more air the engine can take in, the more fuel it can burn, and the greater the power output. An engine's performance is described in part by how many revolutions it is turning in a minute, or rpm. When a motor is turning at higher rpms, it is critical that the internal components are perfectly balanced to the fraction of a gram. If not, the pistons or the valve train or the connecting rod/crankshaft assembly will come apart with disastrous results.

Our crate motors were good for about 7000 rpms, tops. Ford V-8s, and Chevys for that matter, make their maximum torque at relatively low rpms. Torque or twisting power is all that an engine makes. Horsepower is a mathematical measure of how much work an engine can do in a unit of time, usually expressed in foot pounds per second. The formula relating horsepower to torque is simply:

$$HP = \frac{Torque \times RPM}{5252}$$

It should be obvious that if you can increase torque and increase engine speeds, you're on your way to making more horsepower. An engine making 800 horsepower, such as in a NASCAR race car, makes a tremendous amount of torque across a wide range of rpms and has been meticulously built out of the finest metals, and has been balanced to the nth degree in order to stay in one piece through a 500-mile race.

We soldiered on with the 351 crate motor for the balance of the second year and all through the third, working on making it more efficient by improving its breathing. We went to larger and larger throttle bodies, did more work on enlarging the intake manifold for more airflow, found better headers, put exhaust temperature sensors in those headers to optimize fuel mixtures, and installed a new exhaust system with three-inch diameter pipes going into big Flowmaster mufflers, which gave it a rich baritone sound.

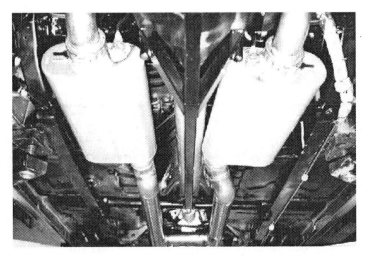

*Three inch pipes in, three inch pipes out.*

With all these changes, we were slowly moving up in the rankings. What a struggle. Every time we made a change that increased airflow, Gary had to recalibrate the EMS. It was fairly easy for him to do (easy for me to say that) because he could vary any of the three resident fuel maps and three spark maps with a small control module that plugged right into a dashboard phone jack outlet that was in turn connected to the EMS computer. If he had to make more drastic changes, he would burn another chip in the lab or at the track.

We knew we were getting closer and closer to winning and did win a race here and there. It was also apparent that we had this car handling better than most of the 'Vettes, but not all. We concluded that our best chance for success was to build a big-time motor that would trump the 'Vettes in the horsepower wars. Hopefully, our greater power would make up for our slight handling deficiency. There is a paradox here in that every time you add power, the car behaves differently. The driver has to relearn the car, has to make adjustments in his technique. Sometimes I would wonder if I had forgotten how to drive. It was just a matter of getting used to more power.

*The moment of reckoning at the end of the black straight.*

I decided to look again around the Detroit area for an engine builder who could build us a 351 that would make major league horsepower and yet be up to the rigors of road racing.

An old-timer at the track introduced me to Greg Coleman who built one engine per winter in his shop down in Carleton, Michigan. Greg had spent a number of years at Roush Racing and was now with Ford Motor Company as a manager in an engine development program. He came highly recommended by a couple of guys who raced vintage Boss Mustangs. His 351 engines were reputed to make nearly 500 HP. That's what we were looking for.

# A Braver Man Might Have Gotten More

## 1994 Mustang Cobra Race Car, Part 2

We got in touch with Greg Coleman and asked if he would build us a Ford 351 that could make us competitive, with competitive defined as bringing 450 HP to Waterford Hills.

Greg said he would take the job on. He needed some up-front capital to get the right block from Roush and other significant parts like top-grade cylinder heads. We were able to obtain an engine block from Roush that was of the quality that could be used as a basis for a NASCAR engine. I shuddered to think what all this was going to cost, but Greg assured me it would be between $15,000 and $18,000, unless component prices from his vendors were increased, and he had no control over that. He was a big believer in two things: ceramic coatings and absolute balancing of the components. He also said he had to have lots of time to do it properly. That's why he only built one engine per winter.

He finished it on time and under budget. We took the new engine up to Brighton to a dyno shop to integrate it with Magneti's EMS and to optimize the power. It took about a day to get everything hooked up and a second day to run the tests. It was a much bigger deal than I had anticipated. The dyno time added another $1500 to the bill. What the hell, it's only money. Nancy was fond of saying that if you could solve a problem with money, it's not a problem, just an expense. I didn't plan to tell her how expensive the solution to my horsepower problem was getting to be.

The guys did pull after pull on the dyno, taking 20 to 30 minutes between each one to change fuel maps and/or spark maps. Talk about a well broken-in engine. The engine was hooked up to the dyno in a sound absorbing room, and we observed the instrumentation and graph printers in a separate control room. Even so, the noise was deafening.

Coleman and Butzke worked well together. They both could see that this engine was going to produce more power than we had ever had before. They were really impressed with the torque curve. It was above 400 ft-lb. at 3000 rpms and stayed there until 6000 rpms. I think the torque peak was in the neighborhood of 450 ft-lb., at an engine speed around 5000 rpms. The engine was designed to live at 8000 rpms and be driven all day at 7500. The torque fell off above 6000, as you would expect, but it still made 475 HP at 5500 rpms. This would give us more HP than any of the 'Vettes. It was quite possible for them to have that much, but they never did build really powerful motors, primarily because they didn't have to. They could win with their handling and be spared the expense we had undertaken. We had spent the money. We had come to play, and play for keeps.

This beast had so much torque we had to put a new T-56 six-speed transmission in it, the same unit used in Dodge Vipers and Corvettes. It would lift the right front tire off the ground under hard acceleration.

We were now in the fourth season with the '94 Mustang. We had electronic scales to optimize weight distribution, good radio communication between crew chief and driver, a fair amount of spare parts, good sponsorship deals, including our long-term deal with Goodyear Tire, who continued to supply us with a new set of tires for each race weekend.

I would like to say that we won right out of the box that season, but it wasn't the case. What we did have was a very competitive car. The Coleman Ford 351 gave us acceleration unmatched by any other car. Waterford Hills is such a short twisty track that you could only speculate what your top speed might be on a track with decently long straights. Later in the year, we did run at Mid-Ohio and reached a top speed of more than 175 mph. A braver man might have gotten more.

Speaking of bravery, I think it's important only when trying to extract the last 2% out of the car and yourself. The first 98% comes from technique, experience and a well-prepared vehicle that I knew I could trust. Once I had successfully negotiated a fast sweeping corner without lifting off of the throttle, I could do it again. I realized that I might be able to go a little bit faster through that same corner, provided I had done everything right just before I entered it, which means I would have had to do everything just right in the previous corner, and so on. Then, when you believe you have mastered the initial braking point, the turn-in point, the line through the corner, the point of initial acceleration, the apex, and the point of full acceleration, I endeavored to be consistent.

What complicates matters is the presence of another car in the corner. I had to decide what to do differently, knowing that this corner would be less than my best. The main things were not to crash, not to be passed under braking and not to mess the corner up so badly that I would be all out of shape for the next one.

One of the competitors driving his own Corvette and not part of the Danny Kellermeyer gang was Kip Wasenko. Kip has achieved considerable fame off of the track for his recent "break though" design work for Cadillac. While he is an up-and-coming executive at GM Design, to us he was just another car to get around. Kip did pretty well at longer tracks like Mid-Ohio but always seemed to be really on the edge of control at Waterford Hills. I think the corners were just too close together for his style.

In any case, when I followed Kip into a corner, he would do anything to defend his position. He wouldn't deliberately foul me, but he would brake a little too late, barely save it, cut across the track in front of me and then somehow recover. I knew that it would just be a matter of time if I kept the pressure on that he would pay too dearly to hold his position, finally sliding off in a cloud of dust. Entertaining to watch, that's for sure. I liked Kip as a competitor, not because we could usually do better than him, but because his car was well prepared, he drove it hard, maybe too hard, and he wasn't one for track gossip or intrigue. There were always lots of head games being played, grudges nursed, old wounds reopened, but not with Kip. He just came to race.

One of the factors in our favor at Waterford Hills was that we seemed to be a crowd favorite, which had more to do with the car than the charm of the driver. There was one other Ford Mustang, my old '88 Ford Mustang driven by Bob Bossche, and a heated-up twin-turbo Mazda RX-8. Everyone else drove a Corvette. So the Ford Mustangs were the underdogs, and the crowd liked to pull for a successful underdog. This helped with both the sponsors and my loyal crew who always had a David vs. Goliath attitude.

Kellermeyer won the ITE championship again in 1998. We were third behind Kris Smith, who drove a Kellermeyer Corvette. We won several races that season and knew we were close, real close. I beat Danny once in the rain. That was great. I was beginning to conclude that Kellermeyer and Smith were just better drivers than me, and that would be difficult to overcome. Yet, hope springs eternal.

We had Greg Coleman refresh the engine over the winter, changed to a more aggressive cam, and hoped this would bring us a bit more power. Always looking for just a bit more. We took the motor up to the dyno shop in Brighton again, going through many "pulls," looking for more steam. We discovered that there was no more power to be had, because there was no more air to be had with the intake plenum we were required to use. I paid the bill, and we took the motor home to be re-installed for the 1999 season.

We made a few more changes to the car to improve its handling. We moved my seat slightly rearward and extended the steering column, so I could still reach it while sitting farther back. We also added a hundred pounds of lead weight under the rear bumper. This was all done to get closer to a 50/50 front/rear weight distribution. The lead made the car heavier, to be sure, which you generally don't want to do. The car handled better, the tires lasted longer, and we went faster.

I knew 1999 would be my last year in a race car. Each year I had to take a driver's physical, and they were getting tougher to pass. The problem was the EKG test. The technician who was monitoring the equipment this last time said, "I think you're having a heart attack." My response was that the equipment was nuts, so we ran another and another. After six or seven EKGs, we finally got one that looked OK. She was shaking her head when I left, but I had my driver's physical form signed.

We felt that we had a real chance to win the championship in 1999. Our engine was strong. The rest of the car, due to Gary's craftsmanship, was bulletproof. Goodyear kept those beautiful new tires coming. Perhaps just as important, the nature of our competition was changing. Kellermeyer was starting to spend more time at other tracks on dates when Waterford races were held; his protégé, Kris Smith, would no longer be driving one of Danny's cars, and we could generally beat almost all of the other guys. The toughest remaining driver was Doug Chynoweth, who teamed up with Roger Mikulas, another formidable competitor.

One of the most important factors in racing is to be ready at the beginning of the season. That may sound obvious, but you would be surprised how many teams don't have it together until the second or third race weekend. Not us. I had learned long ago that first place finishes are a lot easier to come by in May than they are in August when everyone has their cars sorted out. Unfortunately, our first weekend consisted of two middle-of-the-pack finishes. All those suspension changes made the car different. It took all weekend to get it figured out. However, in the next eight races we finished first six times and second twice. When we finished second, Doug Chynoweth was first. He also won both races that first weekend when we didn't do so hot, finishing third and fourth.

The other problem was that my crew chief's family was growing. The countless hours volunteered by Gary over the years were key to the success of the team, but his time was becoming increasingly limited. Without Gary, it would be much more difficult. He would come either Saturday or Sunday, but it was tough for him to swing both days. Sometimes he would bring his little boys along. I have often wondered what two- or three-year-old kids think about at the track. I know they didn't like the noise, but they did like being with their dad.

There was a second race weekend in May that year, but for some reason there were no races on Saturday, probably because of the weather. In the Sunday race I was first, and Doug was second, about two seconds behind at the finish.

The June races were exciting. Doug qualified on the pole on Saturday with someone other than me alongside him. I was right behind him in the second row on the outside with Roger Mikulas, his teammate, alongside of me. The race began and we made it through the first two corners cleanly. Between the second and third turn there is a short straight, and Roger was right beside me. All of a sudden his car turned left, taking himself and me off the track, across a gravel apron and into the tire wall. He hit the tires head on, and I was spun around, so I backed into them.

We raised such a cloud sliding through that gravel that the cockpit filled up with a grey cloud I couldn't see through. I restarted the engine just as Gary came on the radio, asking if I was OK. I said I was, but the dust was so thick I couldn't see the dashboard, much less out through the windshield. He responded with, "The whole field has gone by. Mikulas' car isn't restarting. I think he's got big problems. Just drive straight ahead for ten yards and then turn left. You'll be on the track, and the movement will probably clear the air. Chynoweth is at least a half a lap ahead, so get moving."

I drove blind for ten yards and gained enough vision to see what was ahead. I certainly had the track to myself, as everyone else was way ahead. I thought briefly about the big dent I must have in my right side door where Roger hit me. I had to put that out of mind and concentrate on how the car was behaving. Everything seemed to be working, the gauges read normally, and I couldn't smell anything leaking or rubbing. Drivers are always smelling things and listening for signs of trouble. So far so good.

Doug was cruising along with his big lead, and I was really flying, catching the slower classes and eventually coming up on the other Corvettes. I still couldn't see Doug, but Gary called on the radio late in the race to say that I was in second place, still about a day behind Doug.

About then, it must have occurred to Doug that while he was going to win this race, there was tomorrow's Feature Race to consider. The first race of the weekend was gridded by our qualifying times, but the Feature was gridded by the fastest lap in the class races. This was a different way of setting the grid, to be sure, but one that had been traditional at Waterford Hills for as long as anyone could remember. We always used to have a class race on Saturday, then another on Sunday, followed by the Feature Race. This season they decided to just have the Saturday class race and only one race for each group of classes on

Sunday and that was the Feature. So Doug knew he had to get moving up to his usual speed to qualify for a top spot on the Feature's grid.

Doug turned up the wick to get a good lap time and was passing a back marker who wasn't paying much attention to his mirrors, and he moved right into Doug's car during the pass. Doug and the back marker crashed.

I won the damn thing. The Last Shall Be First. Seems like I read something like that somewhere in the New Testament.

Afterwards, I went over to see Mikulas. I wasn't as hot as I might have been had I not won. Roger denied any collusion with Doug, claiming that someone had hit him from behind. He probably did get hit in the rear, but it was hard to think that way that afternoon. Roger was a good driver, an honorable but tough competitor, and he wanted to win as badly as I did, so I'm sure he was telling the truth about getting punted from behind. Roger was a buddy of Doug's, but nobody would wreck their ride just to be helpful, so I was probably out of line to go over there all honked off.

Fortunately, the car was OK, other than a stoved-in door, which was no big deal.

As the season wore on, it became obvious it was going to come down to us against the Chynoweth gang for the ITE championship. It got a bit crazy in July and August with more rubbing, nudging and crashing going on than I had seen in years.

Not with Doug though, as he and I could go through corner after corner, side by side, no more than a few inches between our door handles, yet we would not touch. It reminded me of a ballet where the dancers are so close but do not touch. It was a ballet with six thousand pounds of steel and fiberglass and eight hundred horsepower between us.

Doug could generally out qualify us. If he did, we had to qualify no worse than second or third because these were all sprints, and there wasn't enough time to come from back in the field. We got a real break one Saturday afternoon when, just before the cars were to roll off the grid for our warm-up lap, Doug's gloves fell off of his console, and he couldn't reach them. The grid official gave the signal to move out onto the track, and Doug elected not to go until a crewman ran over to retrieve his Nomex gloves. That put him at the back of the pack.

Doug was the class of the field that day. Starting last, he ripped through the cars in the slower classes that raced with us. We were fast too, but he was gaining on us with every lap. We barely held him off at the line, but we had our win, mostly because of a pair of gloves.

While we did 95% of our racing at Waterford Hills, we did make two trips to other tracks with less than desirable results. Going back to 1998, we entered a Speedvision race held at the Mid-Ohio Race Course. We lost our clutch in a pre-race practice session that would have put most teams out of business because you have to have facilities to lift the car at least five feet up in the air, and these were not available to us at the track. Some guy we met at a parts store had a brother-in-law who had a small garage with a lift 20 miles away who would let us come over and rent his garage for $75. We packed everything up, drove over to a town of about 200 inhabitants, found this small repair shop, made some new friends, and went to work. It took Gary and another crewmember about four to five hours of hard work to make the repairs. We all slept pretty soundly that night.

We were ready for the race, no small accomplishment. After the televised preliminary ceremonies on Speedvision, we rolled off the grid. We started mid-pack in a field of 38 cars, not all in our class, and were moving up through the field. Our speed down the back straight was approximately 175 mph. I believe this is the fastest I have ever driven. The race was scheduled to last about an hour, and I could see us finishing in the top ten if I didn't crash and all systems held up. Unfortunately, the engine began to miss intermittently. Then the miss was there all the time. I called Gary on the radio to let him know the miss was getting real bad.

"Yes, we can hear it when you go by the pits. It doesn't sound good. Must be some kind of electrical problem. If you're running the electric fan, turn it off, so that the battery will last longer. If you can't make it back around to the pits, just pull off, so you don't get run over." The motor died altogether before I could get back around, and I had to pull off. Damn, double damn, especially after the heroics the guys went through yesterday to fix this thing. It turned out that the alternator failed, a problem we had never encountered before.

In 1999, we entered another Speedvision race held on the streets of Grand Rapids, Michigan. I was pretty nervous racing on city streets. It's much more claustrophobic than being on a road racing course like Waterford Hills. There, if you went off track on your own or were punted off, you slid across a grassy field until you got the car back under control. You lost ground big time, as it took another 20 seconds or more to get back to the track and going again. On a street course, though, if you went off, for whatever reason, you hit a concrete barrier and your day was probably over.

*Craig Weidner & Gary Butzke at the*
*Grand Rapids Speedvision Race.*

Like the Mid-Ohio Speedvision race, I didn't qualify well, ending up near the back of a 25-car field, all of which were in our class. The race got underway, and we started to make some progress. We were up to thirteenth or fourteenth position when a weld broke at one end of a big suspension piece called the torque arm. The torque arm also had a loop welded on it that encircled the driveshaft so that if the driveshaft broke, the torque arm would catch it and keep it from pole-vaulting the car. When the torque arm came undone, that loop dropped down on the custom aluminum drive shaft and sawed through it in 30 seconds. That's one thing you can't do without, a driveshaft. We were done.

In August, I won the Saturday race and Doug finished in second place, just a second behind me. Doug did win the feature on Sunday, and even though I finished second, I was 11 seconds back.

Doug still had a chance at the ITE Championship, and he wasn't giving up. I really had to respect the guy because the driving was hard on him physically. Doug was an accountant but did some singing with a local band on the side. A few years back, he discovered he had a polyp on one of his vocal chords and went in for a routine operation. The story that we heard was that the medical team botched the operation, and from then on Doug had a small opening in his throat with a trach tube that he breathed through. On hot, dusty days it was real hard for him to breathe. He was a tough guy. There was one more weekend to go, and even though I was ahead in points, he had a mathematical chance to win it.

All during the season a young guy with a good-looking lady on his arm would come by our pit to talk to Gary or myself about buying the car. He had heard that this was my last season and that the car would be available. Each time he paid us a visit he would leave his business card, and we would put it in the toolbox with the other business cards we were given by other guys, who were usually big talkers, flakes, really.

After the August races he came by again, with his pretty lady, to see how we were doing. He said he planned to be back for the final two races in September, and hopefully we could reach a deal. I took his card again and put it on the pile.

Looking at the points going into the final weekend in September, I had 101, compared to Doug's 83, putting him just 18 points behind. First place paid 12 points; second place, nine points.

He won on Saturday. I finished second and had one good lap, so I would be starting near the front on Sunday. We looked like we were close to mathematically securing the championship, but at Waterford, you never know.

I had plenty of new tires in inventory for Sunday's big race. The question was, do we use a new set that hadn't been scuffed in or go with a set that had just one race on them and were about as good as new and that advantage of being predictable? We decided to use the new tires, checked and double-checked everything. We were ready.

Sunday we got off to a great start. It is a lot easier to maintain your position, or improve it, when there are only a couple of cars in front of you and all the mid-pack nuttiness is behind you. The Mustang Cobra was flawless, while Doug's Corvette seemed to be having an overheating problem, unusual for that team who were always well prepared. He finished third. I finished first. We won the race, the 1999 ITE Class Championship and placed seventh in the Top Ten Drivers competition.

We had finally done it. I hadn't won a championship since the early days back in the late '70s in my Austin Healey Sprite. Gary climbed into the right side of the car with the checkered flag for our final lap at Waterford Hills, the victory lap. I had a tear or two in my eye then, and I'm misty-eyed as I write this. It was a long hard season. I wouldn't have been able to do it without my trusty crew chief, Mr. Butzke.

The potential buyer of the car was a no-show after the race. I had priced out what I had to have for the car, race car trailer, and all the parts that we had accumulated over the years that belonged with this car. I put that nicely printed page back in the toolbox. Looked like we wouldn't need it.

We packed the tools and spares, loaded the car into the trailer, and then drove over to the clubhouse for the trophy presentation. We ate our usual fare of hamburgers and fries, bought a few beers for the guys, and picked up our trophies.

We were just leaving when the potential buyer walked in, accompanied by a big guy he was recruiting to be his crew chief for next year. I would have rather seen his lady friend. He apologized for not making the race. He had attended an auction down in Ohio and planned to be back for the feature but got held up.

I went out to the trailer, got the price sheet I made up, and gave it to him. He looked it over carefully, showing no emotion. "I have at least three questions for you," he said. "First, I see there is a spare engine, a spare transmission, extra wheels, all kinds of oil, ten new Goodyear tires and lots of brake parts. I know I'll use the new tires and the trailer, but do I really need all this other stuff to campaign the car?"

I was thinking about how to answer that, when he said, "Let me ask the rest of my questions and you can answer them all at once. Secondly, are there any known problems with the car now that the season is over? Third, I see you haven't totaled this all up. If I take everything, how much does it amount to?"

I looked over at Gary, who had his usual poker face on, and I began to answer the questions. "Yes, you should take all the spares. We paid a lot more for them than I'm charging, and you'll eventually need them. No, there are no problems that I know of with the car. Right, Gary?" Gary nodded. There were no problems he knew of.

"As for the price for everything, here's the total." He didn't blink. "Then I have just one more question. When can we schedule the pre-purchase inspection?"

Man, what a beautiful phrase, the PRE-PURCHASE INSPECTION. I liked the sound of that. We made arrangements to have all the stuff cleaned up and displayed at Magneti's facility the following Saturday.

He and his crew chief arrived at the appointed time and looked everything over very carefully. I ran the car for him. They looked the gauges over. Everything looked OK, the engine sounded great, especially inside the building.

He noticed that I had a pair of custom-made aluminum ramps that we used to get on the weight scales, and had set them off to one side. He said he sure liked the looks of those ramps and assumed they would be included. I really didn't want to part with them and said so. The buyer countered with "I'm prepared to pay your asking price for your car, trailer, and everything else, but I can't see how I can get the car on the scales without those ramps."

Gary went into shock. He asked for a caucus and when he had me out of earshot he said, "Have you lost your mind? If this guy had offered a price $5000 less than what we're asking, we would have, after the usual protests and theatrics, accepted it or something close to it. You know that most of those Corvettes we beat are up for sale for a hell of a lot less than we're asking. Give him the damn ramps. You can buy a new set for less than $300. What the hell would you need them for anyway?"

Like my father, Gary almost never swore. He was livid. I knew he was right. It was just the prick in me that wanted to keep those ramps. I went back to where the other guys were waiting and told him he was the new owner of those ramps.

The buyer said, "Fine, I'll have a check for you on Monday. Now, let me buy breakfast." We went down the street and had a big brunch. Since I didn't drink, the only way I could think of to celebrate was gluttony. I probably had a 3000-calorie breakfast, but who was counting?

I delivered the car shortly after I cashed his check. I asked to keep the trailer for two more weeks because we were moving to Holland, Michigan, and I needed the trailer to haul the wife's books over there. We were paying our own moving expenses, and I knew those books weighed a lot. Out of curiosity, I stopped by a truck stop and had the trailer weighed. When I subtracted the known weight of the empty trailer, it turned out that I was hauling 5000 pounds or 2.5 tons of her books. Talk about heavy subjects.

The Mustang Cobra was a great car, one that owned me for five years, provided some great wins and wonderful memories. I can still hear the rumble of Greg Coleman's

475 HP 351, as I took it up through the gears, and downshifted it at the end of the straights. Thanks, Greg.

I'm not sure I could ever thank Gary enough for all he did on the '88 Ford Mustang and on the '94 Mustang Cobra. All those hours that he volunteered finally paid off with this championship.

Gary worked on that last car as if it were his own, building it from scratch, making it better and better, until we finally won the 1999 Championship at Waterford Hills with it. I used to think I was really driving his car. Either way, his car or mine, this car owned me, and probably Gary too.

# I Lifted at 145 MPH

## 2000 Lincoln LS Sedan

*This beautiful black Lincoln LS belongs to my friend, Dirk Kooiker, in Holland, MI.*

From an engineering perspective, this is probably the most advanced car I have ever owned. Or has owned me.

I was driving a Dodge Ram 250 Super cab with a Cummins Diesel. Nice truck. Noisy, but economical. It had enough torque to pull your cottage.

These trucks were necessary to pull my race-car trailer and were needed to carry the computer systems I often brought to customer sites for demonstrations. These were all shipped about in huge black containers, on wheels, and were a bear to get on and off the tailgate.

In late 1999, I decided to leave Scan-Optics, and went to work for HNC, a San Diego-based software firm that sold fraud-detection software to telecoms. I no longer needed the pickup to haul demo equipment around.

I had been thinking about having a car again for sometime. The last street car I owned was the '94 Mustang Cobra, a great ride but one that I wasn't using that much because almost all of my business travel required the use of the Dodge.

My first choice for a new car was the Chrysler Sebring convertible. I think it had timeless good looks, a great fitting top, and you could get a well-equipped one for about $20,000 at the time. I took several out for test drives and always came to the same conclusion: namely, this pretty car needs a motor. I could live with front-wheel drive, not my preference, but I couldn't have a car with such anemic acceleration. These cars were equipped with V-6 engines that were designed for economy and durability, noble objectives. Yet, the motor always seemed to be working so hard, especially if you were passing someone on a two-lane road and you needed to go from 50 to 65 right now. It wasn't going to happen very quickly.

I had noticed the Lincoln LS coming onto the market. You know, first you see early spy shot photos and articles in *Autoweek*, or in one of the monthlies like *Automobile, Road & Track, Motor Trend,* and *Car & Driver.* Then the popular press will have an article or two about Lincoln's new "sport sedan." This was going to be Ford Motor Company's attempt to tap into the low end to mid-range of the BMW market for four-door sedans that had decent power and better-than-average handling. You could get the car with a V-6 or a V-8, 3 liters or 4 liters respectively. No V-6s for me, thank you.

I drove over to Apollo Lincoln Mercury in Ann Arbor to take one out for a test drive. The salesman handed me the keys to a V-8 model, a dealer plate, made a copy of my driver's license, and returned to his desk. He missed an opportunity to qualify me as either a serious buyer or some guy who was merely curious about a new model. More importantly, he missed an opportunity to present the virtues of the car. He also relinquished physical control of a $38,000 unit that his employer was paying money to have there.

I took it out on to westbound I-94 and noticing a mid-afternoon lull in traffic volume, pulled over on to the right-side shoulder to take a good look at the dashboard and get familiar with the gauges and controls. I liked the no-nonsense layout, although it hardly exuded opulent luxury. The red line on the tachometer was at 6500. I knew it wouldn't have too much off of the line, being a relatively small motor with four valves per cylinder, but I expected it would have strong mid-range acceleration and decent top end. That's the way European builders design their motors, and Lincoln was after the American buyer of European cars.

Over here, we had gotten used to big displacement engines. A Ford 302 as in a mid-'90s Mustang or a Chevrolet 350 cubic-inch motor in a Corvette seems like the norm. The Lincoln LS has a 3.9-liter engine. The conversion of liters to cubic engines is that one liter equals 62 cubic inches, so a 3.9 liter mill is only about 242 cubic inches, 60 less than the 302 in the Mustang and more than 100 less than in the 'Vette. The saying goes that there is no substitute for cubic inches. There is a lot of truth in that, but there are other ways to provide a high level of performance.

One of the ways to do that is to give the engine less work to do. BMWs, Audis, and Hondas always were engineered to be as light as possible so that they would still have adequate performance with a relatively small motor.

These smaller motors make less torque, particularly at lower RPMs. Engines, be they diesel or gasoline, only produce torque. The horsepower number is the output of an equation that says the horsepower available, at the crankshaft, as measured on an engine dyno, is the product of the torque value in foot pounds at a given rpm, multiplied by the RPMs, divided by 5252.

Horsepower, which is a measure of how fast power can be increased, is what provides mid-range acceleration and top speed. Therefore, these smaller engines were designed to spin at much higher rpms to reach peak horsepower and to offset the lower torque output of the smaller displacement engines.

When an engine is turning high rpms, it is difficult to flow enough air to support the high number of combustion events taking place per second. That's why these small high revving motors have four valves per cylinder; two intakes and two exhaust valves, instead of the normal number of two valves per cylinder, one intake and one exhaust.

That's what the Lincoln LS brought to the party, a relatively small, high revving 258 HP motor to give this 3600 pound sedan decent performance. I mention the weight because it is one of the most overlooked of automobile specifications. It is a dogma in drag racing that every additional 100 pounds costs about 1/10 of a second in the time it takes to cover a quarter mile. You're not a drag racer, you say, so who cares? You should. Lightweight design, just like good aerodynamics, provides better acceleration and better fuel economy every day with no maintenance required. The increased efficiency, due to good design, is baked in and remains with the car throughout its useful life.

Lincoln engineers did a number of things to reduce weight. They employed an all-aluminum engine, an aluminum hood, an aluminum transmission case, and aluminum double A-arms for the independent suspension at all four corners of the chassis. They also moved weight around where it would do more good, putting the battery in the trunk. The cabin of the car is set rearward to help move the passenger weight towards the rear. They wanted to have a 50/50 front-to-rear weight distribution for better handling. They elected rear-wheel drive so that the front wheels didn't have to do all the work. After all, the fronts have to steer the thing and do most of the braking work because of the natural forward weight transfer that occurs when slowing down, which makes the rear end lighter and therefore has less traction. Too much rearward brake bias could mean a spin if you do not slow down in a straight line.

Lincoln did achieve a 51/49 front-to-rear bias, a commendable outcome, as long as there were no people in the car. When you added in the driver's weight, with him/her in the car alone, the numbers became 52/48, still pretty good.

I was sitting on the shoulder of the road, thinking about how I might best observe the car's acceleration potential and top speed. I turned off the climate control, waited until the road was clear ahead for about a mile and clear to the rear as far as I could see. I pulled out onto the road and stopped. I took a deep breath and pressed the throttle to the floor. It moved out smartly, winding right to the 6500 rpm red line before it shifted to second, revving up to 6500 before it shifted to third and so on through fourth, and then into fifth. I was doing about 125. Still going faster, it gained speed in a linear fashion. I lifted at 145 mph. That's fast enough. If the High Sheriff had observed me, I might be writing this from the slammer.

I took the car back to the lazy salesman who asked if I had any questions. He should have been the one asking questions.

This particular car was stickered around $36,000 to $37,000. It didn't have the stiffer suspension package or the bigger wheels and tires, but it had all the rest, including a sophisticated traction control system. I decided I would probably buy a Lincoln LS but would wait a little longer to do it. No hurry. I needed the truck a bit longer for our move to the west side of the state.

We were settled in Holland now. It was time. The local Lincoln store had a dark burgundy Lincoln LS on the showroom floor that fit the bill. I stopped in, met Mike the salesman, and attempted to assess the negotiating climate.

Mike was one of these guys who told you only what you asked, nothing more. He wanted the sale, but he was not going to prostitute himself for it by offering a big discount or whatever else might work. I liked his style.

The wife had been making noises about trading her '94 Mustang GT in on a mini-pickup, probably a Ford Ranger with four-wheel drive. Politically, I thought that if she had a new mini-truck, there would be less resistance to me getting a new Lincoln LS.

We stopped by the Ford dealer who told us our pristine five-year-old Mustang GT with less than 15,000 miles on it was worth very little to him, maybe $6000, no more. Biting our tongues, we asked if we could take a four-wheel drive Ranger equipped with their biggest engine out for a ride. He gave us the keys, declined to go along, and we left his lot with the truck.

Nancy was driving. When the light turned green on US-31, she pressed the gas to the floor, perhaps out of habit or maybe some latent anger over the offered trade-in price for her Mustang. Not much happened. We heard a furious noise from the engine bay, yet we weren't changing locations very rapidly. "What am I doing wrong?"

"You're not doing anything wrong. That's all it's got."

"No thanks. I'm taking it back."

Now, you might ask, wasn't that a bit shortsighted? After all, there is a lot more to a vehicle than acceleration. Agreed, but a weenie of a motor is always a putoff. A decently performing car or truck has to have an adequate motor, and the consumer is the one who defines adequate.

This truck failed the first question, as far as my bride was concerned. The test was over. We retrieved her Mustang, and I, taking a bit of a diplomatic risk with her in a disappointed frame of mind, suggested we stop by the Lincoln dealer. It was on the way home.

We walked in, ignored the approaching salesman, and I asked her the $38,000 question. "What do you think of this one?"

"I love the color. Is this the actual car you've been telling me about?" Her liking the color was a big plus. I have to keep reminding myself how important color is to a woman.

"Yes, this is the one I'm interested in. Glad you like the color. I think they call it Autumn Red. Sit in it for a second." She sat down in the driver's seat and looked around.

"I would never be able to drive a big car like this. But it would be nice for you. I see that they want almost forty grand for this one. How would you pay for it? We're not financing anything."

"I have a plan, but let's get out of here. I see that Mike guy coming in from outside right now, and I don't want to appear too interested. I will ask him if he's working tomorrow, though."

Mike said that sure he'd be around. I told him I'd be in late in the morning.

I went back the next day to begin the haggle. I like haggling but don't think I'm very good at it. I'm not bad at it, just never feel I get what someone savvier might have gotten.

First things first. I wanted to drive the car. He had a nearly identical Lincoln LS outside, so I took that out for a drive. He didn't come along. I don't understand that, never will. While I was out, he had the used-car manager size up my truck. I just stayed in town, so there wasn't any high-speed stuff out on the freeway. The car drove fine.

Mike and I sat down to wrestle this deal out. He opened with the announcement that *Motor Trend* had just named the Lincoln LS their Car of the Year, trying to build value in my mind. One of the cards I wanted to play was a Citibank credit card that paid points towards buying any new Ford product. I had $1700 worth of points. The idea was to negotiate the best price and then bring the $1700 credit into the deal. I wasn't sure he was going to mention this, but I certainly planned to. I wasn't sure whose $1700 that was, Ford's or Citibank's.

To do a car purchase right, you have to see the dealer's invoice. You want to start there, not working downward from the window sticker. Retail on this car was about $37,000 and invoice was about $35,000. The dealer pays less than invoice for the car because of an accounting item called the Holdback. This is the amount of money that Ford is going to credit the dealer with after the sale. It is usually between 2% and 3% of the purchase price. So, invoice isn't the dealer's cost. Invoice less the holdback is his cost. Many foreign manufacturers have eliminated holdbacks, which is why it is tougher to get them to come down. The dealer has no cushion. I recently spoke with a BMW salesman who said his dealer had no holdback, and invoice was just 8% under retail. I'm not positive that's true, but if it is, there isn't much room to come down.

In this case, there was a holdback of indeterminate size, likely around $1000. No dealer with any brains is ever going to part with that because it represents his guaranteed profit. Mike showed me the invoice on the car and said he had to have invoice plus $1000. That's the least any LS buyers had paid for the car thus far, he claimed. I was willing to pay invoice plus $250. No deal. He just wouldn't go there. He wouldn't do invoice plus $500 either. I said that perhaps I better shop around. He reiterated the car's virtues and said like many a young lady probably has, "Good Sir, I've never done anything like this before. I will go to invoice plus $750."

He had convinced me that I was getting a better-than-the-normal deal. Who knows? Maybe I did and maybe I didn't. I was about to spring the Citibank card when he beat me to it. "You wouldn't happen to have a Citibank card, would you?" "Well, it just so happens I do," said I.

It turns out the $1700 credit was Ford's money. Therefore, it didn't cost the dealer any profit. He was glad to improve the deal by that much. The only other parameter was the value of my truck. I knew what wholesale was going in, and after a bit of a verbal shoving match, I got about $250 above wholesale. I would have made $1500 more if I wanted to go through the trouble of selling it myself. Usually, I would do the selling, but I was new in town and didn't want the hassle of having strangers come out to the house to show the truck. I think I got about $24,000 for the truck and had to come up with about $10,000 cash, which I had squirreled away somewhere.

The car was ready the next morning. I brought the truck in, took three years of credit card receipts, cassette tapes, and CDs out of the glove box, and picked up the new car.

From the first glance, I liked the way this car looked. It was conservative, sure, but in a blue-blazer way. Do you know how long blue blazers with grey slacks have been in style? Since before you were born. And how long will they remain in style? Until we're all wearing spacesuits on our way to a new planet.

Yes, it had style and that presents a problem for Ford. How are they going to change this thing and still keep the timeless look? Not my problem. I hope they don't change it soon.

I did like to drive this rear-wheel drive car in the winter, in the snow. "Are you nuts?" you say. Not really. Well, OK, a little. This car had ABS (Anti-lock Braking System), of course, and it used the ABS three ways to keep you from messing up your car and yourself. Just to review, ABS prevents you from locking up the brakes, thereby losing your steering and going into a skid. It does this with sensors that watch your wheel rotation speed when you're braking, and when it approaches zero, meaning lockup, it releases the brakes for 1/25th of a second and then reapplies the brakes. It can do this 12 times per second, saving your bacon from the skid caused by wheel lockup and loss of steering.

This same ABS system can keep your powered wheels from spinning as well. When the sensors see that the powered wheels are turning considerably faster than the non-powered ones, it concludes you're spinning the powered wheels, and it applies the brakes on those wheels to stop them from spinning. How about that? This keeps the car from losing traction. This is advertised as Traction Control.

Lincoln and others have taken this one step further by incorporating yaw sensors to help save you when you've entered a curve way too fast and are either going to have the front wheels break loose, so you don't turn but go straight off, or have the rears break loose, so you spin out and slide backwards into the ditch. Yaw is rotation around a vertical axis, spinning, in other words. They call this feature Advanced Traction Control. What Lincoln's sensors do when you're about to spin out is that they selectively apply the brakes to just one wheel out of four in an attempt to get things back under control. This single wheel braking works surprisingly well. Of course, you can beyond the point of rescue, and then it's going to get noisy and expensive.

This ability to save you from your miscues along with the 52/48 weight distribution provides the Lincoln LS with the ability to steer well and get good rear traction at the same time, two essential attributes for winter driving.

Of course, there are those who would abuse these capabilities, just to challenge the car, while driving on snow and ice. It's actually a lot of fun if you pick your spots. Imagine an exit ramp with no guardrails, and no ditch. You're on this unplowed ramp with three to four inches of snow. If you were to slide off, you might have to shovel yourself out or get a push from a passing motorist. No big deal. Therefore, it is a good place to challenge the car.

You approach the corner at a little above a reasonable speed. You turn in and you feel the back get a bit loose. The system notices too, and it applies just the inside rear-wheel brake. This adds side drag and slows the sideways motion, so the skid is stopped. Next time, you'll probably come in a little faster to conduct another test. You're learning the car, right?

If the front end washes out in the turn and the car goes straight, then the system notices that the car is not tracking consistent with how the front wheels are being turned and it quite likely will apply a braking force to the inside front wheel, helping stop the front end's plowing. Neat, eh?

As mentioned above, you can get beyond the car's ability to bring you back from the edge. In any trial-and-error process, there is going to be error, so pick your spot accordingly.

This kind of experimentation is a lot of fun, but it does have a serious practical side. This stuff helps you learn car control. When you know what the car's limits are, you know more than 99% of the drivers out there. Most drivers panic when the car starts moving around. They slam on the brakes, losing the steering and any hope of getting the car back under control.

One other attribute of the Lincoln LS that I've come to appreciate is its fuel economy. You're advised to burn 91 octane premium gas in it, but I always put 87 octane (monkey pee) in the tank, and it ran just fine with no pinging sounds. I suspect it had a built-in knock sensor that retards the timing slightly when it hears what is called premature detonation caused by the fuel igniting before the piston gets to the top of its travel.

Running at 72-74 mph, on cruise control, over flat terrain, with a neutral wind, it would travel 27 miles on a single gallon of gas. I'd say that's pretty darn good. I think the five-speed automatic transmission, the aerodynamics, the relatively lightweight chassis, and the engine management system all contributed to this level of fuel economy.

I've never been one to keep cars as long as I kept this one, four years and change. I think the last street car I had even three years was the '74 Jaguar XJ6L, one of my all-time favorites. The Lincoln LS reminded me of that car in several ways. Both had comfortable rides, firm but not harsh. Both cars had timeless good looks. Both cars offered good value for the money.

I had to replace the BF Goodrich tires with Goodyear All Season Regattas at 50,000 miles. The brakes were replaced about the same time. This was routine stuff. Other than that, I just changed the oil.

Every so often, I would mention to Nancy that the new 2006 long body Jaguar XJ8L appeals to me. She asks what that car does that the Lincoln doesn't do. I try to explain how the Jaguar is so beautiful, so responsive with its 294 HP engine, so economical with its all-aluminum construction and six-speed automatic transmission. She gives me a look of utter disdain. "This Lincoln you're driving is 75% of that, and it's paid for. How can you consider parting with more than $60,000 for a depreciating asset? What the hell is wrong with you?"

She has a point, maybe several. Yet, I don't think she understands why guys, and some women, desire certain cars with a passion that borders on a mental condition that isn't very healthy, and psychologists probably have a name for.

Some folks might conclude there is a desire to show off, to obtain some higher status, to possibly overcome some feeling of inferiority. I plead guilty to all those misdemeanors, but I think it's something more.

I think it's similar to an art lover's desire to own a famous painting, like a van Gogh. The true art lover doesn't pretend that the painting confers any status on him; rather, he just wants to be around a work of excellence.

That's kind of the way I felt when I first drove the '74 Jaguar XJ6L. I couldn't claim to have designed it or built it. All I did was to do something else of value so that I had the wherewithal to acquire it. My accomplishment was in the other activity, namely computer sales. That was my true glory, not the car. The car was someone else's work of excellence. I was just in love with that excellence. To have it in my garage was like having a love affair with an object, rather than a woman.

This, it seems to me, is why all of these cars owned me. For the most part, except probably company cars, I was "in love" with them. And as long as beautiful, powerful cars are built, I know I'll be seduced, willing and enthusiastically. The secret sauce will always get to me.

The miles were beginning to pile up, now approaching 70,000 in the spring of 2005. Gas prices were on their way up and would eventually hit $3.00/gallon here in Holland. The LS would get 27 mpg on the highway, so I was OK there. I guess my big problem was I had never had a car this long. If any sort of temptation came along, I would be vulnerable.

That temptation arrived in the form of a 2003 Honda Accord EX owned by our son Joe down in Columbus. He was moving up to a 2005 Honda Hybrid and planned to trade his Accord in. In Ohio, the sales tax paid on a new car is only assessed on the difference between your trade-in's value and the negotiated price of the new car. The dealer where Joe was to get his new Honda Hybrid was willing to give him $15,000 for the 2003, so he wouldn't be taxed on that much of the new car's cost. The sales tax in Ohio varies a little from county to county, and where he lives it's 6.75%, so that would eliminate about $1013 of sales tax if he traded it in. Joe let me know that if I wanted his car, he would have to have $16,000 plus a $13 lunch, as that's the value of the trade-in.

The Honda had about 16,000 miles on it and was in very good shape. This was the top of the Accord line, the EX model, with heated black-leather seats, alloy wheels, great sound system, sunroof, power everything, and had a nice silver paint job with no nicks or scratches except for one small paint chip on the hood. The engine was the 160 HP four-cylinder V-TEC motor. The transmission was a manual five-speed. That combination made for good gas mileage: 28 mpg around town and 35 mpg out on the highway.

I had driven the car a few times and was impressed with its performance, especially its ability to accelerate between 60 and 80 mph. Here was a car that was "younger" than the Lincoln LS by three model years and 55,000 miles. A few more phone calls and emails and a deal was done. The only unresolved detail was when to come and get it. We had planned for some time to attend the christening of Joe and Karla's new son, Erick, in May and that would be the perfect time to pick up our "new" car in Columbus.

Off to Columbus we went in our 26-foot Lazy Daze motor home where we would rent a tow dolly to haul the car back to Michigan after the ceremonies and celebrations of little Erick's baptism.

Now, we had to find a new home for the Lincoln LS that would prove to be far more difficult than I imagined. Our house in Holland was a bit off the beaten path, unlike our house in Ann Arbor on Stadium Boulevard that had 15,000 cars pass by per day and double that when Michigan had a home football game. Almost all the cars and trucks in this book were sold off that corner over a span of 23 years.

Without that drive-by exposure, I relied heavily on the Internet, posting the car on AutoTrader.com and several other similar websites. I got a few flaky phone calls but no strong interest. After about six weeks of no apparent progress towards a sale, I moved the car to a Rent-A-Spot lot out on the main bypass around Holland, US-31, which had considerable traffic each day. You paid $100 and your car could sit there for a month, along with other sedans, pickup trucks, and an assortment of motor homes and boats.

I got a call one day from a guy who noticed the car and said he was looking for a Lincoln LS for his wife.

"Could you come down to the lot, so I could take your Lincoln out for a test drive?"

I was down there in about 15 minutes and met my prospect. He was driving a Chrysler Crossfire Coupe. I took that to be a good sign, an indication that he was into cars and would appreciate the LS's athletic attributes, not to mention its good looks. Before we drove it, I walked him around the car, popped the hood and the trunk, talking about the features and things he wouldn't know about, like the battery in the trunk and why it was there. I think it's important to set the stage before the demo ride. The demo ride is always a subjective emotional experience, and you want to deposit the general information in his brain before the ride because most folks aren't listening to you when they drive a different car for the first time, they're listening to the car and forming their emotional reaction to the car.

I fired it up, backed it out of its parking space, and let it idle for a minute. I wanted him to see how quiet it was outside the car, signifying that the mufflers and exhaust system were in good shape, pointing out that it did have dual exhausts. Now, it was time to have the demo ride. This would make him a salesman for the car or not.

He got in the driver's seat, adjusted the mirrors and seat position, looked over the gauges, put it in drive and got us out of the lot and out onto US-31. We had to stop for a red light, and while we waited for it to change, I suggested that he nail the throttle when it did. And he did. The car leaped forward, and that wonderful pressure on the small of your back was there.

A relatively small V-8 like the Lincoln's was designed for mid-range acceleration from 50 to 80 mph and beyond, rather than for a stoplight Grand Prix. Still, it was a fairly lightweight car and it moved off briskly, getting up to 60 in seven to eight seconds. As he let off, slowed down and drove about the speed limit of 55 mph, I could see a bit of a grin forming. We had to slow down for another light. As we were coming to a stop, I told him to nail it again when the light changed and not lift until I told him to do so. The light changed, he stood on it again with the motor winding up to 6500 rpms, then smoothly shifting to second gear where it climbed up to 6500 rpms and shifted to third, at which point we were approaching 80 mph. He lifted without me telling him to. I said that the point of those two exercises was to demonstrate that this car was no poser. He agreed it was considerably quicker than he imagined.

Since the car was going to be for his wife, I suggested he bring her to Holland and see how she liked driving the car. "Do you think she'll like it?" I asked. "Yes, she'll like it, except for one thing, the color." Oh crap, I thought to myself. Color is a very big deal to women, my wife in particular. "What color does she like?" said I. "White," said he.

Somewhere along the way, I learned that the first thing you do is agree with the other guy's opinion, and then slowly try to turn things around. You have to agree first; otherwise, he won't be listening.

"White is a great color for a car. I have had two white Lincolns, a white Camaro, a white Audi, a white TR-3 sports car, and two white pickups. I always liked white cars." Now comes the turnabout. "The only problem with white is that you miss out on one thing that makes a car pretty and that's a good shiny paint job. You just can't get much of a shiny surface with white. You wash it and wax it, and it looks better than it did, but it's not going to knock you out like a medium- or dark-colored car will that's been freshly waxed. Look at the shine on this car. It's deep. Lincoln calls this color Autumn Red. When my wife saw this color, she liked it so much; her normal resistance was reduced by at least half. I knew I had a chance to acquire this car without the usual domestic warfare. You know what I mean?"

"Yes, I know exactly what you mean. We have a car fight about every other year. OK, I'll see if I can get her up here sometime this week to take it for a drive. I see you're asking

$13,500. I don't think we're going to spend more than 12K if we can help it."

"Well, get her up here, and we'll see if she likes it enough for you and me to arm-wrestle over the price. She just might like the color as much as my wife did."

"We'll probably come over some evening this week, as she doesn't get home from her job in Kalamazoo until about six or so. We live just this side of Allegan, and I drive by here every day going to my job on the North side, so I'll know if it is still here."

The week went by and no call. Another week passed, and a third, without a call from him or anyone else. Nancy said that we had better get realistic about this car sale. "Why don't you take it around to a few dealers and see what they'll give you for it wholesale?" I knew this was going to be an exercise in hurt feelings because the average used-car buyer at a dealer is a ruthless individual. He has to be, in order to be able to make a slight profit if he decides to wholesale the car out at a dealer's auction if he can't move it. He must pay less than wholesale. That's the only way he can still make a few bucks if and when he sells it at wholesale. He hopes to sell it at retail and make a killing, and he generally does. So the sub-wholesale value offered for this fine automobile ranged between $8000 and $9000. Ouch!

Back at the house, Nancy said, "Here's what I think you should do. You know you can get $9000 from the one dealer. Try a little harder to find a buyer and anything you get over $9000 is yours to keep and spend on your sailboat or whatever. Say, what about that guy from Allegan?"

"I don't have his number, and if I did, I'm not sure I would call him 'cause it makes me look too desperate." She said, with a bit more emphasis than I wanted to hear, "You are desperate. I'll try and find his number on WhitePages.com. Give me his name and town again." Five minutes later, she had the number. "Now, call him, damn it!"

I got the guy on the phone and asked if he'd found a car for his wife yet. "No, not yet, although we looked at a lot of Lincoln LSs, some nice, some pretty rough. Everybody wants a fortune for them, so we've just kind of tabled it for now."

"Tell you what, if you can bring your wife up to Holland, so she can drive this car, and it turns out she likes it, I'll make you a deal you can't refuse."

"Are you saying twelve thou or lower?"

"That's what I'm saying."

"Just a minute." He put the phone down and went back into the kitchen where his wife was fixing supper. A couple of minutes passed. "How about we meet you at the lot tomorrow afternoon around 5 o'clock? She gets off work about 3:30, so we should be able to make five although we could be fifteen minutes late if the traffic is bad."

"That's fine. Bring your checkbook because she's going to love the car, and I'll be asking for a deposit."

"If we do buy it, we're going to have to visit the credit union and that usually takes two to three days for those loans to go through. How big a deposit do you want?"

"One hundred dollars will hold it for a few days. Do you just want to meet at 5:30, so you don't have to rush?"

"Hang on... Yes, she says that would give us time to grab a bite to eat, so 5:30 will be better. If there is some problem, like she's got to work late, we'll call you on your cell phone, OK?"

"All right. I'm probably going to get there around 4:45, as it rained last night, and the car probably has some rain spots, so I'll take it over to that quarter wash by the Shell station and get it cleaned up. She is going to fall in love with this car. You'll see."

They did show up the next day, right on time. I really had to hustle to get it washed and dried by 5:30. I had it looking good. We did the walk around, and he helped with the presentation. She didn't want to drive it, so I did. She said she was impressed with the quietness and the smoothness of the ride. I guess they had taken that Chrysler Crossfire to Florida last winter. She said it was pretty hard on her fanny, but this Lincoln was very nice.

We're back at the lot, and she keeps walking around it but not saying much. He presses a little, and seeing some resistance to make a decision then and there, he says they really like it but want to go home and talk about it.

I couldn't let that happen. It took three weeks to get him back here with her. On the other hand, nobody wants to be pressured, which is the way I was sure she was feeling. I let them caucus for another five minutes and decided it was time to make my pitch, which was addressed entirely to her. As far as I was concerned, he wasn't there.

"Here's the deal. When I first showed the car to your husband, I was asking $13,500. I arrived at that price by looking around the Internet at the various car sites for 2000 Lincoln LS cars with similar mileage. They ranged from $13,000 to $17,000. Your husband indicated that he couldn't go more than $12,000, and he said that he hoped to find one for even less than that. You haven't bought one yet so maybe that's going to be tough to do. Now, I could offer this car to you for $12,000 or $11,750 or even $11,500. I'm not going to do that. Here's what I will do. If you make up your mind, here and now, to buy this car, and give me $100 to hold it until your loan at the credit union is approved over the next few days, I will sell it for $11,000." No one spoke for 30 seconds. They looked back and forth at each other, trying to gauge the other's reaction. Finally, she said, in a soft voice, more to him than me, "OK."

Two days later, we concluded the deal but I still had one unmet obligation. I promised them a sailboat ride but didn't get that done last summer, so I'll have to make a definite plan to do that this summer in my new Alerion Express 28.

Bottom line: the Allegan lady is driving a fine ride; my private fund increased by $2000; $9000 was sent with another $6000 from savings down to Columbus for the 2003 Honda, and everyone lived happily ever after.

# A Car This Good Is a Keeper

## 2003 Honda Accord EX

*Silver perfection.*

I bought the Honda from son Joseph in May of 2005 as a replacement for the 2000 Lincoln LS I had driven for the last five years.

Gas prices had been rising all through 2005, and I thought myself to be quite clever, anticipating they would continue to increase. I would be burning a lot less gas with the Honda five-speed than with the Lincoln LS that was not bad on gas. If I kept it in the low 70s on the highway, the LS would go about 27 miles on a gallon of gas. Not bad, really, for a big car. In the city, though, there was no comparison, as the Honda got 28 to 29 mpg while the Lincoln fell to 17 to 19 mpg.

Out on the highway, the Honda has really shone. Gas mileage is consistently around 35 to 36 mpg. I like its 50 to

80 mph acceleration capability. Obviously, it does that better if you downshift to fourth gear, but even leaving it in fifth, its acceleration is impressive.

Some folks think of cars as appliances and have no more affection for them than they would have for their stove. Sometimes I think of the Honda Accord as an appliance too, but in a positive way. For example, we have a Fisher & Paykel washing machine and clothes dryer, plus a double-drawer dishwasher, all three built in New Zealand. They are all very quiet, particularly the dishwasher, so quiet that you hardly know they're running. They all work so efficiently; you would be hard put to consider another brand when these units eventually wear out. That's the effect a well-engineered well-built Honda Accord has on you. It's highly unlikely you're going to switch brands. Every time you get in the thing, it works its magic and you're sold on the brand all over again. That's where customer loyalty is born and nurtured.

I'm told that most folks keep their kitchen and laundry appliances between ten to fifteen years. I probably won't be keeping this 2003 Honda Accord that long. It now has 40,000 on the clock, an addition of 24,000 in the last eighteen months. I do hope I keep it until it has at least 100,000 miles on the odometer. That would be a first. Never have had a car that long. Could be a sign that, now that I've had my 67th birthday, I'm beginning to grow up.

There are three more cars I would like to have, but I'm in no hurry to part with the Honda Accord. A car this good is a keeper. Even if I move uptown to a Jaguar, I might keep it around for one of the grandkids, so they would learn on a stick shift, like their grandpa did on a 1953 Nash, so many cars and so many years ago.

The siren's song that has called to me, tempted me, still reaches me after all these years. The next and last section, the epilogue, tells of cars still lusted after. I imagine this will continue until they're shoveling dirt on a plain pine box.

# Epilogue

If you look at the actual number of days a person living to eighty-five years old has, it comes out to something close to 31,025 give or take a few days, depending on how many leap years there are. Then, if you assume that your last three years are spent trying to stay alive, you end up with a lifetime of about 30,000 days.

As I approach my 68th birthday in April of 2007, my optimistic guess of useful life left is a little over 5000 days: 82 years old minus 68 years old times 365 days of the year equals 5110 days to go.

So, what conclusion might one draw from that little bit of predictive arithmetic? Life is just too short.

Before I leave, I'd like to add to this collection of cars and stories. I want to have a few more cars that possess the "secret sauce."

We know I'm a big fan of the Jaguar marque. I have had three thus far: the 1974 XJ6L sedan, the 1970 XKE roadster, and the 1976 XJC sedan.

I really would like to have another, possibly a 2007 XJ8L. Perhaps, I should wait until the 2008 or 2009 models are out because I suspect there will be some significant changes in style.

The successor to the current XJ will have a hard act to follow. The current model offers an aluminum engine, six-speed ZF transmission, aluminum subframes and a beautiful aluminum body wrapped around an elegant interior with soft leather seats, full instrumentation, responsive controls—in other words, a driver's car. Owners are reporting 30 mpg highway mileage from a very strong alloy engine.

After that car was safely in my garage, I might look to acquire an older classic. I think I would be torn between two cars, quite different from each other. One would be a large American car, the 1956 Lincoln Continental Mark II. I think it is simply the most beautiful car I have ever seen. It offers a sculptured body on a massive ladder frame, a beautiful interior, a classic large V-8 engine and timeless good looks. It truly has the secret sauce.

The other older classic would be a restored version of the one English car that started me down the road to perdition, to being owned by many different cars, and that is the venerable Triumph TR-3B. Unique, stylish and fast, this was the first new car I owned fresh out of college. I had it for little more than a year, from June of 1962 to August of 1963.

The Triumph was the car I never really got over. Almost all the cars that followed over the next fifty years could not quite bring the special joy, the excitement, the desire to drive, that the 1962 Triumph gave to me. Maybe it was the times as much as the car. I was 23, single, about to take my first job as a high school math teacher, and found myself falling in love at first sight with the pretty French teacher down the hall at Clarkston High.

As I reflect a little more on that first year out of college, it wasn't all champagne and roses. I was usually broke. My health went south with a serious sinus infection that required extensive surgery to fix. Teaching school was a challenge but brought more job satisfaction than I thought possible. If I could have afforded to, I think I would have stayed with teaching rather than joining the corporate world. I had to take a second job, selling clothes part-time at Robert Hall, or Roberto Le Hall as we called it. I think the Triumph helped to smooth all the rough spots, so I could soldier on in both teaching and the pursuit of Miss Nancy Mouw.

Cars have always done that for me, help me soldier on in the face of adversity and depression, especially the ones with the secret sauce. As I said earlier, the right car was always a psychiatric help and pleasant therapy at that.

If I had to have one more go-fast car, a Shelby Cobra replica with a Greg Coleman-built Ford 351 would be the one.

I think such a serious, menacing car like that should be black. The style is timeless. There is no doubt whatsoever that it has the substance underneath the fiberglass, and it always struck me as a car that wanted to flex its muscles without being dangerous to drive. Not only does it possess excellent acceleration, but it also offers great handling and braking. Many companies offer versions of this car with different engine combinations. My choice would be the South African-built Superformance brand. Their craftsmanship is tops; they have a great reputation, and the only decision one needs to make is color and engine.

I think a built Ford 351 is the right motor. These motors, especially those built by Greg Coleman from the Detroit area, easily produce around 400 horsepower and about the same number of foot-pounds of torque propelling a body weighing less than 2500 pounds. If we put 300 pounds of people in this beast, we're only up 2800 pounds. That's seven pounds of workload for each horsepower. How long does it take to reach sixty miles per hour? Less time than it took to read the last two sentences.

I hope you find the car, or cars, that will own you too. Don't wait too long. Make sure you have your other obligations handled, like family, work, worship and kids. Then, find the car that makes you sing.

They're out there, the special ones, the cars with the secret sauce.

We are dead a long time. Go find that special car. Enjoy.

**For color photos and more information
visit www.FortyCars.com**